Directing the Tunnellers' War

Directing the Tunnellers' War

The Tunnelling Memoirs of Captain HR Dixon MC RE

Edited by Phillip Robinson and Nigel Cave

Pen & Sword
MILITARY

First published in Great Britain in 2020 by
Pen & Sword Military
An imprint of
Pen & Sword Books Ltd
Yorkshire – Philadelphia

ISBN 978 1 52671 441 1

A CIP catalogue record for this book is available from the British Library.

Typeset by Mac Style
Printed and bound in the UK by TJ Books Ltd,
Padstow, Cornwall.

MIX
Paper from responsible sources
FSC® C013056

Pen & Sword Books Limited incorporates the imprints of Atlas, Archaeology, Aviation, Discovery, Family History, Fiction, History, Maritime, Military, Military Classics, Politics, Select, Transport, True Crime, Air World, Frontline Publishing, Leo Cooper, Remember When, Seaforth Publishing, The Praetorian Press, Wharncliffe Local History, Wharncliffe Transport, Wharncliffe True Crime and White Owl.

For a complete list of Pen & Sword titles please contact

PEN & SWORD BOOKS LIMITED
47 Church Street, Barnsley, South Yorkshire, S70 2AS, England
E-mail: enquiries@pen-and-sword.co.uk
Website: www.pen-and-sword.co.uk

Or

PEN AND SWORD BOOKS
1950 Lawrence Rd, Havertown, PA 19083, USA
E-mail: Uspen-and-sword@casematepublishers.com
Website: www.penandswordbooks.com

Contents

Editors' Note

HR Dixon was evidently of the 'pepper pot punctuation' school and we have taken some modest liberties in removing excessive commas and other more glaring grammatical infelicities. He also had a *penchant* for employing capitals at the beginning of words he thought important and for an extensive use of hyphens, common at the time, which we have adjusted. It was then the practice to use full stops in abbreviations and acronyms (e.g. G.H.Q.) and we have rendered these in the modern form without the stops. Otherwise the text is as written by Dixon. Perhaps most controversially, we have changed his working title to clarify the subject of the book; but, as most authors know, after consultation it is the right of a publisher to decide the title. In the case of Dixon consultation, alas, is not possible.

After some discussion, we decided that the best option for the reader would be to insert editorial commentary in italics in the text. Dixon's own handwritten annotations are included, but we have indicated when these originate with the author. These comments are inserted either within the text or as a separate paragraph. Appendix VII provides brief biographical notes on many of the personalities mentioned by Dixon. Some of these people are well known, some less so. In some cases a biographical caption has been added to a photograph of the person concerned.

We have also sought to enhance his work with photographs of people and situations to which he refers and diagrams, illustrations and plans covering some of the situations he describes.

The editors have made every effort to trace his descendants to seek their agreement to publication but without success. Despite this, we feel sure that Dixon would approve of the publication of his work, albeit eighty-five years or so late, with its many tributes to the men with whom he shared the perils of the tunnelling war and those with whom he worked at GHQ and elsewhere.

About the man himself we know little. He was probably born in the early 1890s, in China. He joined the army as a private soldier in the Middlesex Regiment, but his skills as an engineer soon had him commissioned in the Royal Engineers and he was working as a training officer in Shorncliffe before the memoirs begin. He was academically inclined; post war he went on to take a doctorate in engineering from Glasgow University. He spent a number of the interwar years in China, mainly engaged in developing the navigation of the Yangtse River. This involved extensive use of explosives, which would doubtless have made someone who enjoyed the nickname 'Dynamite' a happy man. He got involved to a limited degree in the civil war that raged in that country by becoming a member of the Shanghai Volunteers, a multi-national volunteer unit that dated back to the 1850s, organized by the Municipality of Shanghai, which was responsible for the internal government of the International Settlement in Shanghai. Soon after the outbreak of the Second World War he rejoined the army full time. Promoted to major, he served as a Royal Engineer in India, latterly as Chief of the Ammunition Inspectorate at Poona, a major Indian Army administrative centre, where he was still working in 1946.

He married in late 1917 and had two sons, one born in 1918 and one in 1922.

NB! An asterisk after a name (first mention only) means that there is an entry on that person in the biographical notes section, Appendix VII.

Acknowledgements

Many thanks are due to Major (retd) Andrew Hawkins MBE, QMG, who converted the original photocopied Dixon manuscript into 'doc' text.

We are very grateful to Martin Morton, the son of Captain Herbert Lea Morton of 255 Tunnelling Company, who kindly allowed us to copy all the photographs from his father's album and from which we have taken most of the photographs of tunnelling officers. Lamentably, the album, sent back to Martin by registered post, was lost by the Royal Mail, a misfortune that he accepted philosophically. Fortunately all the photographs had been scanned, but the moral is to always use Special Delivery for uniquely precious material.

Phillip would like to acknowledge the patience of his wife Mary, who had to bear with his frequent absence in his study and also from some social events whilst working on this book.

Introduction

The Lighter Side of a Tunneller's Life is an unpublished memoir of the First World War experiences of Captain Herbert Ridley Dixon MC.

After a period serving as an officer of 255 Tunnelling Company RE, interrupted by a few months with the 23rd Divisional Tunnelling Company, he was transferred towards the end of 1916, in all likelihood in August or September (he is not specific about the date), to the staff of Brigadier General (later Major General) Harvey*, the Inspector of Mines at the BEF GHQ at Montreuil-sur-Mer.

In March 1916 this small, sleepy town, perched on high ground and surrounded by ancient defensive walls that had been renovated and modernized by Vauban in the late seventeenth century, was transformed into a hive of activity when Haig moved GHQ there from St Omer. The reason for this move was the extension in March 1916 of the British line southwards, replacing the intervening French Tenth Army. Thereafter the BEF's line ran continuously from north of Ypres to the northern heights of the Somme. The move to Montreuil-sur-Mer (in reality, by 1914, well away from the sea) had relatively good transport links despite lacking a railway station; whilst its centralised position to both the front and the supply bases, coupled with extensive accommodation, the basis of which lay in the École Militaire, made the new location a sensible choice. It was a small place – yet big enough to accommodate the substantial administrative machine that was required to keep an army that would soon approach 2,000,000 men in the field. Surrounded by walls that provided a clear perimeter and could be held securely, access to and egress from the town could be readily controlled by guards at the two entrance gates. GHQ was to remain there until the end of the war; though it should be stressed that, during a major offensive in a particular sector, GHQ established an Advanced Headquarters for key staff as the operational situation required – for the Somme, for example, at Val Vion and later Haig also used a train to position himself close to the relevant part of the front.

Dixon's posting to Montreuil was as an Assistant Inspector of Mines. His initial role was to handle plans and records; but in time he was appointed as one of the small group of junior, but experienced, officers who operated as the eyes and ears of the Inspector of Mines.

GHQ had a large number of junior officers from all arms who operated in a similar fashion. The Assistant Inspectors of Mines regularly visited all levels of the tunnelling command, from Army HQs down to the tunneling units at the front and elsewhere. All of these officers had experience with a tunnelling company in the field under their belt: in other words they had a very good understanding of the complex issues and problems at the front, many of which were unique to tunnellers. Their reports enabled the Inspector of Mines to comprehend fully what was happening at the front and in the intermediate commands between it and GHQ. This greatly facilitated coordination and through directives, technical advice and tactical notes, dissemination of lessons learned and best practice. In this way the experience gained by the men engaged against the enemy directly and their conclusions from particular actions or incidents, was passed up the line by those who understood the realities of this specialist type of warfare. In turn this led to various types of Army schools (each Army had its own mining school) in France to train tunnellers in a range of activities, such as the use of the latest rescue gear. At its peak, in mid 1916, the BEF probably had about 35,000 men engaged in the underground war, including infantry who were permanently attached to tunnelling companies as required. Personal communication like this provided direct contact between an officer commanding, say, a company of tunnellers working under Vimy Ridge, and the directing masters many miles away at Army HQs or GHQ. It was an important supplement to relying on written reports.

The Tunnelling Companies were almost entirely officered by non regulars; there were only two regular Sappers by the end of the war, one of whom was the General Inspector of Mines. They formed a relatively small group within the huge officer corps that the BEF had by 1916, so a knowledge of individuals played an important role in developing confidence in the command structure within tunnelling. One of the most important outcomes of the frequent visits from higher command (the Controller of Mines, responsible for mining at Army level, would also have his own team of junior officers, though at best only a couple of them) was to identify potential commanding officers for a tunnelling company – and in turn to assess their efficiency. Dixon's job at GHQ, which initially he held in the lowly rank of lieutenant but later as temporary captain, explains the wide range of his experiences during the war. His service was distinguished enough to merit the award of the MC in the King's Birthday Honours of 1918.

From early and primitive beginnings, the British army's engagement in mine warfare became increasingly complex. The war underground played a considerable role in the fighting along much of the length of the Western Front, starting almost as soon as the line stabilised in the winter of 1914 and reached its zenith in June 1917 with the blowing of nineteen mines along Messines Ridge. Mining had been an operational tool in the most recent major war, the Russo-Japanese War of 1904–1905; the Great War was to take it to new levels.

Given how quickly the Western Front evolved into static warfare, commencing offensive action underground was a logical operational tactic to employ, especially given the relative paucity of heavy artillery (and shells for the guns) at this early stage in the war. The different armies organised themselves to manage their mining operations in surprisingly different ways: an indication that no-one had anticipated tunnelling operations on any great scale. Although each of the major combatant armies had considered the possibility of tunnelling and made some reference to it in the tasking for their engineers in pre war directives, none of them was prepared for the scale of the tunnelling effort that grew so rapidly from December 1914. Given that there was no experience of this type of warfare amongst the combatants, the organization of tunnelling activity in the German and allied armies evolved rapidly through experience.

During the Great War the capability of Britain's tunnellers became technically highly developed in a remarkably short space of time. It is an early example of the willingness of the commanders of the BEF (and even the War Office) to adapt to the realities of the battlefield and the new challenges that faced the combatants. Although pre-war the Royal

Engineers had studied tunnelling, and in 1907 had actually undertaken some experimental work, the reality was that in 1914 there were no units designated to the purpose. In any event the field companies were fully committed to other essential engineer tasks. However, both the Germans and the French had been quick to take up offensive mining once the line stagnated at the end of 1914 and impromptu efforts were taken at brigade and divisional levels to counter developing German mining operations on the British sector. However, as the threat from German mining operations against the British line continued to grow through the early winter of 1914–15 the need to develop a counter capability became quickly apparent. It was then that the forceful personality of Major Norton Griffiths*, already in France, came into play. A dynamic engineer, an entrepreneur with wide experience of major projects in Britain and elsewhere in the world, and a Member of Parliament, he had urged the recruiting of civilian miners for the war effort as early as the beginning of December 1914.

The Secretary of State for War, Lord Kitchener, with whom Norton Griffiths had become well acquainted during the Boer War, summoned him to the War Office in January 1915. At a subsequent meeting in early February it was agreed that specialist Tunnelling Companies would be created under the Royal Engineers' cap badge. Within the same month the nucleus of 170 Tunnelling Company had been formed and was undertaking operations in France. Manning these specialist companies, given the urgency of the situation, involved urgent recruiting and deployment of miners and other tunnelling specialists such as those working on excavating great sewerage systems. They brought a wealth of experience, not only of coal and mineral mining as one might expect, but also of working in a variety of geological conditions, not least clay, which reflected the geology of much of Flanders. (A source of contention was the specialist rates of pay that experienced miners and specialists such as Clay Kickers received, much more than their infantry or sapper equivalents.)

Officers were found with civil and, particularly, mining engineering knowledge and thus a substantial number of its officer corps were experienced engineers who had returned from the various far flung corners of the empire, as well as in developing economies such as South

America. Civil mining techniques were quickly adapted to the battlefield situation and the mixed geology over which the war was fought. Specialists were brought in to advise the military. What was effectively a new branch of the army was swiftly created from scratch. By the beginning of 1916, as the mining war grew in intensity, and the number of formed tunnelling companies expanded, an effective command structure had been established, along with several training schools. Despite some set backs, within eighteen months of being first formed the Royal Engineer and Dominion tunnellers largely achieved dominance over the enemy across much of the BEF front. The British system, which developed from localized efforts at divisional level to the formation of the first tunnelling company in February 1915, soon placed mining operations under the responsibility of each Army (whose number gradually grew to five by mid 1916). The Army tunnelling staff had to coordinate, initiate and develop mining operations within their Army area. The task of the Inspector of Mines at GHQ was to set out an overview of mining tasks to each Army, to issue training manuals and develop best practice (in turn disseminated in Army Mining Schools of various types), to present at GHQ the case for the role of mining in the planning of operations – usually expressed through the office of the Engineer in Chief at GHQ – and to manage available resources, most notably in the form of the allocation of tunnelling companies to the individual Armies.

Mining operations were at their peak in 1915 and 1916 on the Western Front; the opening of the Battle of Messines on 7 June 1917 turned out to be the last great blast of major mining operations, at least as such things are generally understood, on the BEF's front. It was a complex, technically challenging war conducted underground, often a cat and mouse situation in which the two sides tried to outmanoeuvre each other, punctuated by mighty blasts in the front line area and a nerve-wracking experience for all concerned. The tunnellers (and large numbers of infantry that were attached to them for greater or lesser periods of time) often worked in challenging geological conditions, cramped, in poor air and with very little concern for safety; often they laboured under the risk of counter strokes by the enemy in the form of camouflet mines. The infantry above them were never enthusiastic about being in a mining area. Although mines that were fired as part of an offensive are well known – think of the blowing of the Hawthorn, Lochnagar and Y Sap Mines as part of the opening of the Somme offensive on 1 July 1916 – in certain parts of the line they were almost a daily routine. This was the case in Belgian and French Flanders in 1915 and 1916, along Vimy Ridge for much of the summer of 1916; and on the Somme front along Redan Ridge, in front of La Boisselle, at Fricourt and before Dompierre, south of the river for much of 1915 and the first months of 1916. It was no less intense along the French front, where substantial operations took place in the Argonne, most notably at Vauquois, but also in the western part of the forest from the earliest days of stagnant warfare to late 1916 and into 1917. The list goes on.

By mid July 1916 the BEF had available thirty-two tunnelling companies (twenty-five 'Imperial', three Canadian, three Australian and one New Zealand, plus a specialist technical Australian Company). A Portuguese tunnelling company came under the control of the BEF in 1917. The companies generally had a higher proportion of officers to men than in other units – usually about nineteen officers to four or five hundred tunnellers. However, tunnelling companies often had large numbers of infantry attached, be it as temporary labour or semi-permanent (the distinction was important, as 'attached' infantry would usually become the rationing and administrative responsibility of the unit to which they were attached), and the effective strength of a tunnelling company sometimes comprised up to a thousand men. We have produced the tables for the composition of two different tunnelling companies, taken a few months apart, in Appendices II and III.

As regards casualties, identification of tunnellers can be very difficult, with the complication of attached or temporarily attached infantry to be considered as well. The post-war Tunnellers Old Comrades Association lists one hundred and eighty-one officers killed or died, including twenty-four from Dominion companies. There are no published figures for the number of other rank casualties, but statistical analysis over various periods of fifteen companies indicates that the ratio of officer to other rank fatalities was about one officer to twenty-one other ranks. That suggests that about 3,800 other ranks were killed or died – see Appendix VIII.

Besides the work on fighting tunnels – that is tunnelling either to attack the enemy or to block enemy offensive mining operations – tunnelling companies also assisted the capability of the infantry by providing secure shelters for front line troops or those under the constant threat of shell fire. Obvious examples of these can be seen by a visitor today in the British sector in the Wellington Caves in Arras, a medieval underground quarry, part of several massive such works under Arras that were adapted for the use of mass numbers of troops; or in the Grange Subway under Vimy Ridge, one of over a dozen on the northern end of the Ridge that provided relatively secure access for the infantry to the front line. The Germans were engaged in similar work – be it the Prinz Arnulf Tunnel on Vimy Ridge or the Kronprinz Tunnel at Mort Homme, to the west of the Meuse, near Verdun; or in the excavation of secure dugouts for part of a trench garrison, such as the Bremen Redoubt in the Ypres Salient.

The tunnelling war was a strange one. The infantry regarded the presence of tunnellers in or near their trenches with disquiet as it almost inevitably meant that both sides were engaged in their own subterranean battle below the infantry's feet and things could turn out to be disastrous for them in the event of a mine going up. The reality was that once either side initiated mining on a part of the front the situation for the infantry was intolerable unless the enemy miners were countered. In many places it became effectively a private war, with very little tactical application to what was happening on the surface beyond defending one's own lines. In a 'busy' mining area, mines could go up very frequently, including large camouflet charges designed solely to attack the enemy systems. Alexander Johnson, a brigade major at Vimy at the time, noted in his diary in mid 1916 that he could almost set his watch by the 7 pm mine going off. Not only were mines an imminent and evident risk to the front line garrisons, but the infantry also had to be trained to act decisively in making best use of the crater that was thus created – or at least denying it to the enemy.

It follows that for much of the time the tunnellers were engaged in establishing defensive systems under ground – situating listening posts in deep saps to identify enemy activity and enable counter tunnels to destroy the enemy galleries and driving deep lateral (transversal) systems running parallel to and ahead of the forward trenches to block the enemy miners. In anticipation, mine chambers were often charged for use in future operations and then had to be maintained and protected. Few were left charged for as long as the mines under Messines Ridge, which were originally considered as part of a diversionary attack to distract the Germans at the opening of the Battle of Flers-Courcelette on the Somme on 15 September 1916 – a full nine months before they were actually fired with devastating effect in June 1917.

The underground war was also a highly technical one; techniques and methods of work evolved rapidly. Once the challenge of 'winning' an underground battle in a particular sector was accomplished, such as along Vimy Ridge by the end of 1916, then the tunnellers could turn their attention to other matters – in this case to the construction or development of over a dozen infantry subways on Vimy Ridge as part of the preparations for the Battle of Arras, which opened on 9 April 1917. On the other hand, although one side or the other might feel relatively comfortable in the knowledge that they had the upper hand, there was no room for complacency. As an example, the German miners on Vimy were still capable of a major offensive mining blow – the Longfellow group of mines remain today as an eloquent example of this, fired only a few weeks before the opening of the Arras Offensive.

The tunnellers' world involved extremely difficult working conditions. To avoid detection digging usually had to be done as quietly as possible although in chalk silence was often sacrificed for speed. Spoil had to be extracted – tons of it – and this could only be done by hand or by the use of fairly rudimentary trolleys, then removed and concealed to minimize the identification of new workings by the enemy. Air quality was often poor, with the risk of passing out through lack of oxygen, so ventilation systems had to be installed and pumping maintained. More seriously, carbon monoxide, given off from explosives and often trapped in the ground, was lethal in even small doses, and the hazard was only partially mitigated by using canaries or mice to detect its presence. On occasion combustible gases were released and serious casualties occurred not infrequently through gas explosions.

The tunnels were secured with the minimum of supports as timber was a scarce commodity and short cuts had to be made, even at the cost of endangering safety. Once a working was identified by the enemy the entrance to the various inclines became a natural target for his artillery – mortars were particularly effective for this job. Shifts tended to be long. The compensation was that the tunnellers, once out of their troglodyte working world, had their transport lines well back from the front and were relatively safe from anything but long range artillery and the occasional air raid.

Although administration, including record keeping, is a far from exciting topic to most people, it was something that took up a good proportion of the time of tunnelling company officers. They had to accurately survey, map and record their work (that sounds easy, but ...); they had to submit detailed returns every week to the Controller of Mines at Army Headquarters; they had to administer, ration, billet and supply their manpower – and this often included five hundred or more infantry attached to them, thus doubling their manpower. They had to source adequate technical resources. They had to liaise with local infantry units and formations, all to some degree resentful of the work of tunnellers in their midst. A Corps or Divisional commander might have definite views about how he wanted the tunnellers to operate and this did lead to clashes at higher command levels. Dixon mentions, for example, that the firing of mines at 'Winchester' in March 1916, described in Chapter One, was ordered by the Divisional commander against the expressed wishes of GHQ. A further constant complication to the administration of the companies was that it was common practice for one or more sections, which collectively formed a company, to be detached from the immediate area of the bulk of a company and to work on some task elsewhere in the sector and to operate separately in most administrative respects. The life of a tunnelling company adjutant was often not a happy one.

Although the firing of mines did notably diminish after the summer of 1917 (it is claimed that the last British deep mine was fired in August 1917, at Givenchy), the work of the tunnellers did not. There was still work underground in tunnelling – a good example of this would be the extensive efforts of Australian and British tunnellers in the Hulluch-Loos area where the elaborate interconnected subway systems extended to over ten miles along the front. The companies became expert in excavating mined dugouts – deep underground chambers, often with a variety of specialist purposes, at the same time as galleries and subways were still being driven and developed. However, tunnelling companies were increasingly used for new (to them) purposes, in particular after the withdrawal by the Germans to the Hindenburg Line in the early spring of 1917. As the BEF cautiously advanced over ground vacated by the Germans, they were confronted by an utterly devastated landscape – not one created by the incessant shelling by both sides, as it was in the battle zone, but by a deliberate and controversial scorched earth policy ordered by Ludendorff – a policy that was so brutal that it led to two of his senior commanders, Prince Rupprecht and von Gallwitz (the latter no shrinking violet), seriously considering resigning. Tunnelling companies involved in the advance over a substantial amount of French territory had to replace bridges, repair roads that had been mined and defuse numerous booby traps left by the departing German army. By the end of the war certain tunnelling companies had become expert in other fields new to them – for example, the New Zealand Tunnelling Company became well known for its expertise in bridging. Thus Dixon's memoirs cover a much broader range of engineering activities that came under the Inspector of Mines than might have been thought.

His manuscript, produced originally in 1932 or 1933, and offered for comment to his old chief, Major General Harvey, and then by Harvey to the Official Historian, Sir James Edmonds*, for his work on the Official History of the War, was intended for publication. For reasons unknown it remained no more than a draft. It was a time when the book-buying public (or the commissioning editors of the publishing houses) seem to have grown weary of the torrent of post-war memoirs; perhaps its rather light-hearted approach to the ghastly reality that was the war did not fit with the mood of a population that was battling the economic and social realities caused by the Great Depression. The version that we have here was typed in 1946; and even to this he added a number of further handwritten annotations.

At one point in his draft he comments:

> These digressions must be forgiven. Mark Twain, in his autobiography, claims that the only way to write is to put down whatever comes into one's mind at the moment, leaving the reader to sort it all out into proper order if he is sufficiently interested; and his method has a lot to recommend it, more especially when all one's diaries and records are 10,000 miles away.

It may be said that he has been faithful to this viewpoint as he frequently digresses and at times may be said to be rambling. In many respects this is a part of the charm of his script as he is in effect writing 'from the heart', looking back in retrospect and not unduly concerned with a structured tale.

He makes another telling remark: *the carnage and horrors of war have been deliberately omitted, for enough and to spare has been written about these aspects by countless others*; this reaction to many of the published war memoirs, it seems, determined how he would want to remember the war. He is primarily concerned with writing of the people he worked with, of the many personalities amongst all ranks and of his work on the staff at GHQ. This mainly concerned those involved with directing mining operations; but it included some of the other senior GHQ staff and characters with whom he had dealings. His often enthusiastic musing on individuals is richly leavened with anecdotes. This is a big part of the value of his account because it provides extensive insight into the overall conduct of mining operations and work at GHQ; a counterbalance to those who, writing of the sharp end of the Great War, tend to neglect, or be critical of the organization and work of the staff, without a full understanding of the complexities with which they grappled, and the daunting administrative and logistical complexities.

Phillip Robinson and Nigel Cave

The Lighter Side of a Tunneller's Life

By 'Dynamite'

(Assistant Inspector of Mines – GHQ)
(France 1916 to 1919)

Written in 1932

Read and approved for publication by
the late Major General RN Harvey, CB CMG DSO and
Brigadier General Sir James E. Edmonds CB CMG RE (Retired) 1933

('Dynamite' is still playing with Ammonal in August 1946!)

MS submitted by :-
Major HR Dixon
c/o Lloyds Bank Ltd. Bristol Street Birmingham

Note for Official Reader

'The Lighter Side of a Tunnellers Life'

This MS was sent home from Shanghai to the late Major General R. N. Harvey CB CMG DSO, who read it and passed it on to the Official Historian of the War, Brigadier General Sir James Edmonds. The latter also read it and sent it on to Messrs Peter Davis, who, quite nicely, declined it, as there was no market for war books at that time, 1933.

Since then it has not been offered to any publisher, though a Tientsin editor wanted to publish serially, after seeing the copy my brother had shown him. At that time I did not desire any further attempts at publication, and it has accompanied me on my wanderings back and forth across India and Burma and many thousands of miles in China.

It is referred to in 'Rocks to Remember – An Upper Yangtse Diary' which is at present in my bank at Birmingham pending an offer to Glasgow University for the benefit of Chinese students there, together with my thesis and application for a Doctorate of Engineering, 'Ten years of Conservancy in the Upper Yangtse'. It is also referred to in another nearly finished book, 'Tributary – Some Rivers and Some Men' for the Katharine Hunt Memorial Fund for the Ammunition Factory Hospital, Kirkee (Poona, India).

Apart from eliminating my own name where it occurs in conversations, the MS is in its original form, except for revision of punctuation in places, and one or two subsequent minor alterations.

It is suggested that even a poor cheese improves with storage, and may later be valuable as a contribution to the larder. Containing only some 30,000 words, it may be suitable for serialising in Blackwood's.

Parts of it were used by permission at General Harvey's request by Captain W Grant Grieve*, of my old Company, for his official book 'Tunnellers', which was published in 1936 by Herbert Jenkins.

This MS was returned to me in Shanghai by Messrs Peter Davis, in 1933, through the two generals.

'Dynamite'

Chief Inspectorate of Ammunition
Kirkee, POONA, India. 9th August, 1946.

Major H. R. Dixon R. E.
November 1932

To all Tunnellers and to their Inspector of Mines

"SALVETE!"

Out, upon the River, ships are swinging in the tide:
Casting off their moorings, drifting out to sea:
We are on a voyage, ending in a joyous ride
Right across old Flanders, as it used to be.

Dodging all the Minnies, bringing up the ammonal:
Pushing down the handles, listening for Fritz:
Writing it in triple, or yarning with another pal:
Bluffing on a pair, or packing up our kits.

Off to catch the leave-boat, lorry-jumping lots of it:
Back into the billets, and up the line again:
Cursing at the weather, caring not two jots for it,
If the jobs are tough enough to need our men.

Come from the Homeland, from your wide Dominions,
Tried and tested comrades of a long gone day:
Roam o'er the Front, aloft on memory's pinions:
Travelling together in the Tunneller's way.

"Hope Cottage"
K'unglint'on
Dec 1932

Preface

This book is an account of days spent in France by a young civilian, drawn, like millions of others, into the maelstrom of the war years. It does not pretend to be other than a personal record of events, great and small, in which he shared so long ago, and of the varied activities of one branch of the Corps of Royal Engineers. Neither is any claim advanced for exactitude of detail, though the events are described exactly as he remembers them, omitting those ghastly aspects of war we would gladly forget.

Many of the men he met will remember the instance in which they figured, and in doing so will doubtless recall a thousand others. No attempt has been made to give their full military rank and titles, for if they were Regulars they will be readily identified in Army circles, and to Tunnellers at least the Man always meant more than rank or gold braid.

They will understand the feeling of legitimate pride which the writer has always had, in that he was privileged to see their great work carried forward to the end.

The writing has been a labour of delight, all the better because life has again swung full circle, and the book has been written in various offices, ships, and houses secreted along the Yangtze, from Shanghai to the Gorges, and has been completed only a few hundred miles from the writer's birthplace, amid the towering limestone cliffs overshadowing the rapids of the Upper River.

With level and tape and compass ready to hand, he and the River Inspector, R. G. Everest, an ex-naval participant in the Jutland battle, are waiting for the river to fall, so the rocks now covered may be tunnelled and blasted, and the Channel, freed from excrescences, may became a little safer for the navigators of these treacherous waters.

In place of our one-time enemies, many of whom are now our friends, are the wiles and whirlpools of the Mighty River. Perhaps it will prove too strong for us, but at least we shall try, by the usual manner customary among sailors and tunnellers, to find a way of doing our job as negative architects, and we hope it will be possible to utilise the 8000 lbs of high explosive, now on its thousand-mile journey upriver from Shanghai, in a single blast. Memories of days long gone by inspire still and, if we are successful in our work, perhaps the time spent in the Grand Fleet and the mud and chalk of Flanders and France will contribute its mite to the better development of this ancient land of China.

Dynamite

24 Yuan Ming Yuen Rd.
Via Hankow and Ichang
Shanghai.

K'unglingt'an
Hupeh

November 1932

December 1932

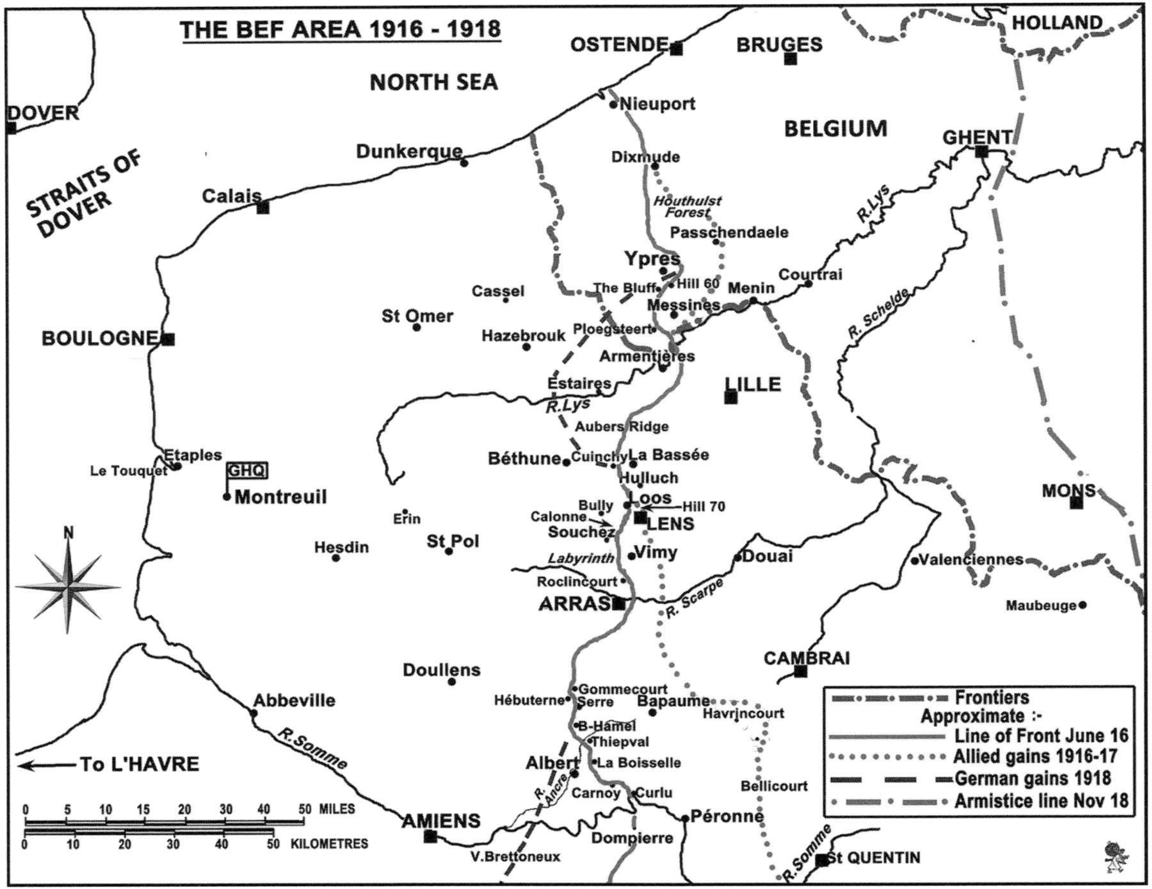

The BEF's area of operations from spring 1916, with some place names of notably intensive mining activity indicated. See also Appendix 1.

Chapter One

255 Company RE

Lead on MacWilliam, English and the rest,
Bring us to 255, One of the best.

My first acquaintance with tunnellers was at Chatham, to which delectable spot I was ordered to report from Shoreham, where for many months I had been a brigade bombing officer, instructing younger officers in the rudiments of explosives, the manufacture of hairbrush and jam tin bombs, and the elementary ideas on trench fighting that were all that could be gained by anyone who had not been overseas.

The transfer was only effected by disregard of the orders of my Brigadier, General Waters; he gave me permission to see the Secretary of the Institution of Mining and Metallurgy, provided that I did not go to the War Office.

Having satisfied the Secretary, Mr McDermid, as to my qualifications for tunnelling work, I was sent by him to a back street off Whitehall, and in an office there the matter was fixed up. It was actually a branch of the War Office, but on this point I successfully pleaded ignorance when, in due course, my orders came through, and I was carpeted for disobedience by the General. Actually he was always very good to me, and it was only after I left his command that I discovered I was listed as a permanent instructor and was not to go to France. He may remember the large tree in his garden, which he blew to pieces on Christmas (1915) as he said it was too big to break-up, and he asked my advice. Needless to say I recommended gunpowder, and was relieved to see him return safely to camp after the holiday. My assistant at the time was an excellent fellow from South Africa called Morphy, and the details of the scheme were largely his.

At Chatham there were a number of other South Africans, MacWilliam*, English* and Alan Bloom* among others, all of whom were in 255 Company RE with me later on. They had been in the German Southwest Africa Campaign, which had recently ended, and were looking for more trouble, like the stout fellows they were. John Brass was another name I recall, perhaps because he gave me a Dunhill pipe, which I treasured for many years after the war and it is still, I believe, tucked away under my bed.

Captain KJ MacWilliam, 255 Tunnelling Company, standing outside one of his company's mine rescue stations. These stations were located at approximately every thousand metres of mining front; for any rescue, speed was of the essence.

We left for France within ten days, going via Southampton and Le Havre, and up the Seine to Rouen, where we put in a week or so in the base camp. It was here that we had our first experience of a French bath, with a Mademoiselle (of uncertain age, be it said) to bring in the towels after we were in the bath.

[*From the meagre evidence offered by the War Diary of 255 Tunnelling Company, it would seem likely that Dixon crossed to France in late February 1916. The Company was formed on 6 January 1916 at Estaires by 'infantry', from some forty different units'. The Company took over the work previously carried on by the 173rd Company RE opposite Aubers Ridge in front of Neuve Chapelle to le Tilleloy. It spent much of the war in French Flanders. Dixon joined it when they were in the Neuve Chapelle area and to the south of that well known place. By the time that he left them, around December 1916, they had side-stepped south to the sector between Calonne and Souchez, taking over a part of the line that had been held by the French Tenth Army until that was withdrawn in the early spring of 1916. One of the unfortunate aspects of 255 Tunnelling Company is that its War Diary is distressingly short – for some reason or the other it only has details (rudimentary*

No. 32 (Tunnelling Officers) Class at Chatham.
Back row: 2nd Lieut A. Walker, 2nd Lieut G. K. Podd, 2nd Lieut O. C. Harwin, 2nd Lieut J. A. Jameson, 2nd Lieut C. E. Bailey
Middle row: 2nd Lieut J. M. Moubray, 2nd Lieut J. F. Smith, 2nd Lieut P. S. Blunden, 2nd Lieut C. K. Thomas, 2nd Lieut F. T. Marley, 2nd Lieut C. C. Arnell, 2nd Lieut G. R. Bernard, 2nd Lieut W. R. McKim
Front row: 2nd Lieut A. E. Painter, 2nd Lieut R. F. B. Burnett, 2nd Lieut G. E. Preece, Lieut G. H. Greenwell, 2nd Lieut F. L. Simpson, 2nd Lieut W. W. de Mattos, 2nd Lieut H. L. Morton
[Of the above, GR Bernard MC (254 Tunnelling Company) was killed on 8 April 1917: Bethune Town Cemetery, III.K.55, 'One who never turned his back'; and AE Painter (171 Tunnelling Company) died of wounds on 14 April 1917, Trois Arbres Cemetery, Steenwerk, I.H.5, 'To live in the hearts of those we loved is not to die'.]

at that) from October to almost the end of December 1916. Why this should be is unknown – there was a weeding of records post-war but even the second copy, at Chatham, is no better than the one held in the National Archives. We have included, as Appendix II, the Field Return for the composition of the Company on 18 November 1916; by way of comparison, and illustrating the evolution of tunnelling companies, we have included the composition of 3rd Australian Tunnelling Company for March 1918 as Appendix III.]

Then away by train to Estaires, a long weary journey, but relieved by a bit of tunnellers' luck. There was only one decent carriage on the train, labelled 'Reserved for TCO', and in our innocence we took it to mean 'Reserved for Tunnelling Company Officers', and boarded it accordingly. The Train Conducting Officer, whose carriage it was, proved to be a good sportsman, so we travelled in comfort, regaling ourselves with biscuits and paté de fois gras on the way.

On reaching Estaires we found a Company lorry and went out along the La Bassée road to Company HQ, which was in a farmhouse. It was getting dark as we arrived and in the far distance we could see the Very lights rising and falling, while the sound of guns and the chatter of machine guns made us realise there we were at last at the front.

The OC, Major French, put me into Captain Wing's section, and in the evening of the next day I went up by lorry to the section front, which was at a part of the line called 'Winchester'. It was a wonderful time to arrive, as five mines were due to be blown the next night; and all that day was spent with AW Runciman* in examining our workings and testing the mines in position. At 9 o'clock the OC and Wing arrived, and while the former looked after one mine further along, we took on the four near our dugout. This by the way was no real dugout, but merely a roofed shelter in the front line trench adjoining our shaft. There was a magneto exploder for each mine, and it was arranged that Runciman and I should turn the handles of the exploders while Wing pressed the buttons at the proper moment.

At 10 o'clock we duly fired them. The last one seemed a bit obstinate and I can still hear Wing's excited, *Turn, you blighter! Turn!* However it went off, and the guns opened for the barrage to protect the raiding bombers. We sat on a plank halfway down our mineshaft, congratulating ourselves on having such a nice cushy spot to retire to; for in that area the water level was so near the surface that it was not possible to dig down for ordinary dugouts. Our complacency was to be rudely shattered, for our eyes began to water freely, and though we tried the rubber goggles we carried, we soon found that the shaft was filling up with tear-gas from the German shells, and we scrambled into the comparative clear air of the trenches. Partially blinded, I soon lost my way, and in the glare of our own gun flashes and the rain of whizz-bangs from the enemy guns, wished heartily that I was back in the security of Shoreham. But at last, more by

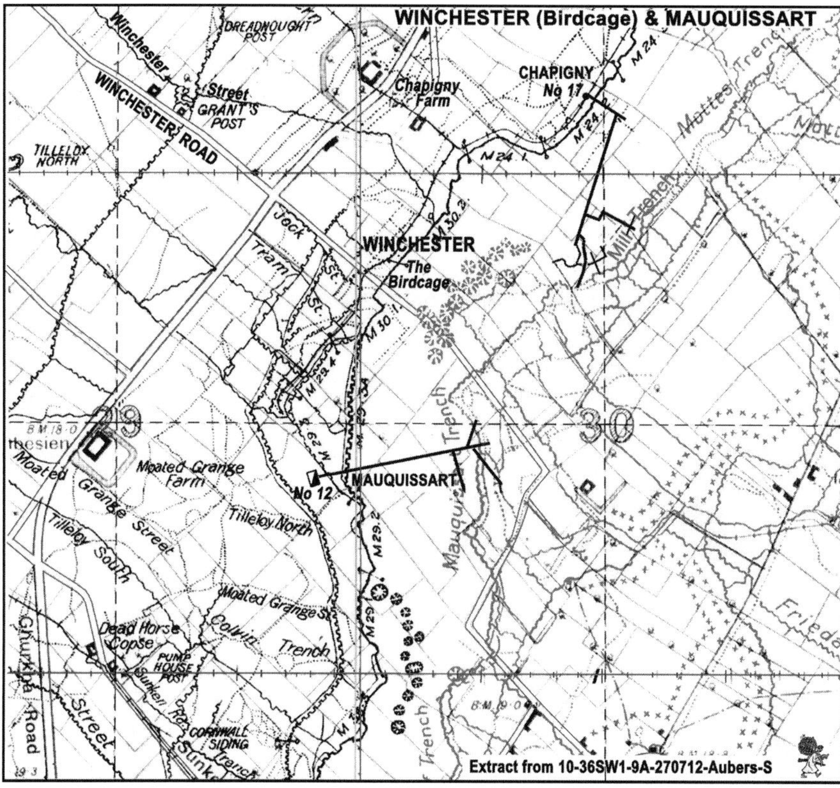

Trench map showing the location of the mines blown on the evening of 20 March 1916. The location is to the north east of Neuve Chapelle.

good luck than management, I found my way back to the dug-out, where Runciman found me a job to do. It was 4 o'clock in the morning before I got back to HQ and tried to find a drink in the mess. The only thing I could discover was a bottle of port. The indignation of the Adjutant, White, at the idea of anyone drinking port before breakfast left me cold, for I felt I needed it.

It was the year later that I heard from General Harvey that these particular mines were blown by order of the divisional general, against instructions from GHQ. It had been intended to reserve them for a contemplated attack on Aubers Ridge.

[*First Army Mining Synopsis for the week ending 23 March 1916 has an entry for the Winchester Road mines: 'On evening 20-3-16 we exploded 5 mines under enemy parapet and works. Charges: 2000, 2000,*

A tunnelling officer and a senior NCO are carefully testing the firing circuit for a mine charge. It was customary to have back-up means of ignition in case of the electrical option failing.

1200, 1500 and 2000 lbs. The left mine is thought to have destroyed the German shaft from which galleries were being run on the left flank of our defence system. Defence gallery on both our flanks now being pushed out. No signs of enemy mining since 20-3-16.']

This terminated my connection with 255 Company Royal Engineers for the time being, as the next day I was ordered, as the last joined officer, to report to the 23rd Divisional Tunnelling Company, which was being formed for special work on a sector to the north of Vimy Ridge. But I was to see a lot more of 255 Company later on.

[*The formation of 23rd Divisional Tunnelling Company was in response to the British taking over the Artois front from the French. The French Tenth Army came out of the line here, in part as a response to the German assault on Verdun, which had commenced on 21 February. This move marked the end of the series of major offensives, collectively known as the Battles of Artois 1914–1915, the major British contribution to which was the Battle of Loos in September–October 1915.*

Divisional tunnelling companies and brigade tunnelling sections were by the end of June 1916 more or less phased out, their functions (and quite often their mining manpower) absorbed by tunnelling companies. These divisional units were often ad hoc creations to deal with a particular tactical situation. It is easy to forget that the length of line held by the BEF increased quite dramatically through the summer of 1915 to the early spring of 1916. There were simply not enough tunnelling companies to take on the extensive mine warfare activity in which the French army had been engaged under these sectors of the line. An example of this can be seen south of the Somme, which the British held for a few months in the late August and autumn of 1915. In the preceding months there had been a quite ferocious mining war there, with a lunar landscape of mine craters now dominating the line, most notably from Fey and to the immediate west of Dompierre, stretching on towards the heights above the Somme at Frise. 1st/2nd Wessex Field Company Royal Engineers were initially despatched to deal with the problem before they were replaced by 183 Tunnelling Company, one of no less than five formed in October 1915 in Rouen, and sent to the southern Somme Front. This is indicative of both the paucity of tunnelling companies in the BEF and of the substantial mining threat here at the time. It was not until July 1916 that the last Tunnelling Company, 256, was formed.

The Controller First Army produced a report, dated 25 March 1916, detailing the mining issues that had been inherited from the French when the British took over the line in Artois on 17 March. This is reproduced in full in Appendix V and shows the extent of the challenge that First Army faced when its southern flank was extended so significantly to an area that had seen some of the most substantial fighting of 1915. For the purposes of Dixon's narrative, the key passage relates to the 23rd Divisional Tunnelling Company: 'At sectors Nos. 2, 3,4 and 5, the work is being done by the 23rd Divisional Tunnelling Company (300 men) assisted by 200 Infantry from the 2nd Division. Until this Divisional Tunnelling Company is approved as a proper Tunnelling Company, it is liable to have to move with the Division and leave this sector without any miners.']

Before joining the new Company, I was sent to Béthune to the First Army Mine School for a course in Mine Rescue work and the use of the special oxygen apparatus. Albu from 255 Company was there also, and at the Globe Café in the Grande Place we met many of the First Army Tunnellers. Albu had a narrow escape here at my hands. I had been showing him my automatic, when it went off and sent a bullet through the floor, close beside his foot. The dear old French couple living in the room below were quite unperturbed. 'N'importe M'sieu, ce n'est rien!'

The new Company were short of a surveying officer and the OC, Captain Williams*, asked me to take on the work. We had extended our line a long way to the south, and the front allocated to us for mining defence work was about three miles long, covering an important part of the line in front of the village of Boullay [sic – Bully] Grenay. The line ran in among colliery pit heaps, through the mining village of Calonne, and then away to the chalk hills forming the northern flank of Vimy Ridge. The French had apparently handed over no details of their own mines, and even trench particulars were lacking. Therefore our first work was to survey the three miles of trenches; and in my Batman, Alfred Round, a moulder from Wigan, I found an excellent man with the tape, accurate, patient, indifferent to the worst weather that the wet spring could produce, and one who combined attention to his tape with a wonderful ear for rifle grenades, 'minnies', and other little interruptions. We often had anxious moments and it was to his eye and ear that I owed my life on many occasions. He belonged originally to the 2nd Worcesters and remained with me until the summer of 1918.

In the course of our work we discovered three French mines, running from abandoned dugouts, and quite unguarded. The exploration of these with Captain Williams was an eerie job, as we could not be sure that they had not been discovered and entered by the Germans. Luckily this was not the case, and they soon formed a part of our mining defences. The enemy had not shown any sign of mining activity on this front, but it was such a suitable one for it; and the French, having blown three small mines previously at a spot known as Bully Craters, we were on the lookout for trouble.

One night Thomson and I detected enemy working under one of the old French galleries at Bully Craters, and listened to them passing

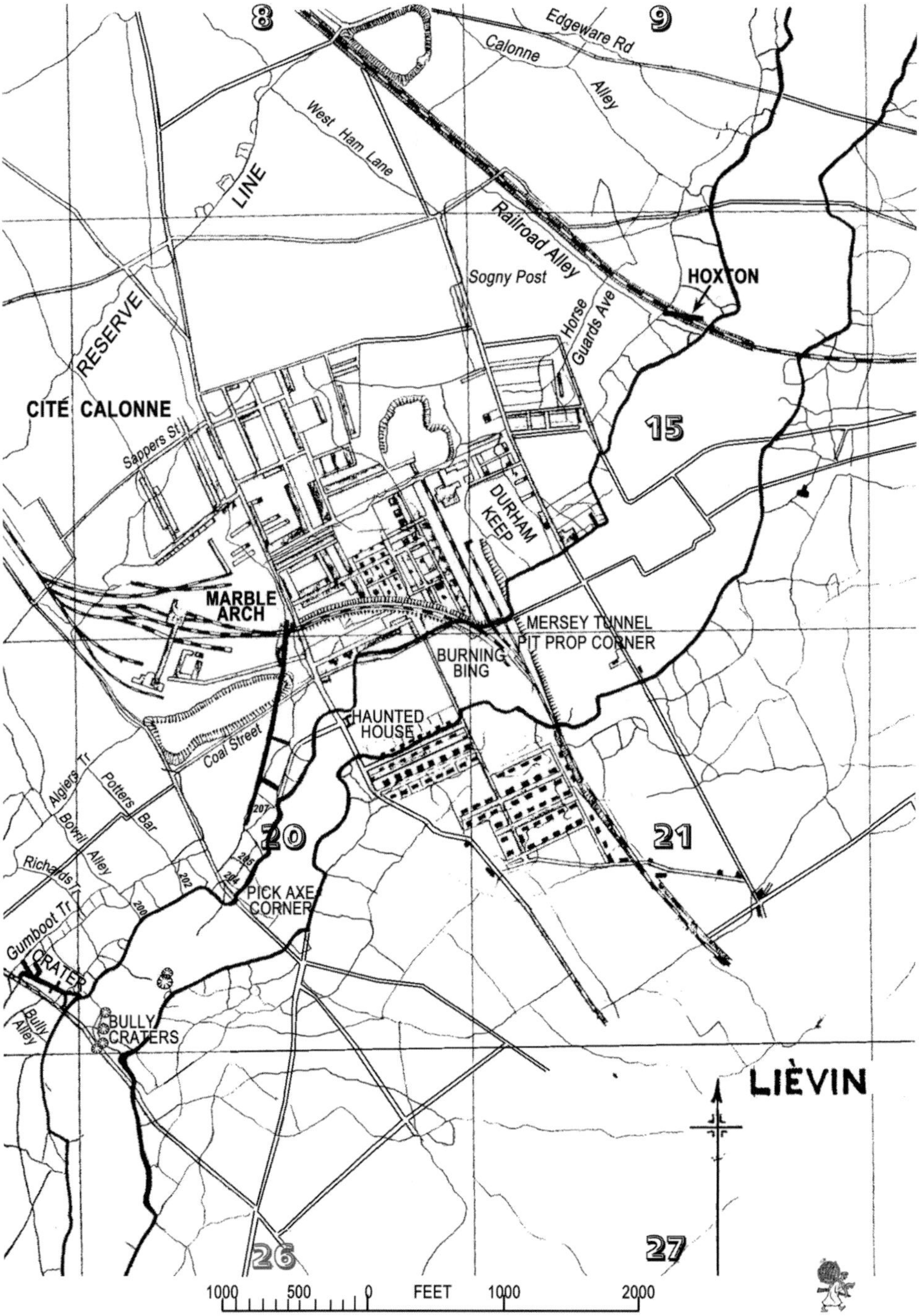

Extract of a First Army mining plan dated March 1917. The mine blown on 25 June 1916 was near Bully Craters, at the bottom left of the map.

ROYAL ENGINEERS
Tunnelling Officers' Mines Rescue Class, Dudley Rescue School.
20 July 1916.

J M Moubray, R F B Burnett, G R Bernard, F L Simpson, G K Podd, A Walker, C K Thompson, W W De Matois, F G Marley, W H McKim, J A Jameson, O C Harwin, G H Greenwell, J F Smith, K Howl Esq, P Hancock, P S Blunden, G E Preece, Capt W C Hepburn DSO, H L Morton, C C Arnell, *Ast Instr* A E Painrer, F Hancock, C E Bailey, Sergt Instr

backwards and forwards, and even heard them talking. The OC was on leave, but Colonel Williams, the Controller of Mines, First Army, decided that we should blow a charge of 4000 lbs of ammonal in the gallery the next night.

The preparations lacked the guidance of the OC, very sadly. Thirty men were in the gallery on their knees passing explosives and bags of earth up to us for laying in position, and it was not long before the air was very bad, as no air pumps had been provided. However the work was done by about 5 o'clock, the charge laid, and 60 ft of gallery tamped with sandbags behind it. It was tested, and great was my relief when at the appointed zero hour, 6.00am, the mine went up.

A mine rescue squad in training, learning to use the Proto breathing apparatus. The squad had to be fit men, as the equipment was cumbersome and made working very difficult in what would be in any case a restricted and dangerous space.

By 2 o'clock of the same day we had a series of excellent photographs from the Flying Corps, showing that nearly a hundred yards of the German front line had been obliterated, and for a while we had no further trouble from them on this part of our front.

[*First Army's weekly summary, dated 29 June 1916, notes: 'We exploded a mine on 25/6/16 near Bully Craters. Otherwise this front has been very quiet. The 255th Company will take over the whole of this area on the removal of 23rd Divisional Company.' The 23rd Division as a whole had begun its move away from the sector in mid June, preparing for its role in the Battle of the Somme; it was replaced by the 47th (London) Division, a territorial formation. Incidentally, the same mining report records the heroic action in the Givenchy sector of Sapper William Hackett, 254 Tunnelling Company. On 22 June, after a German mine was sprung, he insisted on staying with a comrade until both could be evacuated, despite the fact that a rescue party had reached him after two days and Hackett could have escaped. The collapse of the 'running ground' meant that the two men were lost. Hackett was the only tunneller to win the VC in the Great War whilst working underground. A recently erected memorial in Givenchy now commemorates his heroic sacrifice.*]

Shortly after this the 255 Company took over the whole of our front, and the 23rd Divisional Company was disbanded.

Other mines were blown by us on various occasions, but a part of our front was handed over to my old Company, and we thus became close neighbours. At Calonne they experienced a catastrophe; for, having broken into a German gallery and found it charged, they arranged to steal the charge, but for some reason the Germans were aware of the discovery, and blew. Major French* and many others were caught, either by the mine or by the heavy trench mortar barrage put down by the Germans.

An example of a mine explosion, the location unknown. It was quite likely fired as part of a training exercise or demonstration. The picture illustrates clearly the risk of falling debris. As a general rule, the Germans were considerably better than the allies in occupying the mine craters that resulted from these blasts.

[*This incident took place on 1 July 1916, before Dixon had completed his transfer to 255 Company. First Army's weekly mining summary, dated 7 July 1916, noted: 'At Calonne on 1/7/16 we entered an enemy gallery which was found to be charged and tamped and before it could be withdrawn the enemy exploded it, killing ten Sappers. During subsequent shell fire directed on our shaft head, the OC of the Company and another officer were killed.' Laconically, it goes on to observe: 'On 5/7/16 we exploded a charge from an adjoining gallery, smashing the enemy lateral from which talking could be heard.'*

The editors have traced the commemoration place of most of those killed: Killed by mortar bombardment: Major C J French, 5th King's Shropshire Light Infantry, attached Royal Engineers, buried Noeux-Les-Mines Communal Cemetery, I.L.3; and Captain Matthew Roach, Royal Engineers, age 28, commemorated on Bay 1 of the Arras Memorial. Junior ranks killed and buried in the Loos British Cemetery: Lance Corporal George Brewer, aged 23; 2nd Corporal W Mc Kenzie; Sappers L Clarke; Thomas Hands, aged 23; T Jones; W Stevenson and J Surgenor. Also killed but not recovered and commemorated on the Loos Memorial, Bays 4 and 5, Sappers James Crozier and Richard J Brown. We have been unable to track down the commemoration place of the twelfth soldier.]

To my delight I remained on the same front and returned to 255 Company, actually handing over to myself in the most approved red-tape manner. Thereafter came a period of section work in the line in company with Runciman and Wing and others, which I shall always regard as one of the pleasantest spells of my life.

We had a few mines to blow, and the rats gave us endless occupation, but my memory of that summer stands out against a background of scarlet fields of poppies, stretching away to Vimy, all aglow in the westering sunlight. [255 Tunnelling Company were nevertheless much engaged with defensive mining. See their Weekly Mine Report for 10 November 1916 as an example, Appendix IV.]

The record of this period would not be complete without mention of one of the biggest, if not the biggest, fright I ever experienced. I was waiting one night for a working party from the Guards, who were then holding the line, and was standing on a duck board leaning against the side of the trench, at the junction of Gumboot Trench, and another, the name of which I have forgotten. [Possibly Richard Trench.] I felt something on my left shoulder, and turning my head I saw an enormous rat! I gave a wild yell and jumped clean into one of the sump holes into which the deep water in the trench drained itself (sometimes!). It was a long while before my horror of rats left my dreams undisturbed, and to this day there is no other creature, unless it is a Yangtze mosquito, for which I have a greater dislike.

Chapter Two

255 Company RE (continued)

Telling of busy days, and merry nights
spent in the Mess far from the Verey lights.

So far no mention has been made of one of the principal factors in making the life in this Company so attractive. On the death of Major French, a worthy successor to a fine leader had been found in Major WH Morgan*, now (1939) County Surveyor for Essex. He had had wide experience in tunnelling in London, and so was exceptionally well qualified for the work in the similar conditions in the northern part of the British front; and later on, in the tenacious, yet almost fluid, blue clay of Ypres and the Passchendaele Ridge. The Company gained an enviable record for achieving the almost impossible. [*255 spent some time in 1917 in the Ypres Salient, notably the notorious area of the Bluff, before sidestepping south and occupying a sector on the Franco-Belgian border.*]

Towards the end of the summer of 1916 he asked me if I would be willing to take on the work of Adjutant to the Company, as White was leaving for duty elsewhere. It should perhaps be explained that the nominal strength of the Tunnelling Company was about 400, but very large parties of infantry were usually attached as unskilled labour, and the total strength was often over 1000 men. It had therefore become the custom to refer to the man in the office who was technically graded as 'Assistant to OC' as the 'Adjutant' . His duties were fairly heavy, as may be imagined, but he could not get up the line except by way of a joy ride.

However, I enjoyed the work with Major Morgan, ran the mess, and paid the rent and the gas bill for our Headquarters. A Tunnelling Company usually contrived to make itself comfortable, and so the billets were sited well back from the line, which was reached by lorry in the case of the men, and by motorcycle by the officers. As the autumn drew on our thoughts turned to rugger, and a series of matches against other

Companies and units provided us with a lot of fun. We had a fine lot of Welsh miners in the ranks, and the South African contingent among the officers contained some of the most prominent of the interstate players.

Our pack was a very heavy one; in fact the biggest man in the company, 'Big Dickson', weighed over 15 stone and, being tall in proportion, he was really rather a drawback to decent packing in the scrums. So we decided to bring me up to centre three-quarter from my favourite place at full-back, to which I would only agree if 'Big Dickson' was brought out of the scrum and put on my wing. The result was a distinct success, as he scored four or five tries in the next match. The first battle in which tanks appeared had just been fought, and it was not surprising that when three or four opponents failed to bring him down, our supporters raised the cry of 'Go it the TANK'. [*Captain EJQ ('Birdie') Dickson RE* was killed by a sniper when serving in the Ypres Salient on 26 October 1917; he is buried in Lijssenthoek Military Cemetery: XXVII. A. 19.*]

Major Morgan had come to us from 170 Company, and he and the new OC of that Company, Major Manning*, received their majorities about this time, and it was decided that there should be a joint dinner in our

The original and unusually elaborate cross and surrounds of 'Birdie' Dickson's grave in Lijssenthoek Military Cemetery (XXVII A 19). He died on 26 October 1917; to his right is Second Lieutenant Ofield RE, who died a couple of weeks later.

mess to celebrate the double event. As this was the one occasion that I can ever remember of a really uproarious night in France, it may be worth describing.

Officers normally did 48 hours of duty in the line, and came back to billets for 48 or 72 hours off, as the available strength permitted. Consequently there was a goodly gathering from both Companies, reinforced by a strong contingent of guests. It was clearly up to me as Mess Secretary to make adequate provision, regardless of the size of mess bills that month.

After the cocktail stage had been safely negotiated, some ambitious person (it was not English) suggested a champagne competition, full glasses on the table, emptied down the throats of the competitors, and replaced on the table. Each competitor paid an entrance fee of 5 francs, and there were no non-starters. The first, second, third, fourth, and fifth rounds were won by English, after which Sammy Shepherd* went quietly to sleep at the end of the table. The dinner went well, to the accompaniment of songs of wide variety, and I can remember being so rude as to interrupt a conversation with Major Morgan in order to rush to the windows as though it were the side of the ship. Thereafter the noise grew in proportion as coherence diminished, until a dozen stalwarts were singing Kaffir songs, dancing to them on the long mess table. This had been specially made by the Company carpenter and was a work of art, but its strength proved insufficient, and it crashed at last among the ruin of smashed glasses.

Soon after this I went to bed, but was no sooner asleep than Runciman, the most abstemious man in the mess, woke me up. He insisted that he was not going to sleep until he had kissed me, and being nearly twice my size, he did so after a struggle. Not feeling satisfied with this, he turned me face downwards on the bed and spanked me good and plenty. In the morning his recollection of the incident was none too clear, but I can assure him that it was so. When I went across to the orderly room in the morning our Sergeant Major, he was a regular, remarked to me, 'Well Sir, I've seen some sick looking folk in my time, but I can't ever remember seeing anything like you gentlemen this morning all my life.'

Writing as I am with no notes or records available, it is not possible to recall the names of all those in the mess that night, but I expect that most of the following were there from 255 Company: Dickson, McWilliam, Albu, Percy, Grieve, Conner*, Morton*, Rees*, Rogers*, Richards* as well as those whom I have mentioned above.

[*Alas, Major RC Manning DSO MC Légion d'Honneur was killed in action on 6 September 1918, aged only 29, during the opening day of the Advance to Victory on the Flanders Front. 170 Tunnelling Company War Diary notes on that day: 'Major Manning wounded in the morning whilst on the Cambrin – La Bassée Road; died at 7.15 pm at 22 CCS Pernes.' He was a northern Irishman from County Down and left a widow at home in Anglesey. He is buried in Pernes British Cemetery, VI A 38. He had had the distinction of commanding the very first of the Tunnelling Companies for over two years.*

Second Lieutenant Percy Rogers RE of 170 Tunnelling Company was killed on 27 May 1918 at the age of 20; he is buried in Noeux les Mines Communal Cemetery Extension, III C 13.]

A group of officers of 255 Tunnelling Company outside their billets in Arques at the time of the Armistice. Pictured (left to right) are Major WH Morton, Captains HL Morton, KJ MacWilliam and S Shepherd; Lieutenants AE Young, J Christopher, GB Lambie and F Haywood. (M Morton)

Captain HL Morton and Captain EE Rees of 255 Tunnelling Company in late 1918. It is interesting to note that they are still wearing their badges of rank on the cuffs of their tunic sleeves, which appears to have been the practice of all of the Company's officers. (M Morton)

Some few of them I have met since the war at the only Tunnellers' Old Comrades Association Dinner I have been able to attend; but I am glad that I can still recall that merry night; and perhaps gladder still that it can never be repeated!

During the summer I had been able to get in touch with an old stable companion of mine at Gravesend, Colchester, and Shoreham, in the energetic shape of Norman Venner, who has since become well known for his magazine stories and novels. He was still in the Middlesex Regiment, and was in the line near me at Vermelles. I had dinner in his mess more than once, and was shocked to hear one night that he had been hit in a raid, and was in hospital at Lillers. Rushing there on a motorcycle, I was told by the sister in charge that he was under chloroform, but that he could not have been hit in a safer place, though sitting would be out of the question for some time. Later on we met again at Caterham, but since the war our paths have not crossed, to my great regret.

Another old friend had been located in Jim Buchanan*. He had lived in digs with me at Glasgow for two years before the war, and great was my delight to find him in the mess of 180 Company one day when I was calling there. He had been a bombing officer with the Cameronians for eighteen months, before transferring to the Tunnellers, hoping perhaps for a somewhat quieter life after the rough time he had been through. But his Company were up at Hulluch and the Hairpin during one of the most active mining spells, and those who knew the front in those days will agree that it was no health resort, even for a Tunneller. We dined together at the Le Paon d'Or in Béthune thereafter.

Jim was perhaps the greatest friend I ever had, and it was a sad blow to learn long afterwards that he had passed out in a railway accident at Edinburgh, when on leave from the front. [*He was killed in a railway accident on 18 February 1918, at the age of 25, and is buried in Cathcart Cemetery C 12 A.*]

For the benefit of any readers who may perhaps feel that I'm blowing a trumpet of the tunnellers too loudly, I will mention that though casualties in the Companies were high, particularly during the active mining periods of 1916 and 1917, they never approached those of the infantry. I recall my feelings on this point after conducting an infantry officer round our mines at Boulay [sic *Bully*] Grenay. He remarked that he would not have our job for the world, to which I naturally replied that I would not swap with him for anything on earth, that I had never been over the top and never wanted to, and that I thought the infantry were the finest lot going. After all we did have our dugouts and mines to retire to when shelling was hottest and though many miners fought as infantry on occasions of emergency, and won undying credit in every instance, their ordinary job, while calling for a class of cool courage, which, fortunately, is always found among civilian miners, was in reality far easier than that of our patient foot slogging comrades, who, let us never forget it, really won the war.

* * *

The asterisks represent a spell of trench fever during which I was unconscious. It was not long after my return to duty that the Controller of Mines, First Army, Colonel GC Williams, called to see Major Morgan. He later sent for me and told me that General Harvey, the Inspector of Mines at GHQ, had asked him to find an officer to take charge of plans and records in his office, and that he wanted to recommend me for this post.

At this time GHQ was to me a remote abstraction, and figured in my imagination only as a place where red tabs were plentiful, and where nothing was ever actually done about the war, which was of course really being won on our own little sector of the seventy-mile front. If the thunder of the guns on the Somme had not taught me any better sense, it was probably because I had never thought about the matter at all, being too busy.

But Colonel Williams was so insistent that I finally told him that while I had no desire whatever to leave the Company, I would abide by Major Morgan's wishes in the matter. The latter advised me to go, encouraging me by promising that if ever I wanted to get back to the Company again he would do his utmost to get me. So it was left at that for the time being. Soon after this a peculiar incident occurred at Headquarters, which nearly got a faithful old miner into serious trouble, apart from the injury he suffered. We had in the old farmyard that formed our billets an incinerator. One old miner was in charge of it, and he had given a false age on enlistment in order to be admitted to the army. However in due course his age became apparent, and he was given this job to keep him out of the hardships of the front line. As he had eight children, there was already reason for this course in his case. All the sweepings from the billets were put into the incinerator every morning, and on rare occasions a live round of rifle ammunition would get swept up off the floor and explode later in the incinerator. One day the Sergeant Major reported to me that the old man had been wounded in the hand. At that time orders were very strict that any man wounded in the hand or foot was liable to be arrested for self-inflicted injury, unless he could satisfy his OC as to the origin of the wound. In this case it looked obvious that the wound was of his own making, as we were three miles and more from the front line and there had been no shelling in our neighbourhood. Careful inquiry, however, proved that the man had indeed been shot by the incinerator as he claimed. He went to hospital, and his successor was no doubt more careful to see that live rounds did not get put in for the future.

By this time I had acquired a rudimentary knowledge of both poker and bridge. After leaving the company I never again played cards in France, not because I was unwilling to do so, but because of lack of opportunity. But in the 255 Company there were many expert players of both games. Poker was the more popular of the two. Most of the little I learned about it was taught me by Big Dickson. It was said that he had played for years in Mexico, had frequently won, and had always got home safely with the money. No higher testimonial to his ability at the game could be given. But of course the very little knowledge that I did acquire cost me quite a lot of money.

At the same time there is a lot to be said for the theory that one never knows a man until he has played poker with him. Big Dickson was to fall to a sniper's bullet in the advance on Passchendaele a year later, but I can never play or watch a game of poker without thinking of that strapping figure getting well away on the wing at rugger, or lolling back in a chair in the mess, bluffing all the pair holders out of a big pot with a hand only ace high.

In due course my orders came through to report to GHQ and I handed over to Conner, who not many months after lost his arm when the billets were heavily shelled, on another front. My kit was packed and Private Round and I sallied forth in the box car into the unknown.

Chapter Three

First Days at GHQ

Of a strange city, set upon a hill,
Of scarlet tamped ones working with the will.

As we sped along in the box car, I could not help regretting my decision to exchange the known and pleasant existence with the Company for the terrors that no doubt awaited me. All I knew of Brigadier General RN Harvey was that he was a regular RE of the strict type, and after Major Morgan's kindly discipline I did not expect to enjoy the change over much. At the same time there can be no denying that there was a certain thrill in the feeling of getting to this mysterious GHQ, especially for one who less than two years before had been a private in a Middlesex battalion, a cipher among the toughest variety of raw London recruits.

We passed through Lillers and Hesdin, and so to Montreuil-sur-Mer, which I was not to leave, except temporarily, until a couple of months after the Armistice. The ancient walls, built by Vauban, frowned down at us, and we drew up at the Boulogne Gate while the HAC [*Honourable Artillery Company*] sentry examined our passes. At length I found myself reporting to Major Stokes*, who informed me that the General was away, and would see me in the morning.

Smythe* [sic – Smyth] and Major Logan* took me along to their mess for dinner and I turned into my billet feeling very lost. In the morning a thunderous rap on the door woke me up, and in came a sergeant of the HAC. 'Sorry, Sir,' he said, 'I've come to tell you that your batman is in the guardroom for being drunk last night.'

Here was a pretty pass. A General of unknown, but believed, great ferocity to be met, and no Batman! I asked the sergeant if he could not be sent over under guard to do his job, and soon after a very shame-faced and miserable looking Round went through the motions of cleaning belts and buttons and boots, until they would not have disgraced the C-in-C himself. With quaking heart I set out, and in due course was shown into the General. My first impressions of him are as vivid as ever. A sturdy figure was surmounted by a head of dark hair, receding slightly from his temples. His jaw was square, and a military moustache, tinged with grey, added a touch of ferocity to the strong face. His voice was harsh and his manner abrupt.

'Well, what have you been doing before? Oh you've been an Adjutant, have you? If I'd have known that I shouldn't have had you. How much do you know about plans and surveying?'

I told him what my experience had been. Grunt. A pause, another grunt.

My heart was trying to escape from my boots.

'Well we'll give you a trial, but you've got to work here, do you understand? Major Stokes will tell you what you have got to do.' And with that I found myself dismissed from the presence, and shortly was established in a cubicle office a few doors down the corridor from the General's room.

At the time of the photograph, General Sir Douglas Haig. He was promoted Field Marshal in the New Year's Honours List of 1917. He held the post of Commander in Chief of the BEF for all but a month of the three remaining years of the war; he was appointed in mid December 1915 to replace Sir John French. No other commander of the combatant armies on the Western Front with similar responsibilities survived so long in post. Dixon was a great admirer of Haig.

I should perhaps explain that GHQ France was a vast organization, of which the main combatant departments were grouped under 'First Echelon', and this was then, and indeed until the end of the war, at Montreuil. The Commander in Chief, the Chief of the General Staff, the Adjutant General, and the Quartermaster General had a chateau outside the town, and the C-in-C was seldom visible for long at the École Militaire, where the offices were. In fact I can only recall seeing him on two occasions during the whole of the time I was there. This was partly because our own office hours were so long that we seldom had a chance of being about at a time when he would be making a visit. Also I regret to say that I never attended Church Parade for the same reason, for there I should have been sure of seeing him. To me Haig* will always remain the fine soldierly figure that I saw one day at the entrance to the École in conversation with the much shorter, but no less soldierly, figure of Sir William Robertson, who was then Chief of the Imperial General Staff, and had been over for a conference. A finer figure of a senior Cavalry officer than Haig presented that day would be impossible to imagine. In the life of Lord Haldane* there is a touching account of how the one-time Secretary of State for War was sitting alone in his room on the afternoon at the great peace procession in London. The thoughts of the lonely man may well have been bitter, when he mulled over the way in which he had been shelved by an ungrateful country because of an unlucky phrase he had once uttered. A knock came on his door; there was an officer to see him. And behind the butler came the Great Commander in Chief, fresh from all the adulation at the crowded streets, and a triumph greater than any Roman ever knew.

General, later Field Marshal, Sir William Robertson. For an army that was accused, with some justification, of being class ridden (not that any continental army was much better in this regard), he retains the unique achievement of rising from the rank of private (trooper) to field marshal. He became Chief of the Imperial General Staff at about the time Haig got command of the BEF. Both men were convinced 'Westerners' and made a harmonious partnership. He was sacked as CIGS in early 1918; he and Lloyd George, to put it mildly, did not hit it off.

'I came to bring you this,' he said, and handed to him a bound copy of all his Dispatches from France. It was inscribed: 'To Lord Haldane of Cloan, the greatest Secretary of State this country has ever known, to whom in a greater measure than to any other man is due the success of the British Armies in France.'

I cannot now check the exact wording of the inscription, but that was the substance of it. My mind went back as I read it to a day twenty years and more ago now, when I had the honour of presenting Lord Haldane with a bound copy of the history of my old school at the prize-giving. He had, as Secretary for War, inspected our OTC in the morning, and his handshake was an honour that I shall never forget.

Richard Burdon Haldane (1856–1928), First Viscount Haldane (cr. 1911). He was Secretary of State for War between 1905 and 1912, holding the post for six months short of seven years and at a crucial time in the evolution of the British army. The position was concerned solely with the army; the admiralty had its own political head, the First Lord, and both post holders were, at the time leading up to the war, members of the Cabinet.

Haldane either introduced or implemented many reforms, amongst these the creation of the roles of the Chief of the Imperial General Staff and the Army Council, the development of the Territorial Force, the planning for a British Expeditionary Force and a host of other reforms. Not without reason, he has been described as the finest Secretary of State for War of the twentieth century.

But it is of Haig that I am writing now, and there could be no truer a key to his inner character than this simple thought for one whom he might so easily have forgotten on such an occasion. It is only the greatest of men who do things like this.

The Inspector of Mines, or I of M's, office was regarded as a branch of the Engineer-in-Chief's department, and at that time Major General Spring Rice was Engineer in Chief. Of him I never saw very much, although his successor, Major General GM Heath*, made use of me directly for various work during 1918, which will be referred to in its place.

The organization of the I of M's office at this time was as follows: Inspector of Mines, two Assistants known as AI of M, a Mine Rescue Officer, and a Mechanical Engineer. There was a Chief Clerk, Mr Collie*, and two other clerks and two draughtsmen. But of all this I then knew nothing. I knew Major

Stokes was AI of M, and that was all. Later I came to know Major Logan as the mine rescue officer, and Smyth as the Mechanical Engineer.

My work consisted of putting into shape and keeping up-to-date the plans of all mining operations along the British Front. In addition I had to read all the daily intelligence reports from the Armies, marking for the General all references to matters that might affect our branch, and examining the weekly reports from the Companies in the same way. Later on we made a series of albums of air photos of the various mining fronts, and early in 1917 a complete aerial strip album of the Hindenburg Line. This was made weeks before the Germans showed any indication of an early retirement to this line, but General Harvey was selecting points for possible mining attack even then.

Major General Sir Spring Rice was the Engineer in Chief of the BEF from February 1916, having previously been Chief Engineer of Haig's I Corps at the outbreak of the war. He was to hold the job for some eighteen months. From the point of view of the tunnellers, his appointment to replace Major General Fowke at GHQ came at a crucial time, just as the new system of the control of the tunnelling branch of the RE was coming into effect. They were fortunate to have a supporter in him, which was not necessarily a given.

I found my first impressions of the General confirmed as the weeks went by. He was indeed a martinet, and at last I was in despair of ever meeting his requirements, and only looked forward to an early return to my Company. About this time the Chief Clerk, Mr Collie, came in one morning with a file, and said 'I thought you might like to see this, Sir'. I looked, and could hardly believe my eyes, for there was the General's recommendation that I should be appointed AI of M (No. 2 of course and junior to Major Stokes), with the acting rank of captain. It was the pleasantest shock I had had for a long while.

But as though to cure any possible tendency to a swelled head, the General became harder to please than ever. But now I was better able to understand what he wanted, and by degrees things were got into a shape that elicited only grunts instead of a rasping, but quite deserved, criticism.

Let me digress here to say that two years ago I was rung up by an unforgettable voice at my hotel in London. 'That you, Dixon? General Edmonds told me you were in town. I've been looking for you ever since the war. Come and have lunch!' And it was with something of the old trepidation that I found him in the Army and Navy Club in Pall Mall. He gave me two cocktails, and he had only himself to blame for the result. He was told exactly what he seemed to be like in those old days to his junior assistant, and of the terror with which I used to listen for his ring. The signal for my presence in his room was supposed to be five rings on my bell, but usually it was about fourteen, and the bell would still be ringing when I was in his office and approaching the judgment seat. On one occasion Smyth, who was a metal miner from South Africa, had been asked by one Company for a supply of 'sylvesters'. He happened to mention it to me one day, and I told him they were a common form of chain-jack used in collieries at home, and that in fact I had seen one illustrated in a catalogue on his desk, under the name of 'Pit-prop withdrawer'.

He went out and not long afterwards the bell rang furiously and I went into

Brigadier General (later promoted Major General) Robert Napier Harvey was Inspector of Mines for two crucial years, 1916 and 1917, when the BEF's mining operations were at their peak. He was the first to hold the job when this branch of the RE was constituted as a separate branch at GHQ. The creation of the appointment was very much his work, as he was able to make full use of his post as Assistant to the Engineer-in-Chief. He presided over what became the most effective tunnelling organization amongst all the combatants on the Western Front and was able to retain its integrity as a branch even after mining operations substantially diminished after the Messines Offensive in June 1917.

the 'presence'. 'Do you know what a sylvester is?' 'Yes, sir,' I answered, and explained. 'Then why the devil didn't you tell me so before?' It would have been a waste of time to tell him that I had not known that there was any call for them, or that they were an unknown article to most metal men. But at lunch that day General Harvey heard this and many other stories, and laughed like the good sportsman he really always was. At the time he had just returned from being Engineer in Chief of the Indian Army, and no doubt had put considerable fresh life into the slower ones among the Indian regulars.

Major (later Lieutenant Colonel) Sir John [Norton from 1917] Griffiths Bt. Without doubt he was the father and inventive genius of the Royal Engineers' tunnelling companies. He led a quite extraordinary life, filled with daring-do; his early years were a mixture of soldiering and mining and developed into politics, when he was elected an MP in 1910. At the outbreak of war he founded, at his own expense, the 2nd King Edward's Horse (The King's Overseas Dominions Regiment). Given his mining background, it is no surprise that he took such an interest in this development in warfare on the Western Front from its earliest stages. His dynamic personality brought results in an astonishingly short period of time: the first tunnelling company (170) was formed in February 1915, within days of its approval in Whitehall.

His work as Inspector of Mines can never be too highly appreciated. From the embryonic and ill-organised service founded by the untiring efforts of Colonel Sir John Norton-Griffiths, General Harvey welded the Tunnelling Companies into the most efficient military mining force ever known in the history of war. That it was largely due to his personal efficiency and dogged enthusiasm that our greatest successes were ever achieved will be admitted by all those who served closely under him. Perhaps the proudest moment of his life must have been when he read a note from [then] Brigadier General 'Tavish' Davidson* of the General Staff after the successful explosion of the Messines mines and the capture of the Ridge. It ran something like this:-

> 'Dear Harvey,
> Congratulations on your wonderful success. I always did say that yours was the finest show in France.'

It must have been some consolation to him for the long days of strenuous work and anxious waiting which the operations at Messines had cost him. If I conclude this chapter by saying that General Harvey has been since those days a real friend to me in difficult times, it may perhaps serve to emphasise the errors into which the hasty judgment of youth is apt to fall; but I will add that long before he left GHQ, at the end of 1917, I had got to the stage of admiring his finer qualities, and of admitting, which was then a great advance for me, that he was 'sometimes a beast, but all the time a just beast'. No real disciplinarian can hope to stand much higher than that in the opinion of a youngster.

Chapter Four

Routine Life at GHQ

Australia's David leaves his rocks behind,
Antarctic blizzards, Flanders shells to find.

Not long after I reached GHQ a great event occurred in the arrival of Major David to join our staff. This statement conveys nothing to those not privileged to know him, but if there ever was a striking personality, it was his.

David was for many years, and still is, I believe, Professor of Geology at Sydney University, and had already been awarded the CMG for his work in tracing out the famous coalfields of New South Wales. He was an FRS, a DSc., and doubtless many other things. At the age of 50 he had been with the first Shackleton expedition to the Antarctic, and had travelled over 1,200 miles on foot with a small party and had discovered the Magnetic South Pole. He also led the first party to climb Mount Erebus, the famous Antarctic volcano.

When war broke out he had been largely instrumental in raising the Australian Mining Battalion. On its arrival in France, this unit became split up into the three Australian Tunnelling Companies and the Australian Electrical, Mechanical, Mining and Boring Company [*commonly known as the Alphabetical Company*], of which more will be said later.

One of the first problems which engaged Major David's attention was the variation of the water level in the chalk areas, a matter of the greatest moment from a tunnelling point of view. In the process of his researches he inspected scores of French wells, and of one at least he will still have a vivid memory.

He had been in the Noeux-les-Mines area, and came to one well which was eighty feet deep. David took his usual seat on a short plank across the bucket, and was lowered away. The windlass was an old one and the wedges fell out, with the result that David hit the dry bottom of the well with force enough to have killed anyone of less tough fibre. He was badly injured and went to hospital in England for some two months. [*In fact he had suffered internal injuries, a deep scalp wound and two broken ribs. He must have looked a bloody mess and been in very considerable pain. Never the less, as he was being hauled back up to the surface, he called up to his rescuers, 'Pull up slowly and give me time to observe the water levels'.*]

Major (later Colonel Sir Edgewoth) David, DSO January 1918), pictured in 1916. Pre war he had already established himself as an outstanding geologist and a redoubtable explorer of the Antarctic. A supporter of Australia's war effort, he lobbied for the creation of a formal tunnelling capability for the AEF, which eventually resulted in three tunnelling companies and the electrical and mining company. In France (by then at the relatively advanced age of 57) he took up a role for the then three British Armies in the field as a roving field fortifications advisor. After his serious accident in September 1916, he was brought to GHQ as the geological technical advisor to the BEF.

However, to everyone's astonishment and delight, he made a quick recovery, and was passed fit. This time General Harvey decided that David's proper place was on his staff, and so he came to GHQ at the end of November 1916 and shared my office.

Later he became better known as Colonel David*, and now he will be found in reference books as Sir Edgeworth David, and no man ever better deserved his honours or carried them more modestly. The special charms of his character were the utter simplicity and humility of the man, his keen sense of humour, and the kind way in which he dealt with all his juniors. It was said that he was the politest man who ever came out of Australia. I can still remember his method of addressing his batman. 'Johnson, I have left my Sam Browne in my billet. I wonder if you would mind stepping over for it, that is if you have time.' The gentle tone of his voice is impossible to explain; but it will readily be believed that David was loved by all who knew him and he speedily became one of the best known characters in the Army.

David was a keen supporter of Antarctic exploration and is here pictured (centre) with Dr Alistair Mackay (right) and Douglas Mawson at the South Magnetic Pole, 16 January 1909, claiming it for the Crown. Although David was the expedition's leader (appointed by Sir Ernest Shackleton), the physical strain of the journey caused mental issues, which resulted in the command being transferred to Mawson for the last part of the return journey. David rapidly recovered and became a prolific lecturer and publicist on the Antarctic region.

A group of Australian tunnellers at the Plumer's Road entrance to the Hill 63 'Catacombs'. The men are almost certainly from the 1st (Australian) Tunnelling Company, whose work in the war was mainly in the Ypres Sector, notably at Hill 60, but also here, near Plugstreet Wood, beyond the southern end of Messines Ridge. The Company erected a memorial on the southern edge of Hill 60 that was replaced by a more permanent structure, which was for many years the only one on the Western Front dedicated to tunnellers (if one excludes the RE Grave on Bellewaarde Ridge). The three Australian tunnelling companies (ie excluding the Alphabetical Company) spent their war almost exclusively in French and Belgian Flanders. It would clearly be unwise to pick a fight with any of these men.

He and I had great fun out of our interviews with the General. He would come back to the office after having been sent for to discuss one of his technical reports, and remark quietly: 'Well, well, it didn't hurt so much that time.' It was a standing joke between us that his attitude to the General was that of a small boy going to see the Headmaster. His reports were at first always written out, and once he came back very sadly, because the report had to be rewritten. 'The General says that nobody on the General Staff knows anything about geology, and I am not to use any technical terms. He asked me if I could expect anyone over there to know what an anticline is!'

His hardships in the Antarctic had seamed and lined his face with the semblance of one of those fissured cliffs he had spent his life in examining. I was delighted to see him in London for a few minutes in 1927, and to hear from General Edmonds in 1930 that he was still hard at work on one of his numerous books.

Sir Edgeworth David – perhaps understandably he used this name for public purposes, as he was christened Tannatt (he was born in Cardiff) – pictured towards the end of his life. He was knighted in 1920 (KBE) for his services during the war, but would almost certainly have been so honoured for his most impressive contributions to the science of geology. He was appointed Professor of Geology in 1891 at the University of Sydney and held the chair until his retirement in 1924.

His career underlined the nature of the BEF's tunnelling companies; the British were able to call on a large number of mining engineers from positions all over the world (many came from South Africa) and this resulted in a branch of the Royal Engineers that had very, very few regular officers: quite probably the smallest number of a branch of any corps of the British army.

It will be appreciated that David stands out as one of the most striking figures of the next two years of my life. Of Major Stokes I saw relatively little. He was constantly away up the line, and when in the office was always smothered in work. Before the war he had been a well known editor of technical mining publications in South Africa. About the middle of 1917 he succeeded Lieutenant Colonel Williams as Controller of Mines, First Army, in which capacity he did excellent work, until he left to take charge of RE work for the Murmansk Expedition [*against the Bolsheviks*] under Major General Maynard in the spring of 1918. In all his dealings with me he was uniformly kind, and the General's opinion of him is summed up in the remark he passed at the lunch already referred to: 'Stokes was the most efficient man I have ever met.' [*Dixon here has added a manuscript note*: 'When I last heard of Stokes, in 1940, he was endeavouring, in vain, to obtain an "emergency" commission as a second lieutenant.' *In fact he was to be successful, as is shown in this photograph, taken in 1940, of him amongst a group of 170 Tunnelling Company officers.*]

He achieved one record, possibly unique among GHQ officers. On the day that the Messines mines were blown he had been with General Harvey, Colonel Stephenson, Major David and others in the special box-

Officers of 170 Tunnelling Company at Chatham in January 1940

J.B. Simpson N.B. Walker

G.A.P. Moorhead, T. Pickering, J.H. Lander, R.G. Laver, D.J. Rogers, L.J. Foss, St. J.H.M. Findlay, J.E.A. Paterson.

A.R.O. Williams, A.S.W. Wood, G.G. McLea, R.S.G. Stokes, G.M. Edwards, N.S. Cowan, D.M. Thompson, R.T. Brandt, T.M. Keillar.

Those underlined served as tunnelling officers during the First World War. The re-forming of a tunnelling company was a short-lived need in the Second World War, especially after the Fall of France in May/June 1940. (Morton) seat on Mount Kemmel, and thereafter had followed the reserve infantry into the old German lines. Descending a deep dugout in the hope that it might lead to a German mine, he encountered a group of a dozen of the enemy, only too anxious to surrender to him. Luckily there was no fight left in them, and by a further fortunate stroke he had his revolver with him, and so claimed a fine bunch of prisoners.

Soon after my arrival I had moved to a billet in an estaminet, at which Smythe and Logan had their mess, and from which we never moved. The constitution of the Mess varied from time to time, but the permanent members of it were Logan, Evans and myself. Smythe went to the War Office about the end of 1917, and his place was taken in the office and the mess by JW Fidoe*, well known in South Wales mining circles as a consulting engineer. Major Dale Logan was a Scots doctor from Lanarkshire, who had made a special study of mine rescue work in collieries, and to whom was due almost entirely the high level of efficiency to which the rescue brigades and Mine Schools were brought. The makers of the 'Proto' and other oxygen apparatus used, Messrs Siebe Gorman & Co, will no doubt remember his visits to them in connection with detailed improvements in the design of the apparatus.

It must be a satisfaction to him that out of the great experience of rescue work gained during the war, there has followed extensive improvement and development of similar work in the coalfields of the world, resulting in much saving of life in many colliery disasters. He later became a lieutenant colonel, and earned his DSO by a remarkable piece of bravery and endurance when the deepest underground fighting of the war resulted in the death of some French soldiers 1,500 feet from the surface, in the grim darkness of colliery workings. This story will be told later on.

Evans was another remarkable person. He was the Chief Clerk to the Chief of the General Staff, ending as a major. He was of the finest type of the old army, and had served for many years at the War Office, knowing, as only a subordinate so placed can know, the idiosyncrasies of all the senior officers of the British Army.

But on current matters he beat any oyster for secrecy. Never once was he known to breathe a word about his immediate work, or to give the slightest hint of confidential matters. When it is realised that every secret paper dealt with by the CGS during the whole war passed through his hands, the record is one he may well be proud of. In the mess he was one of the best, and a great favourite with everyone.

For some months we had with us a colleague of his, Major Skeats*, who returned to the War Office early in 1918. Though of leaner build than Evans, he was equally cheery, and we used to delight to set them talking about old army days at the War Office and to hear their opinions of the great ones of the Army world.

For a very long time the Camp Commandant's Assistant, Bryant*, was a member of the mess. He was an HAC man and succeeded to his appointment under Colonel Thresher* when the previous holder (Ford*) became ADC to Sir Eric Geddes* and went to live at the Hutment Town, which formed the headquarters of the Director of Transport and which was rather rudely known to the rest of the Army as 'Geddesburg'.

Ford messed with us too for some time. I well remember how we pulled his leg when Sir Eric became a vice-admiral overnight, and abandoned

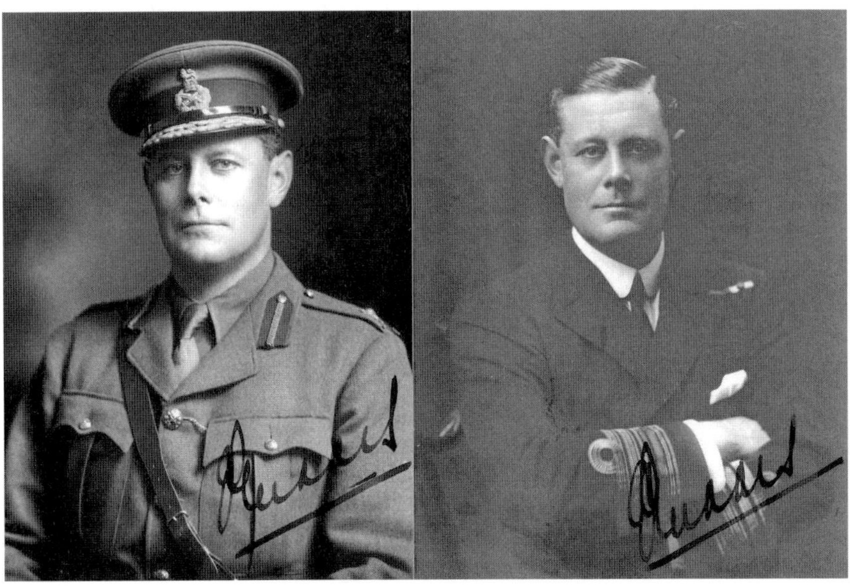

Sir Eric Geddes. He served in both the Army and the Royal Navy, bringing to bear his formidable administrative skills to the logistical challenges that both faced: the army, particularly ports and railways; the navy, shipbuilding in light of the German submarine campaign. In due course Lloyd George made him First Lord of the Admiralty (July 1917). He built up a close friendship with Haig.

his red tabs as a major general; for the newly made sailor wished to transfer him to the Royal Navy as a flag lieutenant, but Ford was too wise to go. It is no secret, and no real reflection on the present chairman of the Dunlop Rubber Company, to say that there was a great deal of jealousy of his rapid rise to favour among the Regulars. That he did wonders in organising railways in France into something approaching reasonable efficiency is well known, but the regulars who were shelved in the process thought that they might have achieved at least equal results had they been given equally dictatorial powers. There was always a feeling, too, that he was pushed on by political influence, and the traditional hatred of the Soldier for the Politician was more than maintained in France.

Bryant was a shipping man from Southampton, and he had some queer cargo to deal with in his job at Montreuil. All and sundry reported to the Camp Commandant on arrival, for allocation of billets or batmen. Among those reporting there one day was Leslie Henson, whose concerts were appreciated so much by the troops up the line. The Artists [*The Artists Rifles, 28th (County of London) Battalion, London Regiment*] and HAC, who always took guard duty at Montreuil, were frequent visitors to the Mess. Among them came AW Hawks, an old schoolfellow, Spicer, another Old Boy, and 'Molly' Royds, of the witty tongue.

A temporary member and frequent visitor was the Reverend Duncan, who was Haig's personal padre, and who conducted the service at his passing in Scotland. Duncan was a fine type of the Scots minister, and throughout Haig's tenure of the command in France and when he was in the Montreuil area the C-in-C very seldom failed to attend church parade on Sunday morning; we all felt Duncan to be a man of real conviction and a fine example of a Christian soldier.

The mess was excellently run for us by 'Madame', her old parents, and by various relatives, among whom 'Berthe', 'Marie Louise', and 'Marie' were the most prominent. We lived like fighting cocks for five francs a day. We were at the office until 1 o'clock, often starting at 8 am, and always returned after dinner, and worked until midnight, and at urgent times to the small hours of the morning. We were expected to take a good walk once or twice a week in the afternoon, in order to keep fit, but it was often impossible to do this. Therefore the heavy work, seven days a week, was a considerable strain, and for me a visit to the line always came as a welcome holiday. For the first year I had few such opportunities, but I spent Christmas [*1916*] with my old Company at Boulay Grenay, inspecting the German mines on this front, for the enemy had retired for a short distance. It was with interest that we compared the exact position of these mines with that surmised from our listening reports.

It was on the way back over the ridge, behind Calonne, [*see map in Chapter 1*] that I was hit for the only time in the war. The heavy batteries had moved up into Boulay Grenay, and the German counter-batteries were pounding away steadily at them. The only method of progress was a wild dash between shells, ending with a complete flattening in the little gutter beside the road as the next shell was heard on its way. As we passed the battery I was a moment too slow in getting down and a small piece of shell struck me on the double thickness of the Sam Browne belt. It cut through the leather, and raised a beautiful bruise. Had it landed anywhere else, my number might have been up.

The visit to the old lines recalls an incident that occurred with the 23rd Divisional Tunnelling Company at the time of blowing the 4000 lbs of ammonal described in Chapter 1. The successful blowing of the mine brought the Divisional General round to our billets in Barlin the next day, and at a formal parade he shook hands with Thomson and myself and congratulated us on the good work. This was in the morning. In the afternoon Private Round and I were surveying along Gumboot Trench. It was pouring with rain, and Round had to scrape the mud off the tape each time before he could read it. Suddenly a procession of officers appeared round a traverse, headed by the Divisional General. I saluted. 'Who are you?' 'The surveying officer of the Tunnelling Company, Sir.' 'Ah. Then you take no active part.' Shortly afterwards they passed us again on the return journey, and the General pointed with his stick at Round's rifle, which was slung on his shoulder. 'Is that loaded?' 'Yes, Sir', replied Round, drawing himself up as smartly as the mud would allow. When the procession had passed on I asked Round if his rifle was really loaded, as by regulation it should have been. 'No, Sir. But I knows Generals.' I felt he had made it all square.

These digressions must be forgiven. Mark Twain, in his autobiography claims that the only way to write one is to put down whatever comes into one's mind at the moment, leaving the reader to sort it all out into proper order if he is sufficiently interested, and his method has a lot to recommend it, more especially when all one's diaries and records are 10,000 miles away.

To revert for a moment to the Mess. It was a custom of Madame's to celebrate New Year's Day by presenting us with a large quantity of oysters and white wine. This was always a great occasion, and there were many 'À votre santé's'. Logan was no French scholar, but in his persistent Scots way would translate his ideas into a literal equivalent, delivered in an appalling accent. One day he decided to have a bottle of wine for lunch, and asked me to have some. On my declining he tried to convey to Madame that I was of a somewhat saintly disposition. His accent cannot be reproduced, but what he said was 'Madame, Monsieur Dixon, il est ong seinte' [*Madame, Mr Dixon is pregnant.*] Madame threw her apron over her head and rushed into the kitchen. We took good care to point out to Logan that as a medical man he should have known that I was unlikely to be in the condition described. We heard shortly after the War that Madame had married again. Her first husband had been killed early on. I cannot recall her name now, or the name of the estaminet or street, but her parents' name was Humbert, and perchance the estaminet still flourishes.

No description of life at Montreuil would be complete without reference to the ramparts. Montreuil was a sea port not many centuries ago, although it is now seven miles from the mouth of the River Canche, where Étaples, the great hospital camp during the war, is situated. The Canche winds around the old town to the north, hugging the citadel, and the great stone ramparts surround the whole town, there being only two gates, the north, or Boulogne Gate, and the south, or Abbeville Gate. It was therefore eminently suited to be the Headquarters of an army. In the old moat were numerous gardens, growing all manner of vegetables in the intensive French way.

It was about a three mile circuit along the top of the ramparts, and this was a favourite walk whenever walking was possible. The valley of the Canche is frequently visited by heavy thunderstorms, and many a wonderful display of lightning we saw on our way back to the mess at night. On the north side were some famous 'Grenouilleries', though I cannot remember whether my present liking for the delicate frogs' legs derives from Montreuil.

A view of some of the ramparts that surround Montreuil sur Mer, the home of GHQ BEF from March 1916. Its relative isolation on the top of a hill, yet proximity to good transport links, both road and rail, as well as its position roughly at the mid point of the British held line, made it an ideal location for the BEF's GHQ. A move from St Omer became increasingly necessary by early spring 1916 as the BEF extended its line southwards.

It was a pleasant spot in which to live, except when the Germans decided to drop bombs on Étaples. Montreuil lay along their direct route, and on a few occasions we had a few bombs too.

I have not so far made much reference to our Chief Clerk, Mr Collie. He was a former Army schoolmaster and after the South African war had married the widow of an old comrade, and he often showed me with pride the picture of his stepdaughter, in whose growth and progress he took the most affectionate interest. [*The Corps of Army Schoolmasters, formed in 1845, was succeeded by the Army Educational Corps in 1920.*] He was amazingly efficient, and could put his finger at a moment's notice on any one of the voluminous papers in the office. He stood with me one night at 12 o'clock, looking out of the window towards Étaples, where the bombs were dropping heavily. After a while I said I would make for the mess before the raiders returned, and he said he would clear my tray before he went. No sooner had I reached the mess than a heavy bomb fell in the town, and a few minutes afterwards Colonel Danford telephoned that Collie had been hit. He must have stayed on to watch the bombing, as he was still beside my desk. He died in hospital at Étaples, and another good friend had passed on.

[*Sergeant Major Alexander Collie MSM Medaille Militaire (France) RE, died of wounds on 3 June 1918, is buried in Étaples Military Cemetery LXV E 26. He probably died of wounds after the first bombing raid on Montreuil on 31 May; Collie would appear to have been the only victim. A second bombing took place on 21 August. It seems strange that the Germans did not expend more energy on bombing GHQ rather than nearby Étaples, although admittedly the huge complex there consisted of much more than the large number of hospitals of various types.*]

Chapter Five

Messines and Vimy Ridge

The Zero hour draws near for eager men.
At last the Ridges are within their ken.

From the time of my arrival until the day of the Battle of Messines, on 7 June 1917, the most important part of all our work was in connection with the great scheme of offensive mines for which this battle will ever be famous in military history. Twenty-one mines had been laid under the German lines, of which only nineteen were ever fired.

[*Dixon's memory has partially failed him here. Twenty-six offensive mines were laid ahead of the attack. A 20,000 lb secondary charge at Peckham was lost when the tunnel was flooded by fluid mud, although the main charge of 87,000 lb was recovered and used. At Petite Douve a 50,000 lb charge was lost to a German camouflet, whilst at 'Birdcage' (Ploegsteert) on the southern flank, four charges totalling 112,000 lb were deemed tactically unnecessary and not employed – see also subsequent note on pages 49 and 50.*]

They stretched from Hill 60 in the north, to St Yves in the south of the ten mile front. Behind the German line frowned the Wytschaete – Messines Ridge, which provided excellent artillery observation for the enemy over the Ypres Salient to the north. The whole hillside had been sown with concrete pill boxes of the greatest strength. The entire area was blue clay and saturated Flanders mud at its very worst, and the surface difficulties seemed insuperable for any attacking force. Underground they were no better, but shafts had been sunk and galleries driven slowly but surely towards the desired objectives.

Digressing again, it should be mentioned that there were at this time thirty-two Tunnelling Companies, as well as the Australian AEMM &

B Company already referred to. Of these, three were Canadian, three Australian, one New Zealand, and twenty-five Imperial. In the latter were a large proportion of South African officers, so that all the Dominions pulled their very full weight in the Service. The Canadians and Australians in particular took a full share in the Messines work. The 'Alphabet' Company, under Major Morse, was mainly responsible for the installation and operation of the many electric lighting, pumping and ventilating sets which the great development of the mines and subways soon necessitated.

Five officers of the Australian ABC Company in September 1916: from the left: Lieutenant George Norfolk MC (Adjutant), Captain Stanley Hunter, Major Richard Morse DSO (the OC), Lieutenants Loftus Hills MBE and William Logie. Note that they are wearing their badges of rank on their shoulders (cf. photograph on page 19).

The Australian Electrical, Mechanical Mining and Boring Company was tasked with supporting the whole BEF, specialising in lighting, ventilation and pumping for the great number of underground systems that were excavated under the British front.

Full details of the Messines Mines may be found in other books dealing more especially with the technical work of the Tunnelling Companies. But a few authentic figures may enable a lay reader to appreciate the magnitude of the undertaking. The total explosive used in the mines amounted to 993,200 lb. The largest charge and deepest mine was at St Eloi, where 95,600 lb was blown from a depth of 125 feet. The longest single gallery was at Petit Bois, and measured 2070 feet. The mine at

Hill 60 took fourteen months to complete, and some of the mines were completed and ready for blowing for fifteen months before the battle took place. The resulting craters varied in diameter from 214 feet in the case of Hollandscheschuur Farm No 2, to 417 feet at Petit Bois No 1 and 430 feet at Spanbroekmolen. [*Dixon has added a marginal note here: 'Taken from my own tables in Military Engineering Pam. IV (1923 Edition) a copy of which was lent to me by Major Mason CRE Shanghai in 1932.'*]

The scheme, like all other war schemes, was not conceived as a whole in the first place. The early mine fighting, which took place in 1915, was mainly at shallow levels, and it was not for some time that the idea of deep mines, running in the blue clay well below the German mine system, actually took shape. Thereafter one mine after another was started, and on many occasions the time was considered ripe for blowing those completed. But the Second Army Commander [*General Sir Herbert Plumer*] was biding his time. An unsuccessful attack would have been disastrous in every way; and General Harvey often told me that the credit for preserving the mines for that great day in June 1917 was almost entirely due to the determination with which Lord Plumer resisted all such temptations.

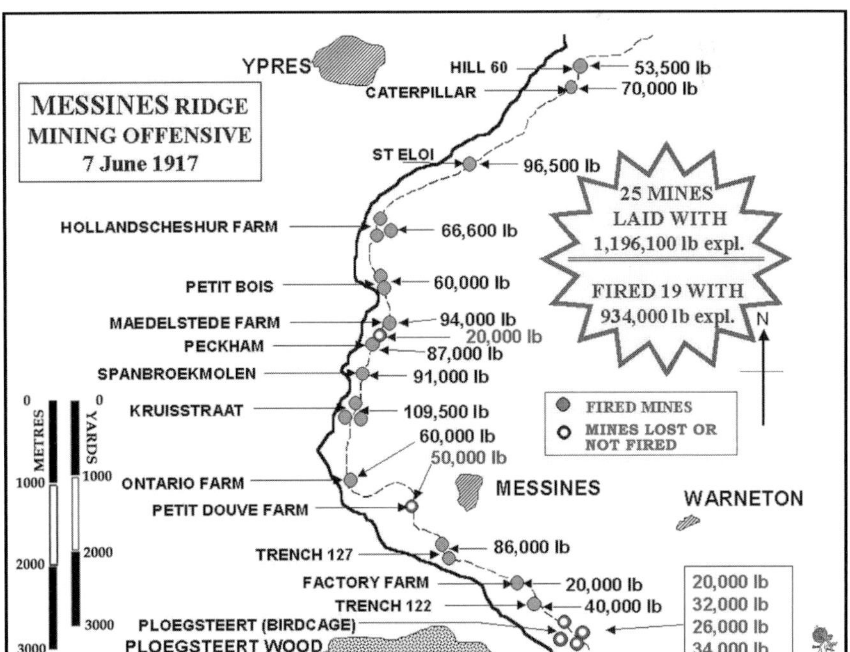

General Sir Herbert Plumer GCMG KCB, GOC Second Army May 1915 to the end of the war, with a few months absence to command the British Force in Italy from mid November 1917 to the end of February 1918. The oldest of the BEF's Army commanders (he looked older than he was and perfectly fitted the caricature of senior army officers), he was popular – not least amongst the Australians – and universally, if discreetly, known as 'Daddy' Plumer. After the war he was promoted field marshal (1919) and ennobled, fittingly taking the title of Baron Plumer of Messines (Baron 1919, promoted Viscount in 1929 – French had already taken the name 'Ypres'). Post war he was GOC Army of the Rhine, Governor of Malta and finally High Commissioner of the Palestine Mandate – a reflection of his multiple abilities.

The secret of the great mines was wonderfully kept, and no inkling of what was in store for them ever reached the German High Command. Although I knew the day was fast drawing near, it was not until the General, Major Stokes and Major David all disappeared together, leaving instructions for me to report the following night to Second Army HQ, that I had any indication of the Zero Hour.

I spent the day following the grand eruption in going over the whole front with General Harvey and Colonel Stevenson*, the Controller of Mines, Second Army. The scene of desolation along that front beggars all attempt at description by me.

What comes back to me as vividly as anything else was our lunch on that bright summer morning in the middle of what had been Wytschaete village. The General picked up some tins of German bully beef, and we found some of their biscuits too. After a hard morning's tramp they went down very well, until the General remarked that he hoped that the biscuits were not made from 'Kadaver' meal! [*This a reference to British propaganda that the Germans, due to shortages, were using human bodies for all sorts of purposes, including the manufacture of glue.*] Away in the distance, two miles beyond the ridge, the battle was still going on, but up there it seemed a place forgotten by the war. So much happens in so short a space of time on occasions, but after a wait of two and a half years, it seemed too good to be true that the Ridge was ours at last.

One of the huge craters created by the mass firing of mines along Messines Ridge; this photograph, with the men standing on its lip, is particularly effective in giving an idea of the scale of the crater that was created. All of the craters that were fired still remain, though they are filled with water, with the exception of the mine blown at Ontario Farm. Peculiar geological conditions meant a minimal crater resulted, though the force of the blast shattered the ground under which it was placed.

There were still two mines of 30,000 lb each unexploded. These lay to the south, and had been reserved for firing on the second day of the battle, to extend our right flank. But the precipitate retreat of the enemy, exceeding the wildest hopes of our staff, rendered them unnecessary, and their subsequent history is not without interest. For the rest of that year, and well on into 1918, we were in correspondence with the Belgian Government, through the Belgian Mission and our General Staff, over the question of the removal of these mines. Now it is one thing to put a mine down into blue clay, but it is even more difficult to recover the gallery and charges months afterwards, when the heavy pressure always experienced in such ground would have broken up all the timbering. It was therefore agreed that a careful survey should be made of the position of the shafts and that the charges would be removed later on, when the pressure of work on the Tunnelling Companies should be less heavy. Neat concrete bench-marks were erected, and everybody was happy. But when the Germans made their great drive on Hazebrouck in 1918, we naturally took the opportunity of declining any further responsibility for the twins, as we called them, and as far as I know these babies are still beneath the sod, and may they ever remain there.

[*It is curious that Dixon not only refers to only two mines but also to them as 'the twins'. Four charges were actually laid with a total of 112,000 lb of explosive. The configuration may suggest two pairs, hence presumably the reference to the 'twins'. As they lay outwith the immediate front of the attack they were not employed but kept 'in reserve' against the*

Birdcage Mine No. 3, which had a charge of 26,000 lb, blew during a thunderstorm in July 1955, to the east of Plugstreet Wood and the tiny hamlet of Le Pelerin. The mine was possibly detonated as a result of a lightning strike on a recently erected pylon. Fortunately there were no casualties and this photograph was taken shortly after the explosion and before the resulting crater was filled in. (Permission of A Prada)

possibility of the main offensive failing. Subsequently they were retained on a 'care and maintenance basis' until the area was overrun in the German Georgette offensive in April 1918. One of them manifested itself dramatically in July 1955 when it exploded during a thunderstorm, creating a crater 250 feet across and 60 feet deep, since filled in.]

Prior to the Messines offensive, the other great attack in which the Tunnellers took a vital part, the capture of the Vimy Ridge, which occurred on 9 April 1917, had also given us much very interesting work.

For this scheme a number of large mines were prepared, all of which were also blown without a single failure when the day came; but the principal role of the Companies on this front lay in another direction.

[*Vimy Ridge. Dixon's memory is again at fault. Although the Tunnelling Companies set out to lay seventeen chambered offensive mines and nine wombat (bored) mines, only three of the chambered mines were used to support the attack on the Vimy Ridge, along with two wombat mines. Two chambered mines were employed prior to the attack. Eight of the others were not employed for perceived tactical reasons, leaving one unaccounted for. Three of these have been investigated by the Durand Group, who made two safe and found one had been salvaged. One Wombat mine chamber was destroyed by a German blow, the situation of the other six Wombat mines has not yet been resolved. The main contribution of the Tunnelling Companies was the construction of infantry subways along the line of the front down to the River Scarpe, along with the Arras subterranean systems.*]

The line ran in a blunt salient to the east of the fine old town of Arras, from which the ground rose at a steady gradient to the summit of the famous ridge. The ground was all chalk, except for a few feet of muddy top soil, and it was decided to construct subways in the chalk, which would enable troops to reach the front line without crossing the open country, in which all the communication trenches were constantly under heavy shell fire. Once again the Tunnellers luck came to their aid. The first subway [in Arras] started from an old sewer tunnel in the town, and had not gone far before a cave was struck. As it progressed others were met with, and it was soon realised that the whole area was honeycombed with them. They were actually the old underground quarries from which the hard chalk had been obtained for the building of the town. An elaborate system of connecting tunnels soon grew up, and the caves were transformed by careful timbering into dugouts capable of housing many hundreds of troops and giving perfect protection against the heaviest shells.

The subways were taken right up to the front line, and a number of shallow headings driven out under our wire, from which, during the night before the attack, the Tunnellers broke through to the surface. There was therefore a complete safe approach from the town to the middle of No Man's Land. On the day of the attack over 10,000 troops were brought up through the subways in perfect safety, and they were able to emerge from them and to assemble for the attack in front of our own wire. [*Most accounts state that 20,000 troops could be accommodated safely in the Arras caves.*]

The total length of tunnels and subways constructed for the attack was over 15,000 feet. The New Zealand Company, together with Canadian and many of the Imperial Companies, played a great part in the work involved. The Caves became the stock joke of that part of the front. A local Corps Commander would ask for increased accommodation for troops, and the OC would enquire 'east, west, north or south, Sir?' Within two or three days a cave would be found in the required direction and the necessary accommodation provided. It was largely as the result of the work done at Arras that the construction of subway defences on other parts of the front was developed to a point far in advance of anything previously attempted by military engineers. Undoubtedly they were the means of saving thousands of lives in the subsequent stages of the war, and enabled the long-suffering infantry to live in a degree, not perhaps of comfort, but of less discomfort, than was ever thought to be possible in the front line.

In another chapter reference will be made to one of the later subways constructed under the ill-famed Hill 70 at Loos. New Zealanders will recognise the handiwork of their own Company in the names given to the caves of the St. Sauveur Tunnel. Russel, New Plymouth, Auckland, Wellington, Nelson, Blenheim, Dunedin, Christchurch, all represented caves at Arras to our minds in those days. [*Once more, Dixon's memory has*

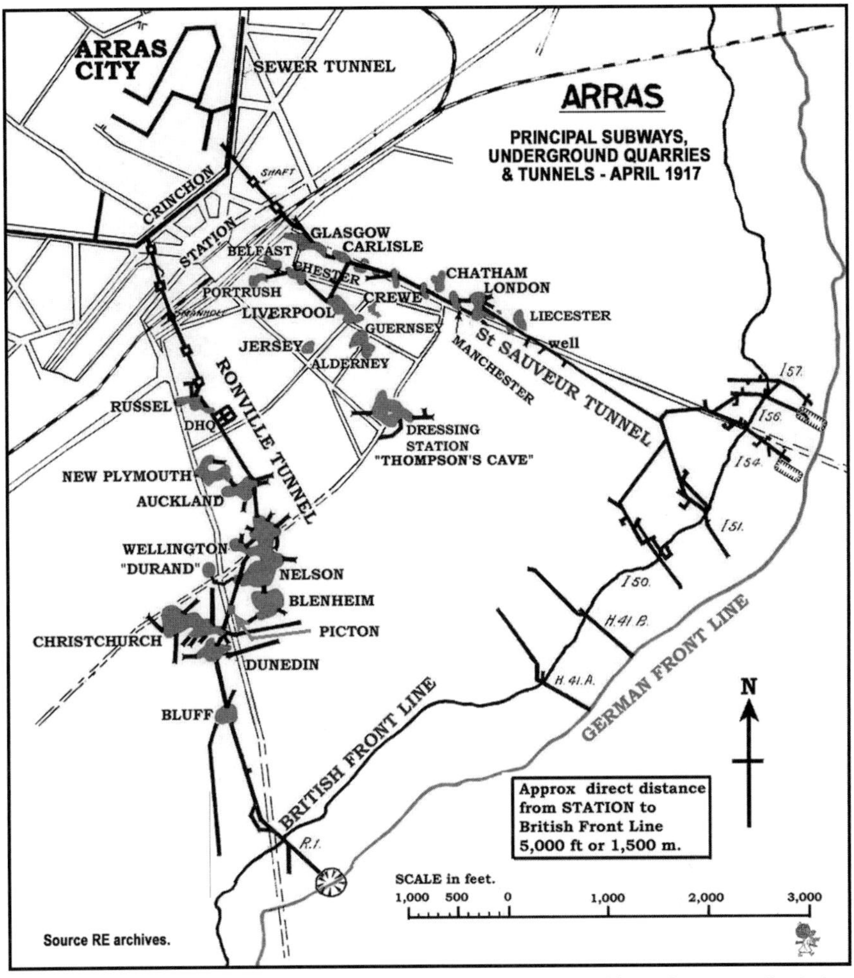

The extensive nature of the underground work under Arras, taking advantage of existing caves, is clearly illustrated by this map.

played him false on several points. The New Zealand Tunnelling Company were primarily responsible for developing the Ronville System, as is evident from the names given to the various caves. The St Saveur System was initially developed by 184 and 179 Tunnelling Companies, the caves being named after cities in Great Britain – see the plan of the Arras subways and caves above. The NZ Tunnellers took over St Saveur in about February 1917. If the connecting passageways and those constructed within all the caves are included, the total passage length was about 37,000 feet (11,300 metres). The subways along the front north of Arras, essentially along the full length of

Views of the Arras Caves and Souterraines. Clockwise from top left: A wartime Easter Sunday service, 8 April 1917, in Wellington or Blenheim Cave; a view of Blenheim Cave, taken in 2003, some years before the Wellington Cave was opened to the public; soldiers relaxing in one of the Arras caves, quite secure from the perils of enemy shelling; basic accommodation, typical of that provided in the caves.

Central Artois Subways as at 9 April 1917

<table>
<tr><th>Sector</th><th>Subway Designation</th><th>Length (Feet/ Metres)</th><th>Tunnelling Company</th><th>Corps – Div Front</th></tr>
<tr><td rowspan="2">'S' Souchez – Calonne</td><td>Rotten Row</td><td>500 / 150</td><td rowspan="2">255</td><td rowspan="3">1 Corps
24th Div</td></tr>
<tr><td>Bois en Hache</td><td>350 / 107</td></tr>
<tr><td rowspan="3">'R'. Carency</td><td>Souchez</td><td>1,700 / 520</td><td rowspan="3">176</td></tr>
<tr><td>Coberg</td><td>1,335 / 407</td><td rowspan="6">Cdn Corps
4th Cdn Div</td></tr>
<tr><td>Gobron</td><td>870 / 265</td></tr>
<tr><td rowspan="4">'Q'. Berthonval</td><td>Blue Bull</td><td>1,530 / 466</td><td rowspan="4">182</td></tr>
<tr><td>Vincent</td><td>1,665 / 508</td></tr>
<tr><td>Tottenham</td><td>4,611 / 1,408</td></tr>
<tr><td>Cavalier</td><td>3,360 / 1,024</td></tr>
<tr><td rowspan="2">'P'. La Folie</td><td>Grange</td><td>4,029 / 1,228</td><td rowspan="3">172</td><td rowspan="2">Cdn Corps
3rd Cdn Div</td></tr>
<tr><td>Goodman / Pylons</td><td>5,649 / 1,722</td></tr>
<tr><td>'O'. Neuville St Vaast</td><td>Lichfield</td><td>1,590 / 485</td><td rowspan="2">Cdn Corps
2nd Cdn Div</td></tr>
<tr><td>'N'. Ecurie North</td><td>Zivy</td><td>2,523 / 789</td><td rowspan="10">185</td></tr>
<tr><td rowspan="3">'N'. Ecurie Central</td><td>Bentata</td><td>2,229 / 680</td><td rowspan="3">Cdn Corps
1st Div</td></tr>
<tr><td>Douai</td><td>2,118 / 646</td></tr>
<tr><td>No 33 Subway</td><td>900 / 274</td></tr>
<tr><td rowspan="6">'L'. Lille Road</td><td>L. 29A</td><td>250 / 76</td><td rowspan="5">XVIII Corps
51st (H) Division</td></tr>
<tr><td>L. 28B</td><td>400 / 122</td></tr>
<tr><td>L. 27 Subway</td><td>1,700 / 518</td></tr>
<tr><td>L. 26 Subway</td><td>600 / 182</td></tr>
<tr><td>L 21A Subway</td><td>1,300 / 396</td></tr>
<tr><td>Barricade</td><td>1,194 / 364</td><td rowspan="2">XVIII Corps
34th Division</td></tr>
<tr><td>'K'. Roclincourt</td><td>Fish</td><td>1,000 / 305</td><td>184</td></tr>
<tr><td>'J'. Blangy</td><td>No subways ?</td><td>N/A</td><td>184</td><td>XVIII Corps
9th Division</td></tr>
<tr><td>'I'. St Saveur</td><td>St Saveur</td><td rowspan="2">37,000 / 11,280 of passageways.</td><td>184, 176 & NZET</td><td>VI Corps
12th Division</td></tr>
<tr><td>'H'. Ronville</td><td>Ronville</td><td>NZET</td><td>VI Corps
3rd Div</td></tr>
<tr><td>Southern Arras</td><td>Not known</td><td>Some short subways but 'neutralised' by German withdrawal</td><td>Not Known</td><td>VII Corps
14th, 56th, 30th & 21st Divisions</td></tr>
</table>

Excluding Arras the total length of subways is approximately 39,400 ft (12,000 m). With Arras included, the subways total is 76,400ft (23,000 m)

A 'shift' of New Zealand tunnellers, working in Arras at the time of the photograph. With mining activity substantially reduced from the summer of 1917, the New Zealand Tunnelling Company became particularly adept at bridge building, although they also carried out other engineering tasks, such as neutralising booby traps. (JC Neill)

Vimy Ridge, were constructed by Imperial tunnelling companies, with some input from the Australian ABC Company. The total length of these subways was approximately 39,400 feet (12,000 metres).] There was no Company of which I stood in greater awe than the New Zealand Company. From Major Vickerman* to the last sapper, they were all over six feet, and it seemed surprising they could ever get into mine tunnels at all. They were a splendid body of men in every way, and made history at bridge building later on, of which more will be said.

General Harvey took me up to this front for a couple of days immediately after the attack. We saw the tunnels and caves, and many of the mine craters along the ridge, and also spent a long day in the Scarpe Valley beyond St Laurent Blangy. I recall the German mines we descended in company with Capt Yuill*, then Assistant Controller of Mines First Army. Arras itself presented a dismal picture in the pouring rain. A long string of mules were tethered outside the billet where we were having a hasty meal before returning to GHQ. They were peaceful enough for a while, until one of them reached across the rope to which their halters were fastened and seized a companion's ear. Then the fun really started,

A subway and a souterraine under the Vimy Ridge area. Top: A view of the publicly accessible Grange Subway, as it was in 1930 and then, after reinforcing measures had been taken, as it is today. Bottom: The interior of the souterraine near Maison Blanche in 2008. Bottom right: The Goodman Subway. Note the many cables on the floor. Originally these would have been attached to timbers.

and it took a dozen men over half an hour to straighten out the mess. Shepherd of Punch [*magazine*] would have been in the seventh heaven if he had been watching them.

Vimy Ridge was never again held by the enemy. It remained an impregnable bulwark on our left flank when the great attack on the Somme drove our Fifth Army back in the following year. The subways again proved their value on that occasion, and those who worked so hard at their construction for many weary months may well be proud of their share in securing the final victory.

With these two great adventures the active period of military mining in France came to a close. Thereafter the Companies gradually found employment of a variety and interest greater than most other troops ever enjoyed. Their further achievements only enhanced the wonderful reputation they had established by their outstanding successes at mine-fighting.

Chapter Six

The Art of Uplifting

How moles contrive their devious ways to take
Beneath the Surface, making mountains quake.

This chapter should be skipped by any reader who has already read enough about mines in the war. But before turning to other matters it seems worth while to answer the query of my two small boys. 'Daddy, what is a mine? What was it really like?'

A mine gallery was what an Irishman once described as nothing at all, being merely a hole. The size of gallery varied according to the conditions, but usually was about 4ft x 3ft in section, though wherever possible it was made rather higher to give greater comfort in walking along it. Except in hard chalk, it was timbered with mine casings of 2″ or 3″ planks fitted together. The methods of work differed from those in use in civil life, because it was very necessary to avoid giving any hint to the enemy listening in his own tunnels for sounds of our working. Therefore the essential atmosphere of mine galleries was their silence. In clay it was a question of scooping out the ground in front with special tools, and Sir John Norton-Griffiths was the first to introduce his system of 'clay-kicking' in the early days of 1915 in the Ypres Salient. Men lying on the floor of the gallery, with their backs partly supported by a plank wedged across it, would push their scoops into the face with their feet. In this way really silent working was possible, and screws were used instead of nails for fastening timbers.

The clay or earth was filled into sandbags and hoisted up the shaft or incline to the surface, where it was dumped at night, wherever possible in a site secure from the observation of enemy aeroplanes. A visible accumulation of bags would always give the game away to the enemy and bring retaliation in the shape of heavy shelling of the shaft head or counteroffensive by the enemy miners. Men and officers worked in

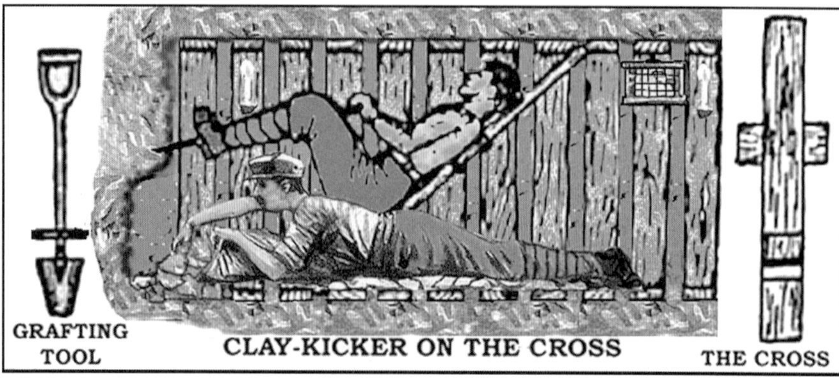

The technique was developed in the late nineteenth century in Britain for excavating sewers for several British cities (notably Manchester and London) in similar geological conditions to those found in Flanders.

their socks as often as not, and the quietest whisper was the only form of speech allowed. The laying of a charge was a considerable undertaking in the case of a large mine. We were fortunate in the choice of the principal explosive used. Ammonal was an Ammonium Nitrate explosive containing some 18% proportion of T.N.T., and about an equal quantity of powdered aluminium. The effect of the aluminium was to raise the temperature of the gases caused by the explosion so that the lifting effect was enormously increased, while the shattering effect of the Ammonium Nitrate and TNT was not reduced. It was therefore particularly suitable for blowing large surface mines, while its crushing effect on any enemy galleries within a given radius could be relied upon. Also it was a powder which was convenient for packing into petrol tins or sandbags, and would not be exploded if struck by a bullet, but only if fired by a proper detonator.

If a charge was to be left in position for a long time it was always laid in petrol tins to protect it from the damp. Otherwise it would be put into sandbags, double ones, in a dry gallery. [*Only occasionally in sandbags. Generally it was decanted into waterproof rubber bags which held 25lb of ammonal and was then sealed with a clamp. See diagram on p.59.*] The electric detonators were often protected further by being placed in small rubber bags [*usually condoms*], and taped until thoroughly watertight. All tins were sealed with pitch in the case of a wet mine. It will be understood how carefully these details were carried out, when it is remembered that

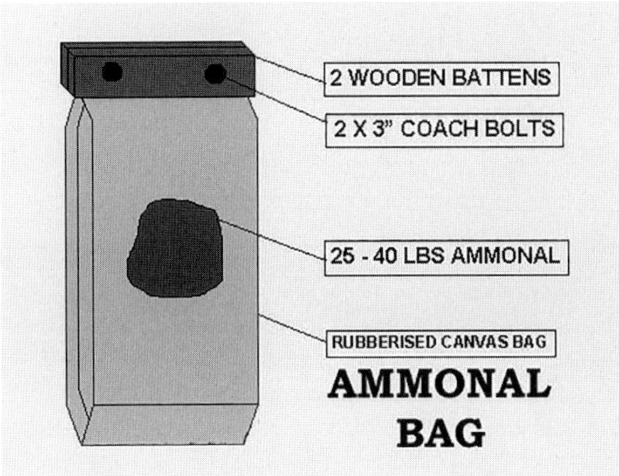

An ammonal bag, used for mine charges and as found by the Durand Group in the Durand Mine under Vimy Ridge. Alternatively, the ammonal could be placed in wooden boxes (as, for example, in the abandoned Broadmarsh Mine on Vimy Ridge).

some of the Messines mines were actually under water for more than a year, and yet not one of them failed when the day came.

Firing was usually done by a push-down exploder from a dugout in the support trench, but sometimes current was taken from the electric lighting plants of the 'Alphabet' Company. The successful explosion of the mine usually produced rum or whisky from the appreciative infantry. On one occasion I had laid my valued watch beside the exploder and missed it later on and all my satisfaction was spoilt by the apparent theft. But a little while later the faithful Round produced it, having taken the precaution to pocket it for me, and great was my relief.

Listening for the enemy was naturally one of the most important duties of a Tunneller. In chalk it was never possible to do the actual excavation in silence, and the sound of working could be heard a long way off. Special listening devices, of which the best was the French geophone, were of great help. This instrument was an adaptation of a donkey's long ears to the doctor's stethoscope. Two microphones placed on the floor of the gallery were connected by two rubber tubes to a headpiece fitting over the ears. These were moved about on the floor until to the listener the sound appeared to be coming from straight in front of him. It was then clear that it was coming from a direction at right angles to the line joining the two microphones. The compass bearing of the noise was noted and another bearing obtained from an adjacent gallery. The intersection of the two lines on the plan would indicate the position of the working enemy.

A German Pionier (Engineer) officer, probably in a posed photograph, firing a mine charge whilst his colleague looks to witness the result. They are probably positioned at the entrance to a mine shaft.

Various tricks and devices were used by both sides to confuse their opponents. Dummy picks, operated by strings from a safe distance, were employed by the Germans, but their lack of imagination caused them to work these so regularly, and with such an even rhythm, that they were always detected. The main idea was to draw the opponent's attention away from the gallery where offensive work was really going on. When a charge was to be left in position for some time it was usual to leave an electric microphone [*seismomicrophone*] buried in the charge, the listener sitting back in the workings out of all danger. At Hill 60, a few days before Messines, the electric listener in the charges indicated that the enemy was within a few feet of them. Very careful tests were made and it was decided that by the Zero hour he would be within three feet, and he was heard at this distance just prior to the blow. Accurate estimates of the German rate of working enabled us on this and many other occasions to predict his position by a given time.

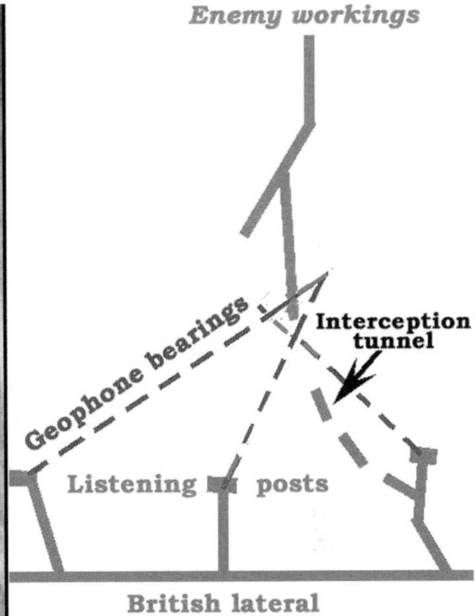

A listening officer at work with a geophone and a bar compass (sometimes known as a trough compass). To the right is a diagram illustrating interception geometry that enabled the pinpointing of the enemy's workings.

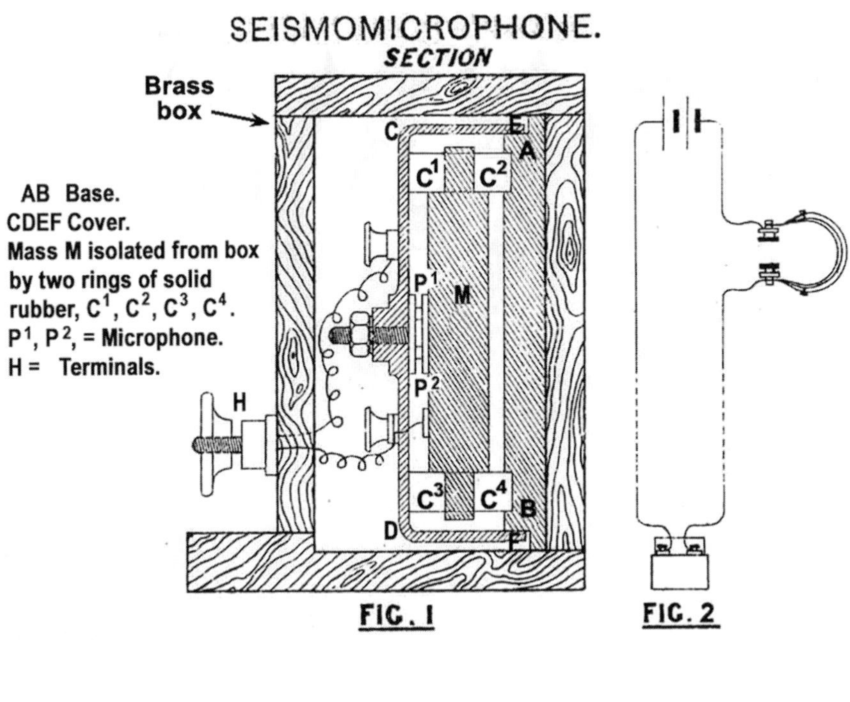

It was all rather like a blindfold game of chess in three dimensions.

Once at Bully Craters I discovered that the enemy were very close to our gallery. We were then on the defensive on this front, and had laid a small charge at the end of the old French gallery discovered when we took over. There was fifty feet of solid sandbag tamping between me and the charge, but the enemy had apparently come across diagonally from a flank and seemed likely to break in to the open part of our gallery within less than twelve hours. Fissures in the chalk often led to a slight miscalculation of distance, and it was quite possible that he was really nearer than this, so I at once sent word to Major Morgan at Company HQ, cleared everyone out of the gallery, and prepared for a long lonely vigil in the dark. I had borrowed a revolver, but it never occurred to me till years later that a bomb or two would have been more than useful. About three hours later I heard footsteps coming along our own gallery. It proved to be a messenger with a telegram for me from home. The history of that telegram should warn all senders of non-vital messages in wartime. It had been sent by the Army post office to the Company billets, from which some poor tired fellow had been sent up the line to find me. He had two miles of communication trench to traverse before reaching my dugout, and a further mile under Private Round's guidance to get to the particular mine. Another man thereupon took off his boots and brought it down in the dark to me! However no harm was done beyond that, and a few hours later Major Morgan, having obtained permission from Division, sent word to me to blow the charge already laid, and we had no further trouble from that direction for some time.

> [*First Army Weekly Summary for the sector Double Crassier to Vimy Ridge dated 5 to 11 August 1916 states: Enemy activity underground has very much increased along this front, and it almost appears that he has put in another mining company. We exploded a mine at BULLY CRATERS on 8/8/16 against close enemy working.*]

Whenever a mine was blown by either side, one of the most important things was to ascertain at once the damage to our own galleries. All underground explosions give rise to heavy fumes, of which the most deadly constituent is carbon monoxide. This gas is the same weight as air and, having no smell, cannot easily be detected. Even 0.1% of this gas is dangerous after some minutes and it was never safe to enter a gallery immediately after an explosion except when wearing oxygen apparatus.

For many years this was the only memorial to the 'Miners' Friends', mice and canaries, which forms a small part of the very large and impressive Scottish National War Memorial in Edinburgh Castle. In recent years a number of memorials to the animals of the Great War have been built. (Trustees of Edinburgh Castle)

On the wonderful War Memorial at Edinburgh may be seen figures of the Miners' Friends, the canary, and the white mouse. Both these creatures are much more sensitive to the action of the deadly gas than a human being, and it was necessary to have a supply available for testing purposes. At the RE stores at Calais a big aviary was maintained.

The white mice occasionally presented the official mind with unusual problems. Most of the ingenuity of people making returns had to be spent in explaining deficiencies, and one officer at least was completely defeated by the white mice, for he had indented for six, and no doubt six were sent, but on arrival there were twenty-seven! There appeared to be nothing in King's Regulations, or other authority, to indicate the correct procedure for such an emergency.

The canaries were naturally great pets and were kept in cages outside our dugouts. There was an amusing incident one day when an infantry major 'won' our canary, and refused point blank to believe that he had stolen an article of RE stores. Reference to Brigade was finally necessary before we got it back.

One bird that perished for its country almost deserved its fate. I had put it into its small travelling cage for an inspection of a gallery, and it looked very pathetic, and aroused my sympathy. But as I watched it, the creature laid an egg and drew still more sympathy, which was however soon withdrawn, for it proceeded to make a hole in the egg and eat it. And the feeding of it had been my special care for weeks!

There is on record a story of another bird that caused the greatest alarm along an important front for some hours. A mining offensive was in progress of which we thought the enemy had no idea, when the canary escaped and fluttered out of the trench onto a picket in our wire. It was of the utmost importance that the bird should not be seen by the enemy, and with great reluctance orders were given that it was to be shot by a sniper. The bullet was almost bigger than the bird, and it is not to be wondered at that the sniper missed the mark. The canary was however sufficiently disturbed to flutter out into the middle of No Man's Land. A staff consultation was held at once, with the result that a well directed shot from a heavy trench mortar put an end to the anxiety. [*This happened with 178 Tunnelling Company at the Tambour, on the Somme, close to Fricourt.*]

By the middle of 1917 the science of mining defence had been brought to a high level, and the danger of the listening work greatly reduced by the establishment of central stations, in connection with as many as thirty projecting galleries driven from a main lateral gallery along the front. The listener had a switchboard similar to a telephone board, and by plugging in to each gallery in turn could detect any enemy working in ample time for protective mines to be blown at the threatened point.

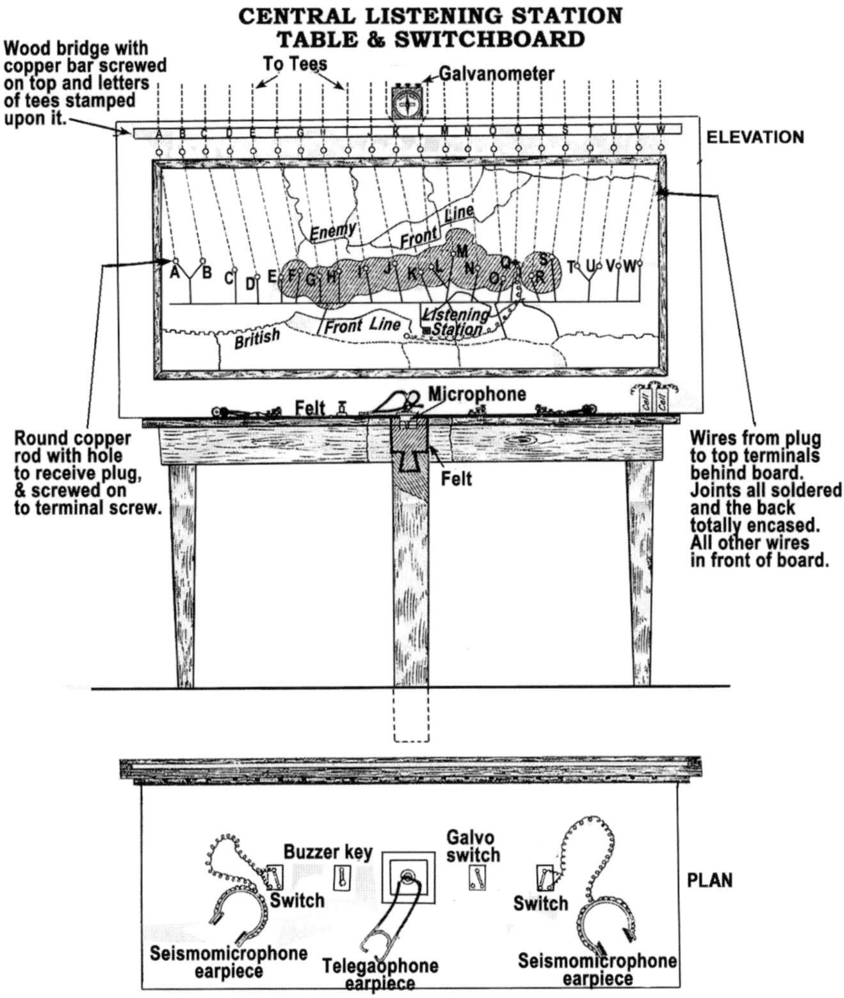

It has often been asked how it was that such a complete ascendancy was obtained over the enemy in underground warfare, and the true answer seems to be that their officers seldom descended their mines, and that much of their mining labour was derived from men sentenced to field punishment.

[*Not fair comment by Dixon. German records clearly show that their mining officers had similar shifts to their British contemporaries and their pioneers were determined and courageous. However mining expertise was much more thinly spread, a high proportion of the men engaged in tunnelling being field pioneers (engineers) rather than mining specialists. The huge amount of engineering expertise required for the development of the Hindenburg Line, whose construction began in the early autumn of 1916, perhaps goes some way to explaining the reduction in German mining operations from about that time.*]

On our side no disgruntled man was kept in a mine five minutes, as he might prove a danger to the safety of the rest. I have no idea of what the rank and file really thought of their officers, but the fact remains that they were prepared to follow them anywhere, and to undertake jobs at their request of the most arduous and dangerous nature, which is certainly a tribute to the men, and probably to the officers as well. Certainly the men were such as any man might be proud to lead. The vast majority were specially enlisted colliers from England, Scotland and south Wales, and no doubt north Wales too. Their military training, such as it was, had to be acquired in the front line.

[*Whilst a large proportion of the qualified tunnellers came from collieries a substantial number were drawn from other forms of mining, for example tin and lead; and many men without mining experience were also drafted in as 'miners' mates'. Furthermore, many miners came from Australia, Canada and New Zealand. The officers were drawn from mining activities all over the then Empire and other overseas territories, the South Africans being well represented.*]

One night I was called up from the bunk I shared with the rats, and was told that we had broken through into a German gallery. I crept along the gallery to the face, and was informed by a husky whisper that 'Ah've put ma pick into a 'ole like, an' thocht ah'd better send for th' officer.' Feeling round in the darkness I found the hole, and explored it with my hand until I was satisfied it was only a cavity in the chalk. My torch was then switched on and I saw a tough old miner of 60 or more sitting on his 'hunkers' with his pick upraised, waiting for 'yon b**** Boche tae pit his heid oot'.

One Company rejoiced in the possession of an exceedingly keen sergeant, who had not had much mining experience. They were driving a gallery at maximum speed through some ground in the neighbourhood of a recent German mine in order to get in a reply to the enemy. The chalk was full of gas from the mine previously blown, and the men were ordered to keep canaries by them and to withdraw at once if the bird collapsed. Up to the face went the sergeant, wielding a pick himself in his eagerness to see the work progress. It was not long before the canary turned up its toes. 'Och', said the sergeant, 'thon birrrd has got nae guts.' They pulled the sergeant out on a stretcher a few minutes later, and brought him to life by administering oxygen, but only just in time.

One of the most interesting examples of mine-fighting tactics, correctly applied, was at The Bluff. This was a point on the Messines salient about a mile south of Hill 60. It was the best place in the vicinity for observation purposes, and was therefore one of the first places in which mine warfare developed. A complicated series of shallow tunnels had been developed

The realities of war meant that ever more ingenious techniques were required by the tunnellers. Here the much decorated Major Alex Sanderson* DSO MC and Bar, the OC of the 3rd Australian Tunnelling Company, is using an ingenious periscope theodolite. (Robin Sanderson)

by both sides, many mines had been blown and the result was a jumble of small craters. But for a while here the enemy was slowly gaining the upper hand and it looked as though we might have to abandon our trenches at this point. It was accordingly decided to drive an incline deep under his defences and to cut off the enemy mine system altogether. The mines were so shallow in his system that careful listening from the surface by night patrols, combined with underground observation, had enabled the Australian Company in the line to fix the exact position of the portions nearest to us. In due course the deep mines were blown, and a party broke through from the surface in No Man's Land, into the enemy workings. They took with them a telephone, paying out the wires as they went along. Owing to the various devices by which telephone conversations could be picked up, special codes were in common use in the front line. But in this instance the Australians, with their usual dislike of normal procedure, produced one of their own. The first message that came to the eager listener was '240 feet Johnnie Walker'. This was probably equally as clear to any German waiter as to the recipient, for they were indeed 'going strong'. [*The company had introduced the slogan 'Born 1820 – still going strong!' in 1909.*] The whole enemy system was captured and added to our own, and the Bluff was secure.

At Cuinchy the line ran through a brickfield, and full use was made of the big stacks of bricks to provide head cover, for the water level was such that it was not possible to get down ordinary dugouts. The Brickstacks was a very active sector, and its near neighbour Givenchy was equally so. Air photos of the line at these and other parts of the front showed one long string of interlocking and superimposed mine craters.

The scale of the mining operations cannot better be indicated than by stating that by the middle of 1917 there were over a hundred miles of British mines and tunnels along the front. The average rate of progress was about 3 feet per eight hours and work was carried on in continuous shifts. Over 10,000 tunnellers, apart from attached infantry to an even larger total, were spread out along the whole front from the sea to the most southerly part of the Somme. General Harvey had good reason to be proud of leading the Tunnelling Service. There were many days at the height of the mining activity when reports of a dozen different mines from all parts of the front would reach our office, and the grand total of mines blown was well over 3000.

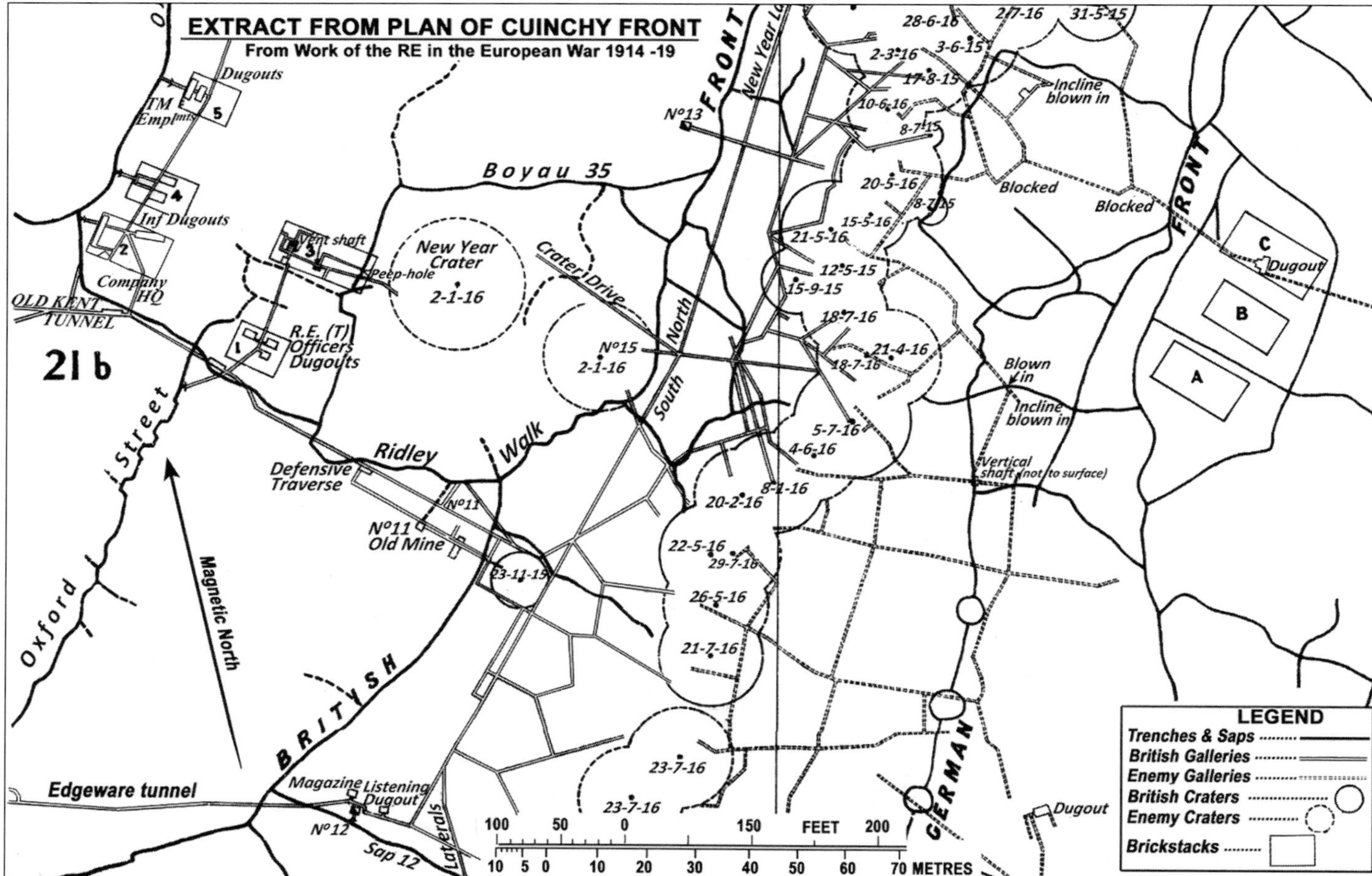
EXTRACT FROM PLAN OF CUINCHY FRONT
From Work of the RE in the European War 1914 -19
21b
Dugouts
TM Empl[mts]
5
4
Inf Dugouts
2
Company HQ
OLD KENT TUNNEL
Vent shaft
3
Peep-hole
R.E. (T) Officers Dugouts
1
Boyau 35
New Year Crater
2-1-16
Crater Drive
Nº15
2-1-16
North
South
Nº13
FRONT
New Year La
Ridley
Walk
Defensive Traverse
Nº11
Nº11 Old Mine
23-11-15
Street
Oxford
Magnetic North
BRITISH
Edgeware tunnel
Magazine
Listening Dugout
Nº12
Sap 12
Laterals
28-6-16
2-7-16
31-5-15
3-6-15
2-3-16
17-8-15
10-6-16
8-7-15
20-5-16
8-7-15
15-5-16
21-5-16
12-5-15
15-9-15
18-7-16
21-4-16
18-7-16
5-7-16
4-6-16
8-1-16
20-2-16
22-5-16
29-7-16
26-5-16
21-7-16
23-7-16
23-7-16
Incline blown in
Blocked
Blocked
FRONT
C
Dugout
B
A
Blown in
Incline blown in
Vertical shaft (not to surface)
GERMAN
Dugout
100 50 0 150 FEET 200
10 5 0 10 20 30 40 50 60 70 METRES
LEGEND
Trenches & Saps
British Galleries
Enemy Galleries
British Craters
Enemy Craters
Brickstacks

[*In a manuscript note, Dixon notes observes 'that in subways where silence was not demanded, a rate of up to 8 ft per hour was often maintained for a gallery 6ft high'. In subways considerably higher daily footage was often achieved.*

At peak there were thirty-two Royal Engineer and Dominion Tunnelling Companies, plus the Australian E.M.M. & B Company, and for a short period a Portuguese Tunnelling Company. With an established company strength of about 550 all ranks, there were around 18,000 men in the tunnelling companies. With the Army mine schools and other training, logistic and staff personnel about 20,000 were employed. Temporarily attached infantry and fatigue parties would take the numbers engaged to well over 30,000.

If small camouflets are included the figure of over 3,000 may be correct. However, where mines are concerned (which includes large camouflets) at peak in June 1916 the British fired 101. Before that there was a slow build up from March 1915 and after June 1916 intensity diminished. Extrapolating statistically, a more likely figure is between 1,000 to 1,500.]

Chapter Seven

Minor Incidents of 1917

Of hospitals and tea, and other things,
Like indigo, and irritating stings.

General Harvey had a bad dose of sciatica that summer [*1917*] and spent some weeks in hospital at Le Touquet, so we led a peaceful life. One day I was told by Major Stokes that I was to go over to the hospital and take some papers to the I of M. and was to take General Harvey's car. The driver of this Rolls-Royce was one of the best in France. The car had originally come to France with its owner, Sir

To add to his natural exuberance and gung-ho character, Norton Griffiths commandeered his wife's Rolls Royce and adapted it for his use on the Western Front. Amongst other things, the vehicle allowed him to carry around a stock of fine port, considerable quantities of which were expended in winning the support of doubting commanders to allow him to have miners from their unit's ranks. When he left the Western Front the vehicle went to General Harvey, who used it as his staff car. His wife seems to have stood the loss of her Rolls well; she died in 1974 at the age of 101.

John Norton-Griffiths. It had been the main means of transport of the original Tunnellers, who had been rushed by him on arrival direct to the line, complete with their tools. It continued to give wonderful service throughout the war.

Le Touquet lies on the south side of the Canche, opposite Étaples, and in the beautiful Casino I found the General. On the way I noticed a couple of staff captains [*in those days staff officers of all ranks wore tabs, usually red ones; nowadays their use is confined to more senior officers*] standing by a stile in the pine woods, but did not feel that a salute was called for, even from an ordinary captain, from such a regal car. As I got out the driver said to me 'Did you see the Prince of Wales, sir?'.

The General was having tea when I was shown into him, and the attractive little nurse disappeared at once. Tea with him was a pleasanter ordeal than I had expected, for luckily he caught sight of a better object for his wrath.

'See that fellow', pointing to one of the orderlies further down the long ward 'he – he – he washes me!' Surely that orderly earned his war medal, for the General in his then condition of chronic pain was well qualified to be considered an untouchable.

It will be recalled that in the spring of 1917 the Germans withdrew on the Somme to the almost impregnable defences of the Hindenburg Line. Their parting presents included the first delay-action mines, the one under the Town Hall at Bapaume being the first to go off [*no less than a week after the German retirement from the town*], killing, among others, two French Deputies, who were visiting their newly recaptured constituency.

It was of great importance to us to discover the mechanism which they were using for this purpose, and I was given strict instructions to keep a close look out in the daily 'Comic Cuts', or Army Intelligence reports, for any indication of the finding of a fuse of this type. One morning, after the General had been away in the Fourth Army area for a couple of days, I saw a sketch of a new fuse found by that Army, which was of the type expected. At once I took the report to the General. His hand went out for the telephone.

'Give me the Central Laboratory at Hesdin at once.' … 'That the Central Laboratory? Did Major Stokes leave a fuse with you this

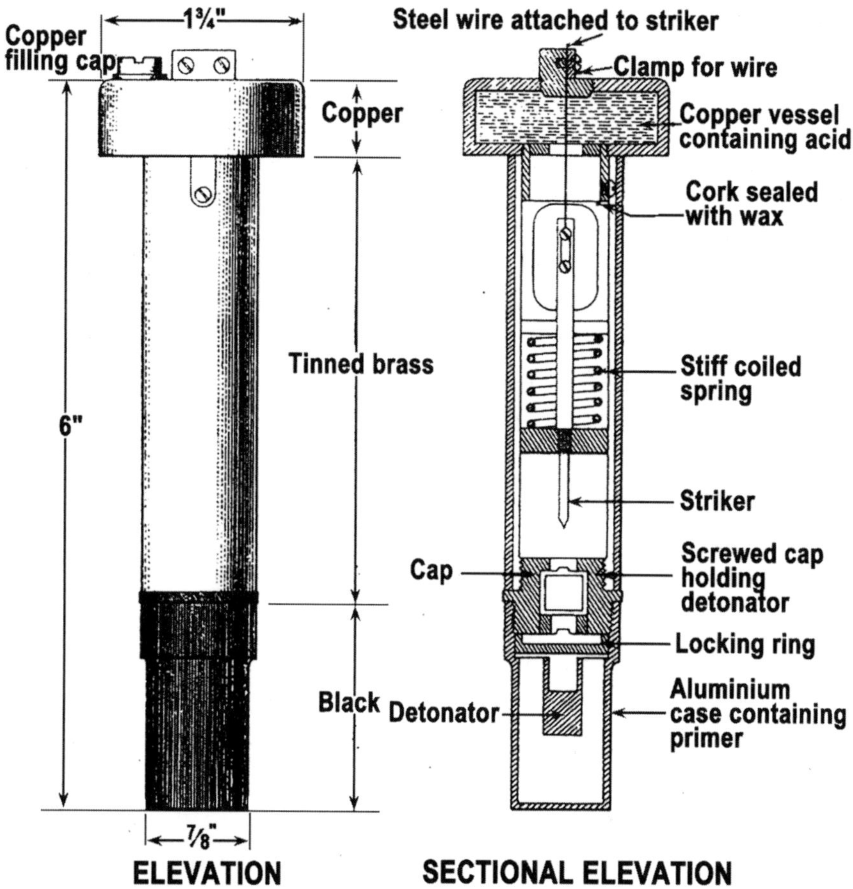

A diagram of a German delayed action fuse. When the Germans made their withdrawal to the Hindenburg Line they adopted a scorched earth policy that was controversial even amongst senior commanders, such as Prince Rupprecht and Gallwitz. As part of the plan to make life as difficult as possible, they also planted numerous booby traps, the making safe or demolition of which was a major occupation for a number of the tunnelling companies.

morning?' … 'Take it out and bury it at once. It's a delay action thing and may go off at any time.' Apparently the fuse had been given to the General the previous day. He had put it in his pocket for the 150 mile trip back to Montreuil, had given it to Major Stokes, who had it lying on his bedside table all night, before leaving it at Hesdin on his way through in the morning.

A fortnight later the Experimental Officer on the E-in-C's staff made some enquiries at Hesdin about it. The fuse was still underground, so

Bellamy* had it dug up, and duly discovered, after very careful inspection, that what looked like a paper fastener in the side was really a safety pin. Furthermore there was no acid in the little vessel at the top, so that the piano wire which held up the striker could not have been eaten through. This was our first acquaintance with these fuses, of which we had far more than enough before – and after – the Armistice was signed.

I am reminded by the story of the visit to Le Touquet of another journey in the same car. General Harvey was travelling that day in company with Colonel Sankey* of the E-in-C's staff. Major David told me of the conversation in the mess that night. Apparently the General had been complaining of the shaking they had had, as another driver was doing temporary duty, and took all the bumps at top speed. Colonel Sankey, who was a son of the world famous engineer Captain Sankey, remarked over the port: 'Well, General, next time we go out with that driver I suggest that you wear a steel helmet to protect your head from the roof. … And, by the way General, wouldn't it be a good thing if the driver wore a gas helmet?' I appreciated this story better after travelling with the General later on. We got stuck behind a lorry, on the back of which sat a look-out man who seemed entirely unaware of the presence of the car. At last the General could stand it no longer and, putting his head out of the window, shouted to the man, 'What the blazes do you think you are? A look-out or a pink mascot?' The road was soon clear.

I do not know whether I shall get into trouble from my wife if I include in this chapter a reference to my application for special leave in September, 'in order to be married'. This was one of my really few courageous actions, for it involved permission from the General. However his very generous wedding present was duly paid into Cox's, and we spent our honeymoon at Bontddu in the Barmouth valley, as far away as I could get from France. Returning to London I left my wife in the care of the Venners at Caterham, but on the way I thought we might as well call in at the Bank to ascertain the extent of the damage.

At the time I thought I had a few hundred pounds there, and expected to be welcomed with open arms accordingly as a rarity. The clerk turned up his books and announced that my balance was £13-7-4! What my wife's feelings were I have never learnt, but a lengthy discussion ensued, and I discovered that another RE man of the same name and initials had been credited for months with all my pay, while under some special arrangement all his Chatham Mess bills had been debited to me.

During the summer there was a mild spy scare at GHQ, with what real basis I never discovered, but it brought about the only physical combat of a serious nature that came my way in the war. I was leaving the office late one night, in company with Logan and Smyth, and we had just reached the main entrance to the École when we heard loud cries behind us of 'Stop that man!' At once the spy story sprang into my mind and I turned sharply round to see a figure in British uniform running hard for the gateway. The sentry was behind me, but I never gave him a thought for here was a man away on the wing, and a tackle hard and low was sheer instinct. He came down on the concrete surrounding the gravel of the main square, and slid clean across it, ending with his head against the wall. There seemed no sign of life as I gathered my own wits together and picked up my hat. The crowd behind me looked somewhat surprised but great was my chagrin to be told that it was a poor batman who had got somewhat tight, and was beating things up. For days afterwards Logan and Smyth would stop on the way in to show me quite imaginary blood stains on the wall. It was a bit of a mystery, which I never solved, as to what happened to him. Bryant told me that there was no man charged with any offence just then, nor was anyone notified as admitted to hospital who might have been the batman. I can only conclude that his persecutors thought he had had enough to sober him up and left it at that.

About this time my brother, CD Dixon*, had returned to France. He came home from Shanghai with a strong contingent of volunteers from China in the spring of 1915. As an expert machine gunner of the Shanghai Volunteer Corps, he was given a commission in the Somersets, and was with them in the Somme battle in 1916, until at Trônes Wood he was buried in a trench and consequently ceased to take any active interest in the war for some months.

Later on he came out in command of one of the Chinese Labour Companies, with headquarters at Val-de-Lièvres, near Calais, and once or twice I had lunch, or rather tiffin, in his mess. This was a complete replica of a China mess, the boys in their long white gowns, the cries of the coolies outside, and the steady throb and swish of the punkah, making the whole atmosphere that of any China port. While I was with him they

Mechanics of the Chinese Labour Corps at work in the massive tank workshops at Teneur (west of St Pol). Thousands of Chinese labourers were recruited, the process picking up considerably after China declared war on the Central Powers in August 1917. Up to 100,000 of these men served with the BEF. Most returned to China at the end of the war; but a substantial number were retained for a while to assist with the clearance of the battlefields. (National Library of Scotland)

were sorting out a train load of salvage from the battlefields. Everything was jumbled hopelessly together, but the patient coolies went through it all, the old boots were sent to the repair shops and were rendered serviceable again, all the copper and brass was recovered, and anything of the slightest use sent home as a source of new material and equipment. One coolie had come across the identification disc of a Chinese among the rubbish. He brought it to my brother with an inscrutable smile. 'Poor Johnny, him gone west.'

At the end of the war CD returned to China, and has since spent five years in Chunking, one in Tientsin, and seven in Hankow. He often says that he has seen more ammunition fired off since the war than he ever saw during it, and he has actually been closely concerned in most of the really good rows in this forlorn country. He was Chairman of the Hankow Municipal Council in 1927, at the time of the handing over of the former British Concession to the Chinese under the Chen-O'Malley agreement, in the negotiations for which he naturally had an important part to play. Since that time, however opposed he may have been to the policy of 'scuttle', then, and for long after, adopted by the British Foreign Office, he has set himself to make the new administration a success. Officers of the Navy who have enjoyed the wonderful hospitality of the Hankow Clubs, and all the many diplomatic and other visitors to this 'metropolis' of Central China, will know best whether his efforts and those of his colleagues on the Council of S.A.D.3, as the old British Concession is now called, have met with success. In February 1932, when there was a first class little war in Shanghai, Hankow remained quiet, and it was my good fortune to be able to represent the family in the Shanghai Volunteers and make an intimate acquaintance with the most interesting defence problems which it presented to the foreign community, and to have at the same time a free box-seat in our block houses during most of the fighting.

But all that is another story, and may perhaps, like the doings recorded in these pages, be described someday after it can be seen in better proportion in the light of the years between.

One of the familiar figures in the courtyard of the École when I first went to Montreuil was that of John Buchan*, then performing the duties of 'Official Eye-witness'. It must have been a strain for him to

John Buchan served as an officer in the Intelligence Corps on the Western Front, where he arrived in 1916 and was attached to Haig's staff to write speeches and communiqués. He was then made Director of Information in London by the newly appointed Minister of Information, Lord Beaverbrook. He was outstandingly talented; a poet and a popular author; much travelled (his early adult years were spent in South Africa; and he wrote two excellent formation histories, on the South African Brigade and the 15th (Scottish) Division.

prepare the bald statements which were all that the General Staff were able to sanction in those days. But perhaps we have all been the gainers subsequently. At least there are compensations for us in 'The Three Hostages', 'Greenmantle', 'Mr Standfast' and his other more solid but none the less fascinating books.

Lord Gort* was on the General Staff for some months, leaving it to command the Grenadier Guards. His record is too well known to need elaboration here, but he was a particularly arresting figure, especially to me, for he had acted as Adjutant to the OTC camp at Aldershot in 1911, and had even then seemed a glamorous personality to us school boys. Since the war his name has become well known in Shanghai as Staff Officer with the Shanghai Defence Force. There are few men who better deserve the description of 'born leader', or who have ever carried equivalent rows of medals as thoroughly earned.

Of Captain Smyth, the Mechanical Engineer on our staff, I have said very little. He was a good friend and excellent mess companion, who went about his work so quietly and efficiently that his services were

John Vereker, 6th Viscount Gort, VC DSO and Two Bars MC, pictured as a lieutenant colonel of the Grenadier Guards. Gort came out with the BEF in August 1914 and served on the Western Front throughout the war, holding a variety of staff appointments (including at GHQ) and field commands, ending the war as CO of 1st Grenadier Guards. It was whilst with them that he won his VC for his actions at the Canal du Nord in September 1918. (S.T. Gill)

General the Lord Gort (Field Marshal 1943), photographed in France when he was in command of the second BEF. In the inter war years his career prospered and from a substantive major in 1919 he was CIGS by the end of 1937. After the retreat from Dunkirk, his finest hour came as Governor and Commander in Chief of Malta for two years, 1942–1944. Dixon was obviously an admirer of this soldier and colonial administrator. Gort died in 1946, soon after he was diagnosed with inoperable liver cancer; and only one month after he was promoted in the peerage to Viscount.

never appreciated to the extent they deserved. When he left to go to the War Office in the latter part of the year he was sadly missed in the mess.

Fidoe, who took his place, came from 251 Company, which had fought a magnificent underground campaign against the enemy at Givenchy-les- la-Bassée, and which played an equally striking part in the anxious days of April in the next year, when Givenchy was the bastion of our right flank, which never gave under the onslaught of the Germans when they made their last drive for the Channel Ports. There must have been something about the post that Smyth and Fidoe held that made for soundness and reliability, for that was the chief characteristic of them both. No doubt Smyth in South Africa, and Fidoe in Cardiff have often found the work they did at Montreuil of use to them in later life. It was certainly of the greatest value to the Tunnelling Companies.

In the late summer of that year we were honoured with a flying visit from Sir John Norton-Griffiths. He was the real founder of the Tunnelling Companies, and his dynamic temperament could not have found a better outlet. Known to all the older hands as 'NG', he was, when

I first saw him, on his way back from his wholesale destruction of the oil wells and granaries of Roumania. It will be remembered that in that year Mackensen's Army swept through Roumania, and it was a matter of great urgency that these valuable sources of supply should not be left to fall into the hands of the enemy. It must have been difficult for even the intriguers of the Balkan states to withstand the fiery enthusiasm of the Allies' special representative in the shape of 'NG'. Once he had been given the official orders for the demolitions by the Roumanian Government, there was no time wasted and the work was done before any secret countermanding instructions could get through. His KCB was well earned. He will be remembered as 'Empire Jack' in political circles of pre-war days, when his powers of rhetoric and political organization found him a place in Parliament. The evening spent with him over our mine plans in the General's office was a memorable one to me, and a good opportunity for studying the strongly contrasted, yet equally forcible characters of the two men, whose names will always be associated with the founding and organization of the Tunnelling Companies. The sad death of Sir John a few years ago in Egypt cast a gloom over the minds of all who had known him. [*He was killed whilst out swimming with a surf board near Alexandria in Egypt on 27 September 1930, aged 59. He was shot in the temple with a pistol at very close range. Whether he was murdered or committed suicide was never satisfactorily established.*]

And here I would pause to justify the few references in this book, which claims to deal with the lighter side of a tunneller's life, to the passing of men he has known. To me it was such a privilege and inspiration to know them, that it will always be the case that their memory lightens the darker days, which come to us all in turn, and I make no apology for writing of them. But the carnage and horrors of war have been deliberately omitted, for enough and to spare has been written about these aspects by countless others.

Shortly after the Battle of Messines [*7–14 June 1917*], Major David and his assistant, LBR King of the Geological Survey, accomplished a notable piece of geological work. Our Foreign Office had long been in communication with the Dutch Government over the question of permitting war material to pass through their waters from Germany to the front. Particularly so was the case of the vast quantities of sand and gravel, which the British Staff claimed were being used for the erection of the reinforced concrete defences, which were the most formidable obstacles to our advance in the northern areas. Careful examination of the heaps of gravel left on the Messines ridge suggested to our geologists that it might be possible to trace their source by detection of their characteristic minerals. Eventually a certain mineral was found for which they were looking, which proved conclusively that the gravel had come from a certain point on the Rhine, as this mineral is unknown elsewhere in Europe. With this evidence in their possession the Foreign Office were able to bring pressure to bear on our neutral friends to place the desired embargo on this traffic.

At the time of my marriage I had been a little disappointed that I had not had a line from my old school friend, Keyser Atkin*. A few weeks later I heard from him to the effect that he was sorry that he had not been able to write in time, because he had only just returned from a

German engineers engaged in the construction of a bunker, using frame work and poured concrete, the only method approved by the German military authorities by late 1916. In the Flanders Front alone the Germans erected some 9,000 bunkers; later, medium sized bunkers could use up to 10,000 metres of reinforcing rods each. However, over time the Germans began to regard bunkers as something of a mixed blessing as allied artillery became both heavier and more accurate. (Fond documentaire Alain Jacques)

six weeks stay in Germany as the guest of their Government. He had been up at Cambridge at Jesus when war broke out, and as a medical student of great promise had been ordered to complete his course before joining the RAMC. As a doctor, he had been exchanged after being a prisoner for some weeks, and soon went back to the line, only to find there a grave which cut short a career of singular promise, and for me, a friendship of over eight years. [*Captain K Atkin RAMC, died 6 June 1918 and buried in Marfaux British Cemetery VIII G 7.*] He was the son of PW Atkin, himself an old boy, who had the unusual distinction of rowing for Cambridge for three years at the time when sliding seats were first used in the Boat Race. At their house in Birkenhead I had often gazed with awe at the collection of oars and the portion of the first sliding-seat boat which adorned the walls. PW Atkin was well known in the northern Circuit for many years, and in Manchester he will be long remembered as the Stipendiary for Salford. His wife was one of the sweetest of American women; she died shortly before the war, and the loss of their only son, Keyser, must have been a bitter blow to his father. During the coal strike of 1921, I was able to call at their home in Manchester, and renew this old friendship with the family. PW Atkin passed on to meet his wife and son two years ago.

General Allenby, GOC Third Army, nicknamed'the Bull', photographed in late spring 1917 with Field Marshal the Duke of Connaught, the third son of Queen Victoria, recently returned from a highly successful five year appointment as Governor General of Canada. (His daughter was the 'Patricia' in the extant Canadian regiment, the PPCLI.) The Duke had also had a notable military career in his earlier years, ending as GOC Aldershot Command. Allenby had a rather mixed war on the Western Front, but his talents bloomed in Palestine, where he commanded the Egyptian Expeditionary Force and led it to victory.

It was one of my duties to take in to the General any telegrams of interest dealing with the progress on other fronts. Perhaps the most memorable of these was the announcement of the capture of Jerusalem by General Allenby*, the former Third Army Commander. Colonel Mackintosh*, staff officer to the E-in-C, was with the General at the time. Mackintosh had previously been ADC to Sir Reginald Wingate, the Sirdar in Egypt. 'Well Mackintosh', said the General, 'what will they make him for that?' Allenby was always known to his Army as 'The Bull', and Mackintosh replied at once 'Bull of Bashan, Sir'.

I should be more than ungrateful if I omitted a special reference to two men on our staff who worked under me during my stay at GHQ. In Sergeant Kearns we had an excellent clerk, who succeeded to Mr Collie's duties in due course. Perhaps he will remember the times we spent together deciphering the General's handwriting when his sciatica was at its worst and he was only able to sit in his office at all because of the relief occasioned by his air cushion whilst amending the numerous weekly mining reports, which we concocted together from the company reports for the edification of the Great Ones.

We were most fortunate, too, in having as our draughtsman Sapper Clark*, promoted to sergeant finally. The amount of work he got through was colossal, and it may be some satisfaction to him to know that in the 1925 edition of the official War Office publication 'Military Engineering (Vol IV) Mining and Demolitions', I saw some years ago a large number of the drawings we made in the war years, taken from 'Mining Notes' and the official technical reports on the operations at Messines and elsewhere. He and I spent long hours in sorting out and piecing together into mosaic form the thousands of air photographs of the Hindenburg Line and the various mining fronts. Later on we took over, under Brigadier General MacInnes*, the Defence Plans for the whole of the British front, and kept them up to date weekly, which was no small undertaking. To these two men I would like to express my special thanks for all the long hours they put in for me. [*Brigadier General Duncan MacInnes CMG DSO, a Canadian serving for many years in the British army, became Inspector of Mines on 1 January 1918; he was accidentally killed when visiting the front on 23 May 1918 and is buried in Étaples Military Cemetery, XXVIII L 2.*] Always cheerful and willing to tackle anything in their respective spheres, they contributed very largely to the efficiency of our office.

Perhaps the principal thing for which all tunnellers should be grateful to General Harvey was his insistence that the main duty of the Inspector of Mines office was to see that the Companies' interests were always fully considered by the General Staff at GHQ, at the Armies, and by all the myriad other departments who had axes of their own to grind. Perhaps it has been made sufficiently clear that he was a strict disciplinarian, though he was stricter with his office staff than anywhere else. Many a Company officer will remember the rough side of his tongue, but few realise in all probability how hard he could fight for them when their interests were attacked from outside.

The best example that comes to mind was the case of a certain OC Company, who shall be nameless, who found himself in serious difficulties owing to an act of 'scrounging' on a scale that even Tunnellers seldom attempted. He had won the MC and DSO, and had a splendid record for tackling tough propositions. The mechanical transport allotted to Companies included a box-car or van for the use of the OC, and for rushing urgent stores up to the line. One day the OC in question found a French car of superior make unattended by the side of the road, and had it taken into his billets, where his mechanical love of a good engine seems to have overcome his sense of proportion, for it was a good motto for scroungers to remember: 'be moderate in all things'. At all events it was not long before the touring body of the car gave place to a boxcar body constructed by the Company carpenter, and with fictitious British army number plates the car gave splendid service during several months, and life seemed very good to the culprit. A mechanical defect developed, however, and the car was sent into the nearest MT depot for overhaul. By one of the queer coincidences that so often outdo the best efforts of writers of fiction, the car happened to stand next to another in the shop, bearing the identical number. The facts came out by degrees, and the DRLS riders began to carry a heavy mail on the subject from Army HQ. A court martial was the obvious outcome, and exactly what took place I cannot remember in detail, but I do know that it was only by the most impassioned appeals and strenuous efforts in many directions that General Harvey was able to avert the impending cashiering of that OC.

[*Major WT Wilson DSO MC was OC of 256 Tunnelling Company at the time. He clearly had a penchant for acquiring beneficial comforts.*

Whilst a captain, acting OC of 185 Tunnelling Company on the Somme, substantial domestic comforts were acquired from damaged shops and buildings, not least of which was a grand piano. These were discovered after 185 Tunnelling Company had been taken over by Major E Tulloch, DSO MC, and resulted in a Court of Enquiry. However the evidence was disposed of, strangely enough, by being removed by 256 Tunnelling Company! That Major Tulloch escaped Court Martial may probably be attributed to General Harvey's intervention.]

It is fitting to close this chapter with the account of a visit which the General paid to the Fourth Army front (it may have been the Fifth Army) about this time in company with Major David. It may be referred to hereafter as the story of the General, the helmet and the wasp. It will be well known to all who wore them that the early steel helmets were provided with a leather lining which was far from comfortable, and General Harvey was then experimenting with a new type, which was secured to the inside of the helmet by a small bolt, and in his specimen this was too long, and projected beyond the top of the helmet for about half an inch. Signallers and Gunners had woven a web of wires along and over every trench, and it was necessary to duck one's head every few yards. The General was in front, and David followed him. It was a warm summer day, and the temperature along the trench rose even more rapidly as each offending wire caught the projecting bolt, and knocked the General's helmet off. After a while he dropped the chinstrap, but the effect was then to half choke him. David would have been an inwardly chuckling, though outwardly sympathetic, observer throughout that long hot walk, but he was not the only one. In the chalk country of the Somme, the wasps had many nests. These wasps, as regards development and élan in the attack, were true sons of France, and a particularly valiant specimen found the Achilles heel of the General in the nape of his neck. A few more offending wires, precipitating the back of the helmet onto the vital spot, completed the first act of the tragedy.

By the time the miles of trenches had been covered and the car found, expletives were exhausted, and silence reigned until Army HQ was reached, and an astonishing vision burst upon the occupant of the Controller of Mines' Office. This was Buchanan. (I believe I once met him before the war at Kilsyth or Twechar, in Scotland.)

'Buchanan! What's good for a wasp sting?'

'Bluebag, Sir.'

'Blue bag be blued and qualified! How the blue blazes do you expect to find one in the middle of this wilderness?'

'Well, Sir, what about some indigo from the drawing office?'

'Get it at once. … Put it on. … Not there you idiot, here! … No, further over!' And by the time the job was finished the facial aspect after that hot walk was put completely in the shade by the gorgeous array of colour on the neck.

David's sense of humour must have subjected him to a severe strain that day, but the honours undoubtedly lay with the wasp.

Chapter Eight

Passchendale

The clouds loom low o'er Flanders' tragic clay,
Halting the mighty dreams, on its way.

The operations at Messines were intended to pave the way for the great offensive in the north, which should free the Channel ports and begin a turning movement which would roll up the right flank of the long German line. It is a matter of history how those hopes were frustrated by the weather, and the final victory achieved a year and more later by other strategy.

The very word 'Passchendaele' seems fraught with unending sadness for us all, and it is with difficulty that one writes of it even now. But it has its own special place in my memories of 1917 and 1918, and this story would not be complete without reference to it.

The start of the great offensive, which was shared by the Second Army and by General Gough's* Fifth Army, specially brought up from the Somme, was delayed again and again, until on 31 July 1917 the costliest advance the British Armies have ever known was heralded by the drumfire of the thousands of guns in front of Ypres. [*In fact Third Ypres was not the costliest; it comes below the Battles of Arras and the Somme and the Advance to Victory in terms of daily losses during offensive operations.*]

I spent some days in the Salient just prior to the great day, inspecting work on dugouts in the ramparts by the Menin Gate, at Sanctuary Wood and other places. Hell Fire Corner was living up to its reputation just then and the whole of the immortal town and its environs would have been entitled to a similar description. 255 Company, with whom I spent the night of the 29th, were then in billets on the 'Canal Bank'. Shelters had been dug in the eastern bank of the Yser Canal, and these gave a certain amount of protection against shelling, but the Germans had the exact ranges of the canal and of every bridge and earth ramp constructed across it. The Company actually lost over seventy men out of their 400 in a single week, most of them around their billets.

The approach to their HQ was over a notorious earth ramp, constructed for the passage of tanks, known as Bridge IV. [*Tunnelling Companies were engaged in the construction of these tank bridges.*] Morton and I, returning from Ypres, were greeted by two 5.9s, which arrived just as we stepped on to the bridge. The taste of the ramp lingers with me yet. Certainly we hugged it to our bosoms, and though I cannot claim a great experience of lip stick, it cannot taste worse than that mud. As we rose and ran before any more shells followed, we passed the entrance to a communication trench called Coney Street, by which there was a gas-alarm station. The usual notice to indicate 'Wind Safe', or 'Wind Dangerous' had suffered with the rest, and all I read was 'WIND!'.

Captain Herbert Lea Morton RE, adjutant of 255 Tunnelling Company, photographed in 1918. South African born but educated in Britain, he was working in southern Africa at the outbreak of the war in the mining industry and returned there after the war. (M. Morton)

The major [*ie OC 255 Tunnelling Company*] told me that their work for the attack was to be the laying of signalling cables behind the attacking infantry, following them as closely as possible through the enemy barrage. It was during this work that Big Dickson lost his life, owing to being too far in advance, and coming under the fire of an isolated bunch of the enemy, overlooked by our infantry [see Chapter 2].

One of our more aged miners earned a Military Medal in this battle. He had been ordered to stay in billets, as his age was so great that he was

Australian signallers (in this case linesmen) laying cable near Westhoek, a small ham- let on high ground east of Ypres that was captured on 10 August 1917. The job of these forward signallers was very dangerous, as the cable (or line) was frequently broken by shells or by troops blundering into it. Repairing these breaks was difficult enough without running the gauntlet of shells and bullets.

not considered fit for the work. However he broke billets and joined his section in the line, where he rescued a wounded comrade under very heavy fire.

During the following year I visited 255 Company when they were engaged in making dugouts near the summit of the ridge, to the south-east of Houthulst Forest. Of all the examples of heavy pressure in blue clay, this was one of the very worst I ever saw. Steel 'elephant' sections were used at first, as timber however thick was broken like matches over night. But the elephant sections closed in like gigantic grab dredges or nutcrackers, and it was only by using 3-inch steel joists, spaced at 18 inch centres, for top, sides, and bottom, that it was possible to make a dugout at all. Of course it was necessary also to hold the girder sets together by means of the special steel clips, to prevent movement. The actual excavation was carried out more easily than many miners would imagine, for it was not until the clay had been exposed to the air for a little time that it seemed to develop its properties as a fluid. The approach to the site of the dugouts was then along miles of greasy duckboards, to step off which often meant being engulfed in the foul slime of waterlogged shell holes. The 'Forest' had disappeared as though Time had bought the largest razor of any nightmare and, disdaining to use it on himself, had swept it over that tragic hillside.

Chapter Nine

'Controllers' and Others

These were the leaders of a sturdy breed,
To them men looked for guidance in their need.

My associations with First Army were closer than with any other. Colonel GC Williams I met first at Béthune in the spring of 1916 and as he was responsible for sending me to GHQ, he must take a large share of the blame for this book ever being written. He was an ideal Controller of Mines, and of Miners, and was held in the highest esteem by all his Companies. In 1917 he was deservedly promoted to the command of a brigade, and for the rest of the war and since then, in India and elsewhere, has continued the brilliant work he did with the Tunnellers of the First Army. [*Dixon has a hand written annotation: 'I last heard of him as a Brigadier and Instructor at the Imperial College of Defence and as a lieutenant general on his way to study New Zealand Defences in about 1941.' He had a distinguished career and retired as a full general, when Military Advisor to the New Zealand Government during the Second World War, loaded with honours – KCB, CMG and DSO. He died in 1959. When Dixon first knew him during the War he was only 35 years old.*]

His successor was Colonel Stokes from our office, and when Stokes went to Murmansk in 1918 the Assistant Controller, First Army, became Lieutenant Colonel Yuill, to the great satisfaction of all who knew his sterling value. He will always hold a special place in my war-time friendships. After the blowing of the mine at Bully Craters with the 23rd Divisional Company, he came round one day to my drawing office in Barlin. There had been some soreness over certain recommendations for honours on that occasion, which had been turned down, quite rightly, by the Controller, on the ground that the work done was the normal duty of any Tunnellers. That it was rendered more difficult owing to poor organization, only confirmed the Controller in his view that no honours could be granted. Yuill at first took me to task because I said I was fed up with it, thinking for the moment that I meant I was fed up with tunnelling, and not merely with the discussion of the incident.

Yuill was a very shy man, more so than any other Canadian I have known, but he could develop a very obstinate streak with any outsider who attempted to interfere with Tunnelling Company rights, and he well maintained General Harvey's tradition in this respect. I had a letter from him a few years ago from Nova Scotia, but I believe he is now a consulting engineer in London.

Of all the Army HQs the one of which I retain the clearest picture is the Second Army Headquarters at Cassel. All those who ever visited it, and the total must run into millions, including all the political and other joy-riders who ever came to France, will remember its lovely setting. Approached along the straight Flanders roads, towering beyond the avenues of poplars, rose the famous hill town, for ever associated with the marching of a Duke of York and his ten thousand men.

The level crossing passed, the road curved in a steep winding ascent to the town, and the office of the Controller of Mines was soon reached. Colonel AG Stevenson was on a level with the rest of Plumer's happy family, as the Second Army Staff always were. To me he was somewhat awe-inspiring and as he too took over the command of a brigade in the middle of 1917, I did not see a great deal of him. It is a curious fact that after the war he followed General Harvey in three successive posts of great importance in the Army; as Chief Engineer Portsmouth, Chief Engineer Aldershot, and as Engineer-in-Chief India. He developed the work begun by General Harvey in all these positions. I was glad to meet him again at the Tunnellers Old Comrades Association Dinner in 1927, when he took the chair, and at which Sir Edgeworth David and Sir John Norton-Griffiths were among the speakers.

Of the other Controllers and their Assistants, whose hospitality I enjoyed at many different times and places, I would like to mention, more especially, Colonel Hyland, Fifth Army, to whom reference will be made again, Colonel LE Hill* of the Fourth Army, Colonel LC Hill*, Second Army and Colonel Laws*, Third Army.

By the end of the war Colonel LE Hill was one of the only two regular officers left in the whole Tunnelling Service, the other being General H

Biddulph, the Inspector of Mines*. It says much for the good start in military organization given to us by the original Regulars that we needed so little help from them later on.

Of Colonel Laws more will be said. His bushy black beard was unique in the Tunnelling Service. Originally an active member of the Naval Division on Gallipoli, he continued (shall I say it?) the barbarous tradition of the Senior Service. As he was the last Controller with whom I stayed before leaving the Army for ever, his kindness to me on many occasions is not likely to be forgotten.

Captain HS Ball* of the First Army Mine School provided me with many a welcome meal after wanderings round the front, and I was glad that his work was recognised by promotion to major shortly before he took over my work at GHQ, after the war was over. The paper he read before the Institution of Mining and Metallurgy later on had a special interest for me, as it had fallen to me, after the Armistice, to collect all the principal data of the work of the Tunnelling Companies for General Biddulph for official purposes, and no doubt the completion of that task was of great interest to Ball.

His assistant at the Mine School, RG Smart*, is a well-known mining engineer in the Cannock Chase coalfield, and his book on mine rescue work is the standard authority on the subject. I had the pleasure of meeting him at his home in 1930.

Two other men on the Engineer-in-Chief's staff were Bellamy, the Experimental Officer, and Hopkins*, the bridge designer. With Bellamy I shared a batman after the departure of faithful Round for more active work in 1918. He was mainly concerned with mechanical gadgets and inventions beyond my understanding, but one thing he did earlier on is of special interest. The armoured cars in France were for a long while proof against the German bullets, but on one occasion it was found that cars were being penetrated by a new type of armour-piercing bullet the enemy had developed. There was no time for proper measures to be taken to protect the cars, as they were needed for an urgent raid. Accordingly the cars were covered with thin sheets of a cement-asbestos fibre, similar to those now sold as 'Poilite' etc, for it was found that if these were fixed on frames about an inch away from the steel plates, they provided full protection, although if close against them they were useless. [*It is interesting to observe that, so far as the editors can ascertain, it was not until the early sixties, with the development of Chobham armour, that this defensive principle was revived.*] If this story seems incredible to any reader, I would refer them to a well-known armoured car leader of those days, Captain FW Poate MC*, who confirmed it in conversation with me a few months ago and, in Shanghai at least, his word goes on anything to do with armoured cars, which are still his pet hobby, and the armoured cars he designed are often in action there.

Hopkins was a great character. Perhaps the least military-minded of all the staff, he had been designing bridges in South America before the war, and at this work was a genius. The thousands of 'Hopkins' bridges erected in France during 1918 were his best testimonial. He produced designs so well standardised and so simple of erection that all kinds of troops were ultimately employed in that work. It was an added point

A 120 foot Hopkins bridge that was built in seven days over the Haute Deûle at le Pont Maudit, north east of Lens and close to Pont à Vendin and Annay. The bridge carried the road between Lens and Carvin. Many of the tunnelling companies were committed to replacing bridges that had been blown up by the retreating Germans during the Advance to Victory at the end of the war. Two civilians and a child have joined the photograph of Chaplain Baird and members of the 3rd Australian Tunnelling Company in front of their handiwork.

in their favour that there was no part which would not go onto a GS wagon. Bolts were used in place of rivets for fitting them together, and the bridges were really large scale examples of the 'Meccano' art, which most of us have been taught by our small sons in their spare time.

One picture of Hopkins may be given here. In the bitter weather we so often experienced at Montreuil, he had been ordered to report at the E-in- C's mess one morning in order to make an early start for the forward areas with his chief. The open cars we mostly used had taught Hopkins a lesson, and he appeared in due course in the mess, with his normal equipment of red thatch and eyeglasses, half hidden by the collar of his British warm, below which appeared a foot of bright purple dressing gown!

There are so many others who should find a place in this account of GHQ and Army life, but there is no room for them all [*Dixon makes an annotation here: 'Colonel Hudspeth, Major Tulloch, Major Brown and all the other Company Commanders must therefore forgive me.*] and it is time I passed on to the story of the doings of the last and, for me, the most interesting year of the whole war.

Chapter Ten

The GHQ Lines

Last hopes they were, and dug in desperate times,
By multitudes of workers of all climes.

The gloom of Passchendaele spread itself over the remainder of 1917, and with the collapse of the Russian front the Germans transferred their divisions steadily to our greatly extended line. It was clear to the most junior student of the position that we were in for a serious year in 1918.

Important changes took place in the E in C's office before the year was out. Major General GM Heath succeeded to the post of E in C. The I of M left to become Chief Engineer to a Corps, where his fighting instincts were more likely to find an outlet, now that active mine warfare had practically ceased. His place was taken by Brigadier General McInnes, who became also Deputy E in C conjointly with General Edmonds. Major Buckingham*, who had come from 180 Company to fill Major Stokes' position in the summer, went away to command a Field Company; and under the new establishment his place was taken by a Staff-Colonel, who was actually almost entirely responsible for the work previously done by the I of M, but who was described still as AI of M. This post was filled by the Controller of Mines, Fifth Army, Colonel BWY Danford, of whom much more anon.

For several weeks before General Harvey left I occupied the trestle table in his office in the place of Major Buckingham, who had gone some time before then. General Harvey may remember that my telephone was an extension line from his own instrument, and it was necessary for me to ask him to remove his receiver every time I wanted to use mine. Eventually I rigged up a system of strings across the ceiling which removed this trouble, and gave him a little more peace. Those weeks were of great interest to me, as I saw the General at closer range than ever before, and lost most of my fear of him.

General MacInnes, and his successor General Biddulph, were responsible for so many things besides the Tunnelling Companies, that Colonel Danford and I had a great deal of work added to our own in connection particularly with the defence work which was now the first consideration all along the front. With the help of Clark, we prepared defence plans for the whole front, and over these many an anxious conference took place, particularly those of the Fifth Army front, where some fourteen weak divisions were endeavouring to develop defences on the line taken over at Lloyd George's wish from the French. Really solid defences were almost non-existent along this front, and the time was short. But men were woefully scarce for such a colossal undertaking, and a whole year would not have been too long to prepare for that overwhelming attack which the Staff so clearly foresaw.

Everything that could be done in the time with the men available was done. At every point along our own old line, save in the north, where

A mixture of allied troops and refugees in the Somme area retreating before the Germans after the launching of the Kaiserschlacht and Operation Michael in late March 1918. Despite causing severe damage to Gough's Fifth Army, the offensive in this sector eventually ran out of steam a fortnight later at Villers Bretonneux, west of the key city of Amiens. The Germans had lost many fine troops and had reconquered a large swathe of largely barren territory, much of which had been devastated by themselves during the withdrawal to the Hindenburg Line the previous year.

the collapse of the Portuguese let the Germans through, our line held fast, but on the Fifth Army front the hammer blows of March drove our splendid troops back to the very gates of Amiens.

From the time the attack broke upon us there was an incessant flow of telegrams announcing our further retreat. It was one of my duties to keep General Heath's situation map up to date, and a miserable work I found it in those anxious days. I asked Colonel Danford to let me go to a Company, but before anything could be done about it we were sent for at 1a.m. one morning, and told that we were to start at once for the Doullens area to construct a line of rear defences. Knowing little else than this, we set out at 7 o'clock the same morning on a memorable ride. Danford became OC GHQ Line, and I was his Adjutant. For a day we took up our quarters at the Fourth Army Training School, while officers and men of all kinds and nationalities began to appear from all over France to help in the work.

It was 'Dan's' job to get the line marked out and to supervise the work on the site. I had my hands much more than full in endeavouring to sort out, to billet, and to feed the 11,000 workers for whom we were responsible. Beyond a chauffeur there was no staff, until I borrowed a typewriter and sent for Sergeant Kearns. Of transport we had none beyond the car we had come in. A few miles to the east of us the greatest battle of the war was rolling towards us. Tools, food, wire and sandbags could only be got by fetching them ourselves, and it was not long before I had commandeered a fleet of fourteen lorries by the most high-handed methods. The driver of any empty lorry seen was ordered off for supplies, under pain of instant arrest, no matter what his own orders were, and so we found a way through those dreadful days. When we received a third telegram from Army about a particular lorry it was released and another one commandeered. Of messages from mere Corps we took no notice, relying on the circumstances to acquit us if court martial resulted.

The whole base areas of France had been swept clean in the effort to provide us with officers and men for the work. From camouflage officers to half recovered wounded, all the white troops available were sent; but apart from Britishers of all descriptions, we had Italian, French and Portuguese labourers, Indians and Chinese; and last, but never least, the energetic Americans.

What Danford did up the line I hardly know, for I never saw any part of the thirty miles that were dug before our very irregular organization was taken over at the end of a fortnight by a complete Corps headquarters staff from the Fifth Army. No doubt they found it a very pleasant rest after all they had been through.

During this fortnight Danford had taken as his field assistant a merry Irishman, Musgrave, who was an ideal man for the work. To hear the pair of them telling Irish stories over their so called dinner was a treat after the day's struggles, for Dan's short pipe would come out and his chuckles would warn us of another one even riper than the ones before.

We returned to GHQ for a few days before being despatched to similar duty behind Hazebrouck, this time with our HQ in St Omer, where we found the most luxurious of billets with a French family. One of the fellows from the base who came up to us there was so delightful a companion, and so obviously unfit for heavy work, that we got him to run our mess. As he was a man of considerable wealth, being a well-known figure in the City, we did ourselves very well indeed, and owed a lot to his open-handed hospitality, for I am sure that the mess accounts he presented could not have represented a half of what he spent. His name was Ralli and I hope he is still able to adorn the dinner tables of his Clubs as graciously as he did that mess in St Omer.

Among the officers who reported to us in the south were two Australians, who were ordered to report to a section officer for work, but whom I did not see again for ten days. When they strolled in they informed me that they had been up to see the war, and having satisfied themselves that the fighting had settled down again after the exhaustion of the German effort, they thought they had better report for duty. What they had been up to in those ten days I had no time to enquire, and was not inclined to, for any kind of Australian was only too welcome to help on the work on the line.

We spent five weeks at St Omer, and the defences were joined on to the great scheme of inundations which the French put into force in front of Dunkirk, and we felt that our left flank was at least safe.

Danford was one of the most amusing people to work for. He was once asked by a certain General whether the Indians were any good at putting up barbed wire.

'Rather, Sir,' he answered, 'Only, when they have finished, the result is mostly turbans and puttees.'

It was a favourite saying of his that no man should get up before the day was decently aired, but he never got a chance to put this maxim into practice. We were fortunate to have in the north a section of a Tunnelling Company for the work, and they proved very useful on one occasion at least as special police.

We had several hundred Chinese coolies among the rest, and they worked splendidly for the most part, as they always did when properly handled. But they caused some trouble one night, which might have proved much more serious than it did , but for the prompt action of the Tunnellers.

One of the officers of the Chinese Labour Company had sent his batman round to a farm to buy some eggs. The old French farmer hated the sight of the Chinese, whom he suspected, not altogether without reason, of purloining his fowls whenever opportunity offered. Accordingly he told the coolie to go elsewhere in forcible French. Not to be daunted, or in his

No 228574 Chinese Labour Corps. Died 10 July 1917. 'A good reputation endures for ever', Maroeuil British Cemetery, close to Arras. Members of the Chinese Labour Corps were simply known by their number. The inscription was one of a number, chosen at random by the IWGC from a list of half a dozen, that reflected an English translation of common expressions used by the Chinese in regard to soldiers.

ignorance of the foreign devil's tongue, the coolie went round to the back door and tried that. Thereupon the Frenchman hit him over the head with a rake and laid him out. The rest of the coolies gathered round and there was much 'Wallah, wallah', but no action was taken until 2 a.m. the next night, when they completely wrecked the farmhouse, the owner and his wife just escaping with their lives.

When we again handed over to a tired Corps Staff, I had the temerity to tell this story to the incoming General, he listened with a frozen face, and then said disdainfully, 'And where were your Military Police?' Danford stood by while I tried to explain to the General that such emblems of red tape and routine as Military Police had never come within our wildest dreams in our emergency organization, and Dan told me later that I had been unlucky in striking the one man in the army known to be entirely devoid of the remotest sense of humour.

The American contingent who helped in the work at this time were fine specimens of men, full of an enthusiasm for any kind of work that was going to win that 'God damned war'. Danford had a lot of difficulty at first because their own officers would site trenches in impossible positions while he was at some other part of the long line, and the trenches would be nearly dug before he could rectify matters. But they were a grand bunch, and my happy experience of their working capacity was repeated in Shanghai this year, when for a while the 31st American Infantry and the 4th U.S Marines showed me what could be done under analogous conditions. The particular battalion of US Engineers who came to us for the work in the north had been in New York less than three weeks before. I hope that none of their passion for digging evaporated during the next six months.

My first experience of Americans in the war was in the summer of 1917, when two of their advanced staff, engineers of great distinction in civil life, came to us to get some idea of our methods of mining. Behind their cigars were two very pleasant men, who were at first a little bit inclined to patronise, but whose interest in the tactics of mine warfare became quite acute when they were shown our plans and heard a few of the details of the Tunnellers work.

One of them said after a while 'Say, how many yards of tunnels have you dug on your front?'

'Something over a hundred miles so far.'

'So far! Say, Boy, that's far enough isn't it? A hundred miles!!'

Thanks to Ralli's help, and the reduction of the urgency of the work as the German attacks quietened down to the east of us, it was possible for me to see more of the work on this line, and even to get over to Boulogne on a motorcycle once. At the officers' club there were many who had been through the fierce fighting on the Somme and in front of Hazebrouck, and mention of that visit reminds me of another occasion when some officers entering the dining room were requested by a sergeant at the door to put out their cigarettes, which astonishing greeting was explained when they entered the room to see, sitting at a table among that collection of gentlemen, temporary and otherwise, His Majesty himself, lunching with the C in C.

Chapter Eleven

Odd Jobs and Happenings

From sand dunes by the Sea southern chalk,
Along the storied duck-boards we must walk.

The most northerly point of our front was the scene of some interesting tunnelling. In the sand dunes near Nieuport one Company drove mines for a considerable distance, the work in the loose running sand being some of the most difficult ever undertaken by our men. Before the mines could be charged, the Germans made a sudden attack along the strip of coast and overwhelmed our troops. Many of the Tunnellers were cut off by the attack, which was a disastrous day for that Company. [*257 Tunnelling Company.* See Appendix VI]

Consideration of this sector had led General Harvey in 1917 to consider the possibility of tunnelling under the canal, which reaches the sea at this point, and among others consulted was Major Morgan, who expressed the view that it could only be done by the use of compressed air caissons, the sinking of which in full view of the enemy would have been an undertaking beyond the bounds of practical possibility. The running sands could not have been penetrated in any other way, and the opinion of some of the greatest of civil engineers in London fully confirmed Major Morgan's report, so that this idea was abandoned.

After Messines the Companies were gradually transferred to duties other than mining. The construction of dugouts thirty and forty feet deep was pushed on, subways were driven at many important points along the line, and the endless work on road construction and the laying of light railways found full scope for the technical skill of the personnel.

In connection with the Passchendaele and later offensives it was necessary to prepare approaches for the tanks employed, and in that country of 'beekes' and canals it was necessary to provide means for crossing them. The usual form of tank bridge, of which many hundred were constructed by Tunnelling Companies, was an Irishman's bridge, for it was not a bridge at all. Possibly this is why Colonel Danford was asked before the close of the war to command one of the new Tank Bridging Battalions then being raised.

Major WH Morgan DSO RE, OC 255 Tunnelling Company, photographed in 1918. He was awarded the DSO in the Birthday Honours of June 1917. The number of officers who received the DSO amongst tunnelling company officers, particularly of company commanders, was notably high.

At any rate the form of bridge made in 1917 and later was very simple; either an earth embankment run straight across a canal or, when it was necessary to allow a free passage for the water, a couple of piers of earth built out from the two sides, with a gap of about eight feet for the tank to 'jump'.

It was of course necessary to build walls of strong wooden piles driven deep into the ground, with brushwood fascines between them held in place by wire. Many a 'Mother' found her way successfully across these only to fall into an impassable bog after reaching the enemy lines. These derelicts lay scattered all over that slough of despond, wrecks of the first land-ships of war.

During 1918 many of our section officers were transferred to other RE duties, and a few company commanders also. Many of the former went to command the Tramway Companies formed to develop the use of light railways. Among these I was glad to see AW Runciman attain a majority after his long service with 255 Company.

To retain a correct sense of proportion it must be remembered that the Tunnelling Service was but one branch, though a very important one

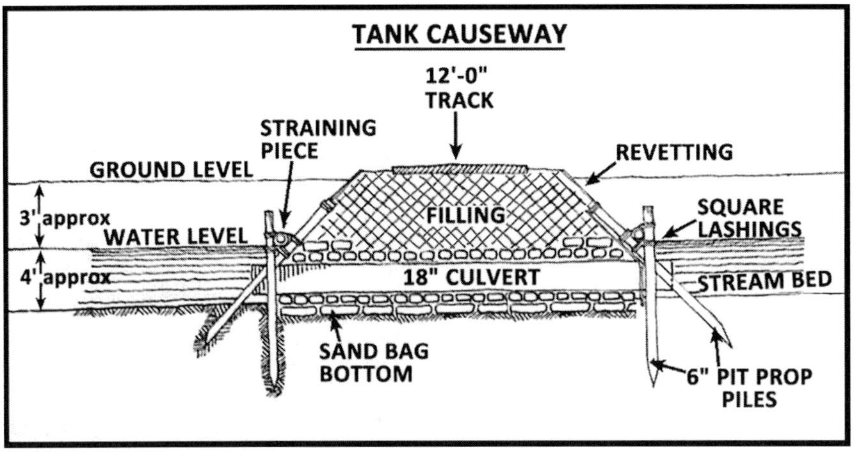

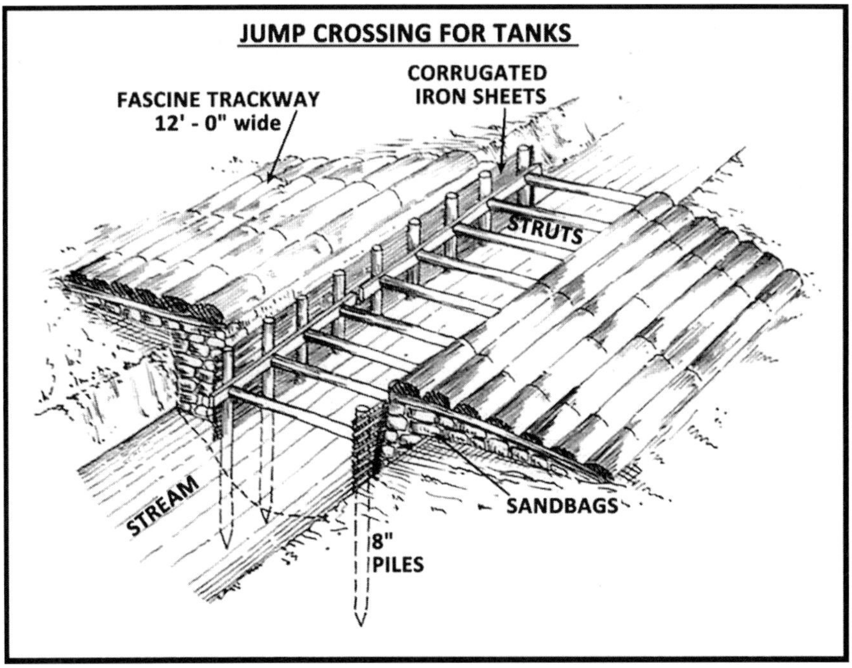

in our opinion, of the Corps of Royal Engineers, the expansion of which during the War was such that over fifty entirely new branches of it came into being. At Christmas 1918, Colonel Mackintosh* took the lead in presenting to the Engineer in Chief, from his staff, a Christmas Card. It took the form of a painting, very cleverly executed, of the old woman who lived in a shoe, with her scores of children depicted as carrying on

A post war photograph, taken by Captain HL Morton RE in early 1919, illustrates a common fate for tanks during the Third Battle of Ypres. This one was photographed near St Julien, in the Ypres Salient. The problem with tanks was that they were heavy, very slow moving, under powered (that apart from the appalling conditions inside them) and were vulnerable to anti-tank guns and light artillery. Throw in the terrible condition of the ground in the Salient and it is easy to see why they made relatively little impact in the battle. (M Morton)

their nefarious trades around her. The dirty little devil that was supposed to be a Tunneller was shown setting light to a fuse, which disappeared under her voluminous skirt. All the other branches found a place in that work of art, from the Inland Water Transport to the Forestry Companies, the Army Troops and Workshop Companies, and so to that main fighting branch the Field Companies. [*The Royal Engineers' manpower in 1918 was almost 296,000, about twelve times larger than it was at the start of hostilities.*]

This brings me to the subject of bridging, which was of the greatest importance in the latter stages of the war. Hopkins scattered his 'Meccano' steel bridges all over that part of France before it was over. There was a reluctance to employ any but Field Company personnel in the work of erection at first, and it was mainly due to General Harvey's knowledge of what Tunnellers could do, and his impatience with wasteful use of valuable technical knowledge on mere labourer's work, that they were given an opportunity which established their reputation as military bridge builders for all time.

The 180 feet span Hopkins bridge across the Canal du Nord near Havrincourt. This bridge was completed on 8 October 1918, eight days after the work began. This was mainly done by the New Zealand Engineers Tunnelling Company, assisted by 565 and 577 Army Troops RE. At the time this was reputed to be the longest single span bridge erected in military history. The scale of the bridge may be judged by contrasting it with the horses who are starting to move across it, coming from the left hand side. The road over the canal is now carried by two different bridges at or very close to this spot, one of which has many similarities to the bridge pictured here. (Inst of RE. Tom Alban)

He was then Chief Engineer of the Corps to which the New Zealand Tunnelling Company was attached. The Germans had blown the only important road bridge over the great gash of the Canal du Nord, which runs near Cambrai through a deep cutting. A detour of some five miles was involved for all our transport, and the provision of a new bridge was an urgent matter. The point selected was necessarily close beside the blown bridge, and here the cutting was 90 feet deep and 120 feet wide. A specially modified Hopkins bridge was sent up, an extra forty feet added to one end, on which all the available scrap iron was thrown to act as a counter- balance, and the bridge was then pulled into position by wire hawsers from the other side. The whole operation was completed by Major Vickerman's [New Zealand] Company in five days. Lest any may think that this was only a light bridge, it may be added that it carried two fully loaded five ton lorries at one time with perfect safety. I am told that

The Havrincourt Hopkins Bridge at road level. Amongst a number of New Zealand officers, wearing what by then had become their distinctive 'lemon squeezer' hat (designed by Lieutenant Colonel George Malone when on service on Gallipoli) are several British, including Brigadier General Harvey (centre), by this stage Chief Engineer IV Corps. The New Zealand Division formed part of his Corps at this stage in the war.

Lieutenant General Sir Aylmer Hunter-Weston, known irreverently as 'Hunter-Bunter', GOC VIII Corps. He was one of the most controversial British corps commanders – and also one of the longest serving, having a corps (VIII) more or less continuously from late May 1915 to the end of the war. He managed the unique achievement of being elected an MP in October 1916 whilst commanding a Corps in the field. Undoubtedly a brave man and certainly not devoid of ideas, military historians generally regard him as inadequate and obsessive about small details.

the bridge is still in position to this day. It was opened by the Commander in Chief, and the Company thoroughly earned his congratulations on their work, while thereafter Tunnellers were in great demand wherever bridges were needed.

Reference was made in an earlier chapter to the subway constructed under Hill 70 at Loos. This was mainly the work of an Australian Company, and was possibly the finest example of this class of work ever executed. Hill 70 is a long hog-back to the north of the village of Loos, and was one of the only gains we continued to hold after that famous battle in the autumn of 1915. [*Not so. Although taken in the 1915 Battle of Loos, it was lost to a German counter attack. Hill 70 was not taken and secured until an offensive by the Canadian Corps in August 1917.*] At the time of my last inspection of this work, VIII Corps, under an old Sapper in Sir Aylmer Hunter Weston, the Hunter Bunter of so many war yarns, was holding this front, and in the detailed development of the subway and its subsequent maintenance the Corps Commander took the greatest interest, with most beneficial results.

An entrance to Hythe Subway at Hill 70, to the south of Loos. Although the scale of tunnelling activity dropped off dramatically in the second half of 1917, this did not mean that it stopped altogether. The Loos sector remained relatively busy.

An incline entrance to Hythe Subway, coming off Hythe Trench at Hill 70.

The rear entrance to the subway was in direct connection with our light railway system, which in its turn communicated direct with the rail head for that area. The tunnel ran under the highest part of the hill towards the front line for some 700 yards. In branches off it were large and comfortable dugouts, cook-houses, wells and water bottle filling stations, various aid posts and a casualty clearing station, or, to be strictly accurate, a forward dressing station. In the forward portion were cleverly hidden trench mortar battery positions, Lewis and Vickers machine gun positions, company and battalion HQs with rocket posts adjoining and, away out under our own wire, was a special observation chamber, from which a large periscope was arranged in among the wire, camouflaged to look like an old tree stump. This instrument was of special design; looking into the eyepiece one had the whole of the German lines in view over a wide area and their working parties were spotted at once if they ventured to do work outside their trenches. Telephone communication with all the other parts of the system enabled swift action to be taken if the enemy were seen.

But the most interesting features of this fortress lay in the measures taken for protection against gas attacks or heavy gas shelling and the

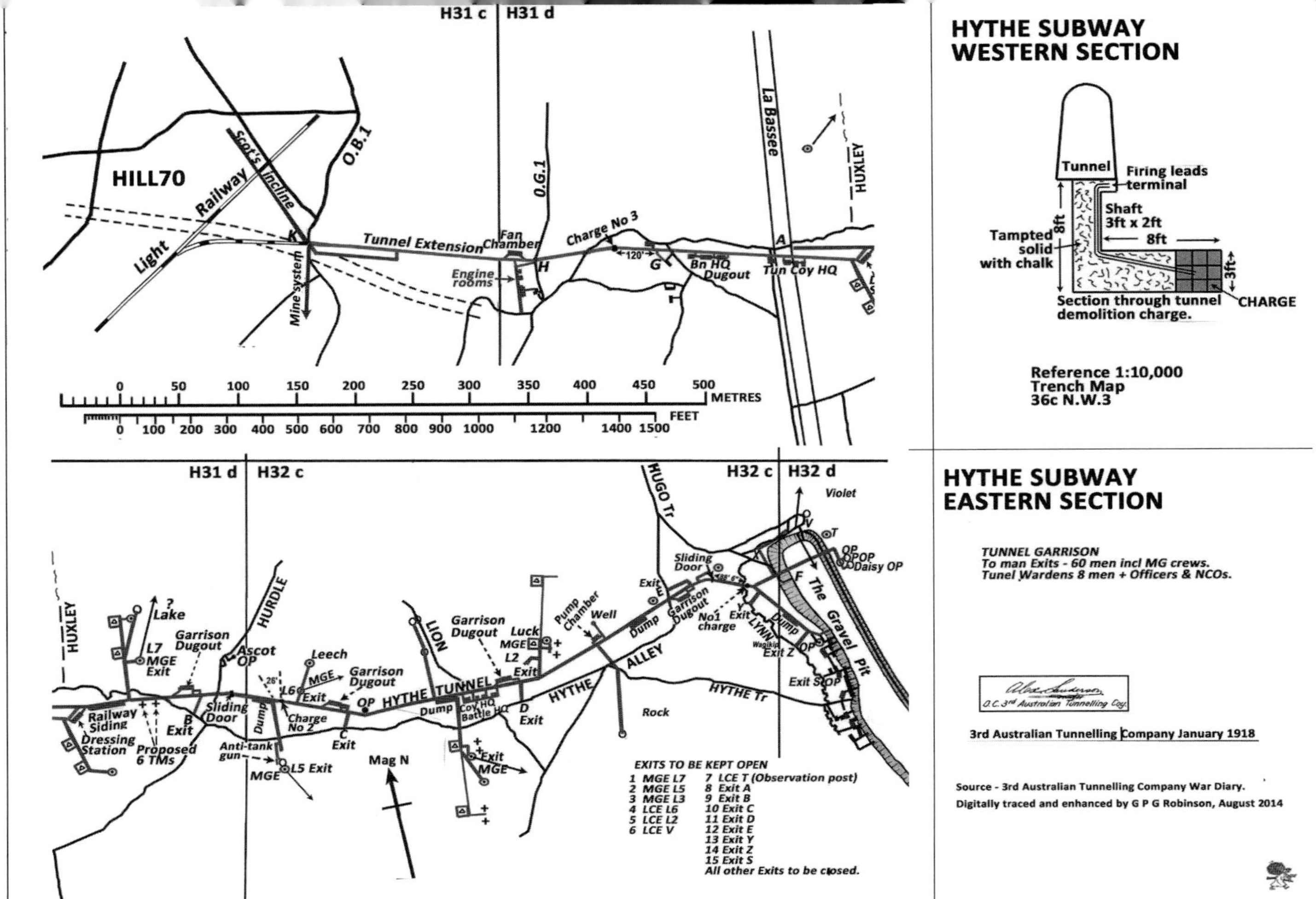
HYTHE SUBWAY
WESTERN SECTION
Tunnel
Firing leads terminal
Shaft 3ft x 2ft
8ft
8ft
3ft
Tampted solid with chalk
CHARGE
Section through tunnel demolition charge.
Reference 1:10,000
Trench Map
36c N.W.3
HYTHE SUBWAY
EASTERN SECTION
TUNNEL GARRISON
To man Exits - 60 men incl MG crews.
Tunel Wardens 8 men + Officers & NCOs.
O.C. 3rd Australian Tunnelling Coy.
3rd Australian Tunnelling Company January 1918
Source - 3rd Australian Tunnelling Company War Diary.
Digitally traced and enhanced by G P G Robinson, August 2014
H31 c
H31 d
HILL70
Light Railway
Scot's Incline
O.B.1
O.G.1
Mine system
Tunnel Extension
Fan Chamber
Engine rooms
Charge No 3
La Bassee
Bn HQ Dugout
Tun Coy HQ
HUXLEY
METRES
FEET
H31 d
H32 c
H32 c
H32 d
HUGO Tr
Violet
Daisy OP
The Gravel Pit
HURDLE
Lake
Garrison Dugout
Ascot OP
Leech
LION
Luck
Pump Chamber
Well
Sliding Door
Railway Siding
Dressing Station
Proposed 6 TMs
Anti-tank gun
L5 Exit
Charge No 2
HYTHE TUNNEL
Coy HQ
Battle HQ
HYTHE ALLEY
No1 charge
LYNN
HYTHE Tr
Rock
Exit S
Mag N
EXITS TO BE KEPT OPEN
1 MGE L7
2 MGE L5
3 MGE L3
4 LCE L6
5 LCE L2
6 LCE V
7 LCE T (Observation post)
8 Exit A
9 Exit B
10 Exit C
11 Exit D
12 Exit E
13 Exit Y
14 Exit Z
15 Exit S
All other Exits to be closed.

concrete work that was carried out. Every entrance to the surrounding trenches was fitted with a gas curtain, made from an army blanket, specially treated to prevent gas passing through it. These were arranged on rollers above a sloping frame, so that a pull of a string would fasten them tightly in position over the door. To ensure that no gas or contaminated air could enter the system owing to damage to, or failure to close, any door, a powerful electrically driven fan could in emergency provide the air for the whole system. This was drawn through an enormous box-respirator, and the pressure caused in the galleries when the fan was at work was such that air could not get in to the galleries, even at an open door. The power station for driving the electric fan and the lighting plant was installed and run by the Australian AEMM&B Company, and was necessarily quite an elaborate affair in itself.

The tactics to be adopted in case of an attack had been very carefully thought out, and the garrison, which comprised a whole brigade of infantry, had very special training in the use of the many new devices

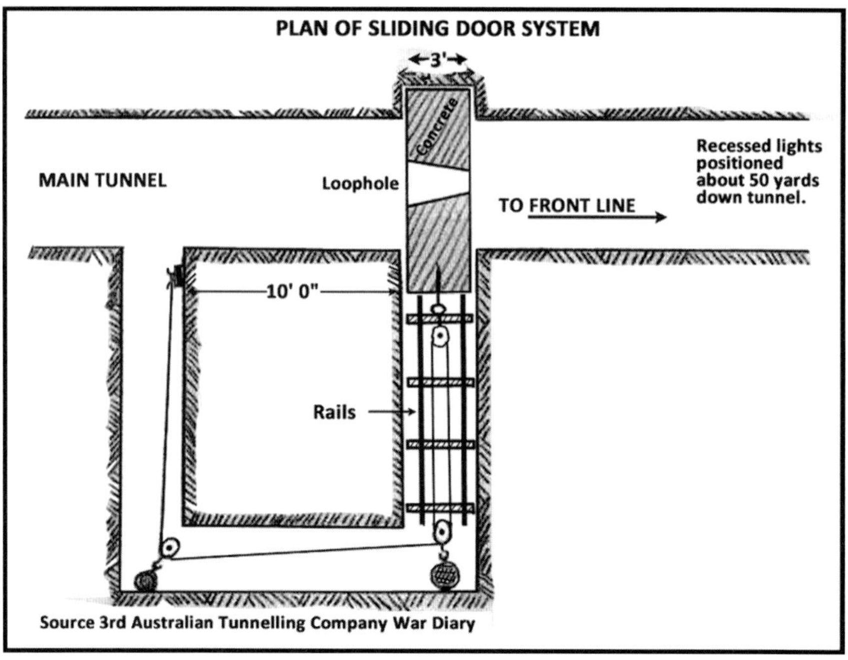

One of the 3rd Australian Tunnelling Company's ingenious additions to the system's defences, a sliding door that aimed to thwart the progress of any German infiltration into the system.

employed. Chief among these was the scheme of concrete doors. In the main galleries were solid doors of concrete three feet thick, mounted on rails. By means of snatch blocks and ropes they were normally pulled clear of the gallery into chambers cut for them in the chalk, but the rails on which they ran were arranged to slope towards the gallery, where they ran below the level of the floor. If the need arose the door could be run into position by a single pull of the rope, which released it at once. These doors were provided with loopholes. All the lights in the main galleries were set in recesses cut in the side, so that while the gallery was clearly illuminated throughout its length, it was impossible for an enemy to see the lamps and shoot them out. [*In 2015 the Durand Group found one of these in position in the Hulluch Subway*.]

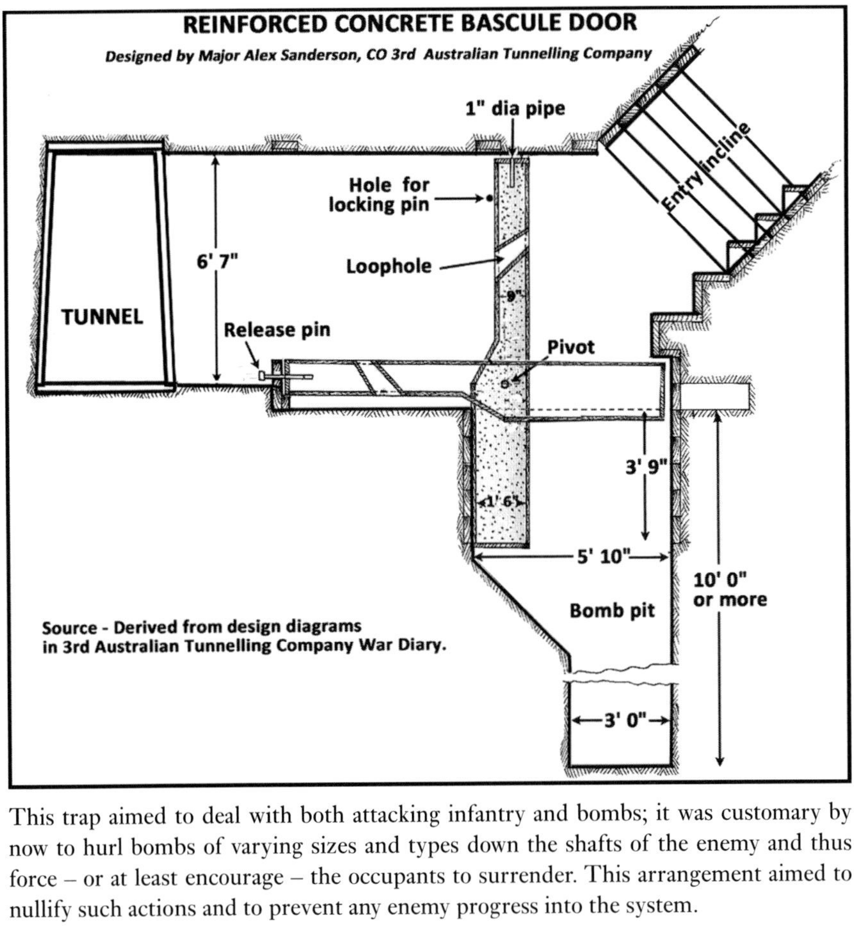

This trap aimed to deal with both attacking infantry and bombs; it was customary by now to hurl bombs of varying sizes and types down the shafts of the enemy and thus force – or at least encourage – the occupants to surrender. This arrangement aimed to nullify such actions and to prevent any enemy progress into the system.

At the foot of the steps leading down from each trench entrance was an ingenious trapdoor, also of concrete, arranged on a pivot across the gallery, so that when a bolt was pulled out the outside end turned downwards into a hole twenty feet deep, into which the pursuing enemy or his bombs could drop, while the inside part of the door rose into place and blocked the gallery. These doors were also provided with loopholes. It was a sad day for the garrison officer responsible if the Corps Commander ever found one of these doors not in working order owing to mud.

Many other subways were constructed at other parts of the front on similar lines, but perhaps Hill 70 was the most elaborate of all. Any visit there ended with a picnic lunch in a ruined cellar in Loos itself, but my host's name has been forgotten, to my regret.

Various attempts had been made in 1917 to obtain machines which would expedite the work of the Tunnellers, and Smyth will remember the many trials of tunnelling machines, or 'Earthworms'. It was found, however, that for mining work they were useless on account of their noise, and for other work they were too cumbrous and complicated, whilst in the softer ground for which they were best suited, the difficulty of timbering more than offset any slight advantage they might claim over hand work. [*Two such 'Stanley Heading Machines' were manufactured in early 1916.*]

This mechanical cutter was briefly employed in the St Eloi area in 1916 and is probably a Stanley Heading machine. There were numerous problems in using mechanical cutters in the Battle Zone – in Flanders, for example, the nature of the clay was one factor that contributed to render them more or less useless.

One was deployed with great difficulty at Petit Bois under the Messines Ridge. There were numerous tribulations, explained in detail in Alexander Barrie's book War Underground. *In March 1916 it was abandoned and remains in situ about ninety feet below ground. The second machine was apparently used successfully for quarrying work and then in the 1920s for a preliminary effort to drive a tunnel under the Channel. It is rumoured that it still exists.*]

Marshal (from July 1918) Foch and General Weygand. Foch was an effective Army commander in the early months of the war. He performed particularly well at the First Battle of Ypres, which likely provided the generally sound foundations of good relations with Haig, who commanded I Corps during the battle. His career seemed to have peaked when Joffre was replaced as Commander in Chief in December 1916; but Nivelle's failures in 1917 brought him back into the limelight. In late March 1918 he was appointed, effectively, the Allied Commander in Chief ('Supremo' was often used to describe his new position) in the light of the opening of the German spring offensives in March 1918. However, the powers of command that he possessed were far from clear cut and it was largely due to his capabilities and tact (and the fact that he got on well with Haig) that he made such a success of the job. Never far from him was his ever-loyal assistant, Weygand, who was a first rate staff officer. At well over seventy years of age, as an act of desperation, he was brought back to command the French armies in May 1940, only to have to approve an armistice, which ceremony took place in the same carriage where he had witnessed the Germans sign theirs in 1918.

At the time of these experiments we received a visit from a notable personality, who has for many years rendered wonderful service to his country. This was Sir John Cadman*, now head of the Anglo Persian Oil Company. As Professor of Mining at Birmingham University he had been one of the examiners appointed under the Coal Mines Act, and in 1914 he had passed me for a colliery fireman's certificate in gas testing and so forth at Hednesford, and it was a pleasure to show him over the plans in the I of M's office three years later.

Throughout 1918, apart from the time spent on the 'Last Hopes' or GHQ lines already described, I was away a great deal on the fronts of the various Armies, and also in connection with a very special and 'hush-hush' scheme of demolitions. Marshal Foch had decided that in the event of the German pressure in the north continuing its severity, the British Armies were at all costs to retain touch with the French Army, and that if necessary the Channel ports were to be abandoned. This would have involved a retreat greater than anything recorded in the war, and the details of this operation were carefully worked out by the General Staff, and orders issued for the necessary preparatory measures to be taken.

This was always referred to as 'Z' Scheme, and it became a constant feature of the 'Secret Box' circulated to the officers concerned. My part in the scheme was the preparation of all the organization for demolition of the roads behind the retreating Armies. There were four principal roads running south from Flanders, and one of these was allotted to each of the Second, First, and Third Armies, the other being intended for the civilian population. Each of these, and all interconnecting roads of the smallest importance, had to be demolished, if the scheme were ever put into operation, at as many points as possible.

The area concerned was about 3000 square miles, covering all that part of France behind the Army areas, and roughly stretching from Dunkirk in the north to Dieppe in the south, as far forward as a line running from Dunkirk through St Pol, and so southwards. Had the scheme ever been brought into force it would have meant that the Tunnelling Companies would have been wiped out of existence, for they would have had the post of honour in the retreat.

The area was divided off into rough squares, one square being allotted to each Company, and a site selected for the HQ and the explosive dump.

Twelve tunnelling officers on motorcycles spent many, I hope, pleasant weeks on the reconnaissance of this lovely countryside, and by degrees we collected in our office a mass of paper which would have rejoiced the heart of any War Office clerk. For every selected site, whether a bridge, a crossroad or other point where useful craters could be blown, a sheet was filled in giving a sketch of the site, and of the proposed method of dealing with it, the map reference of course, with all details for its easy recognition, and a detailed list of the stores and tools required for the job, down to the last sandbag. Some degree of uniformity of method was arrived at, no doubt to the upsetting of the pet ideas of some of those twelve tunnellers, but at least they had the sadistic satisfaction of working out one of the greatest schemes of demolitions ever conceived, and, fortunately for everyone, never needed. Probably they still suffer from my own complaint of never being able to see a big bridge without mentally calculating how much ammonal would be needed to blow the piers and bridge to smithereens. [*Perhaps curiously, Phillip Robinson was involved with a very similar scheme in Germany in 1965 against the anticipation of a Soviet attack.*]

One or two of the fine bridges in Calais and Boulogne were particularly attractive to us. Once Colonel Danford took me with him on a visit to his parents' home on the coast north of Boulogne and the fresh strawberries suffered considerably; but that was a pleasant afternoon for me. His red tabs bent down over the beds remains a vivid memory.

One distinctly odd job that came my way in 1917 was in connection with the air raids, which even then were becoming disturbing to the peace of GHQ. General Harvey had been asked for his views on the arrangements for air raid shelters at the École. He put me on to make an inspection, and I remember giving a very candid opinion on their inadequacy. Below the rectangle of buildings there were arched cellars of no great strength, which would have been readily penetrated by any fair sized bomb. But far worse than this was the fact that one cellar was allotted for each branch of the staff, so that if one cellar had been hit the whole of the staff of one department would have been wiped out.

Thereafter it was arranged to distribute members of the different departments and I was asked to investigate some rumours as to caves below Montreuil with a view to providing accommodation for the civilian population. After long enquiry from many of the inhabitants, all of whom told me that caves were certainly there, though how to gain access they did not know, I was able to get something concrete, and one afternoon at the Boulogne Gate I met a French boy of about 16 who had a knotted rope over his shoulder and who was to show me the caves.

Outside the gate there is a line of shops along the Hesdin-St Pol to Arras road, and into the chemists we went. In the kitchen a stone flag was removed and a circular shaft disclosed, down which we went hand over hand, finding ourselves in a long cavern some fourteen feet wide and about as much high. It ran for half a mile or more altogether, with one or two branch galleries, and we duly surveyed it and reported to the General that while there certainly was a good cave there it would be a death trap in heavy bombing, as the span was so great and the chalk so broken and fissured that it would fall in large sections. The cost of timbering it would have been absolutely prohibitive, the idea was abandoned, and proper dugouts were constructed later by labour under the direction of a section of Tunnellers.

The deadly mustard gas first used by the Germans in 1917 was the cause of another opportunity for work for the Tunnellers. It will be known that this poison only becomes volatile at a temperature of about 60°F, and in cold weather it would often be flung out of gas shells as a liquid and lie dormant for a long time. If it was on sandbags or clothing it was often the case that in the relative warmth of a dugout the effects of the gas were not noticed until long after a man had been contaminated. We had a number of casualties from this cause in the mines and dugouts then being made. Some genius had discovered that the effects of the gas could be prevented, or at least partially so, by exposure of the clothing to the action of an equally unpleasant gas in the shape of chlorine. The problem was how to treat men who had been in gassed areas without giving them a worse dose than they already might get from the mustard gas.

The Mine Rescue apparatus was eventually tried, and during 1918 a number of stations were put into operation and the men affected put through a chlorine chamber wearing it. This treatment undoubtedly saved many casualties from this insidious danger.

In the heavy fighting in April of 1918 two old friends of mine, brothers together in the Warwickshires, came in for all the worst part of the Somme retreat, and were no sooner taken out for a rest as they hoped, on a quiet sector, than they were in the thick of the Hazebrouck battle. One was taken prisoner and spent the rest of the war in Germany, while the other lies buried not far from Estaires. One Sunday, some months after, I was able to find and photograph his grave, and a draughtsman then in our office made a little pen and ink sketch, which hung on the wall of Eric's parents' bedroom until they too passed on after the war. An old school-fellow, Eric Parsons* was a fine cricketer, and had he lived we were hoping he would have appeared for his county at Edgbaston. [*Lance Corporal E Parsons, 8/London Regiment (Post Office Rifles). Died 20 April 1918, buried in St Pierre Cemetery, Amiens. XII E 4, and so in reality was finally buried many miles from Estaires. Eric was not in the Warwicks when he died, though may well have been transferred from a Warwicks battalion to the Post Office Rifles during the substantial reorganization of the BEF that took place in February-March 1918.*]

Chapter Twelve

Tales That are Told

A chapter that contains many a yarn
Told in a dugout, Nissen Hut, or barn.

Of all the reports of Tunnellers' activities that passed through my hands there was one, which in its bare account of fearlessness and audacity, surpassed all the thrillers ever written. It was from a young Australian officer who had then been in France only a fortnight. The main features are so firmly fixed in my mind that I will attempt to reproduce the story in something of the style in which it was written. It should be explained that this exploit took place at a part of the line which was then very thinly held by the enemy, as far as the front line trenches were concerned. The report ran on these lines:

> The infantry having reported that there seemed to be a large dugout at the end of a German forward sap opposite our front, I accompanied one of their officers across No Man's Land and found this to be the case. Inside the dugout there was a mine shaft, and I therefore returned for my compass and tape. With another infantry officer I then explored the German workings, which were unoccupied. A plan of the workings is enclosed. It was then thought desirable to blow in the shaft, and we accordingly placed a charge of 501bs of ammonal in position and exploded it at 4 p.m. The explosion attracted some attention to our lines from the German guns, and in order to make sure that the shaft was demolished I returned to the site and found this to be the case.

The point of the story lies in that 4 p.m. The four separate double crossings of No Man's Land were all made in daylight. He earned his MC rather thoroughly. But this kind of courage, or perhaps lack of fear, was typical of the Australian and Canadian troops, of all kinds. Not that it was not to be found among our own men, but because most of our own fellows would never have gone wandering about No Man's Land in broad daylight without first getting permission. This would seldom have been granted for an adventure of this kind by day.

The Royal Air Force [*The RAF came into existence on 1 April 1918; it is unclear which wit thought of April Fool's Day as the foundation date!*] were of the greatest assistance to us in our mining work, giving us photographs of the German lines, taken often from very low altitudes, within a few hours of the request being made. Some of our officers went to them later on in the war, including English of the cast iron throat and Thompson of the Bully Crater days. But it is probably not known to many of those who served in the Air Force that they once called the Tunnellers to their assistance in their air fighting.

A kite balloon with its observer in position about to take to the air. The balloon was specially designed to provide a steady platform for observation of the enemy lines, mainly used for spotting enemy artillery. The job of the observer involved some skill in managing the balloon.

The kite balloons that formed such a prominent feature along the front were constantly being shot down by the aeroplanes of the opposite side, and certain of our own and of the German aviators seemed to specialise in this form of activity. I can recall a day near Beaumont Hamel when

An observer in the process of jumping out of his balloon basket – another observer can be seen below him and to the right. Observation balloons were a favoured, if dangerous, target for enemy aircraft. Unlike aircrew, it was relatively straightforward to provide these observers with a parachute, as it could be fixed to the side of the basket in a container and attached to the observer by a harness. When he jumped, the bulk of the parachute was pulled out of the container – though, as illustrated, it looks as if it might have been a painful experience. Neither side used parachutes in aircraft – they were too bulky for a cramped cockpit and weighed too much; however, in the last weeks of the war the Germans did start issuing them to airmen.

four of our kite balloons came down in flames one after the other, the skilful enemy pilot escaping to his own lines unscathed. At all events it was a matter of great importance to our gunners that the constant attacks should be discouraged, and with the help of the nearest, 252 Tunnelling Company, it was done. A balloon was sent up with well made dummies in the basket, apparently observing as usual through their field glasses. Along came the same aviator who had been so active hitherto and swooping over the sausage let fly with his incendiary bullets. But there was no need for them that time, for the 500 lb of ammonal which was also in the basket was exploded at the right time, and though I do not think the aeroplane was actually caught, there was a lot more care taken in approaching our balloons in future. The officer who blew the charge told me that when he was testing the circuit he was alarmed to notice relatively heavy currents passing through the galvanometer, which he could only attribute to the atmospheric electricity. It must have been as exciting as catching trout to wait with such a bait, for a nibble from the flying fish.

There was one section officer who rather fancied himself as a surveyor, and who had occasion to criticise the plan of his front drawn up by the regular surveyor. The surveyor was told that the section officer's own plotting apparently differed widely from his and the latter was sure he was right. He was then shown the aeroplane photograph of the line and was flabbergasted to see that his version did not even remotely resemble it. He was asked whether he had been using a prismatic compass. 'Yes, and I took special care to leave my revolver behind … but, oh Lord!, sorry old man, I had my steel helmet on all the time!' (The early helmets were magnetic.)

The previous story of the Air Force reminds me to mention (and here let me say that this book has largely been written for the benefit of my own boys and their cousins in years to come) that my eldest brother served for a year with the Air Force at Corfu in the Mediterranean. This was after his return from the two-and-a-half-year cruise of HMS *Kent*, the predecessor of the fine cruiser of the County class, which is such a familiar sight on the Whangpoo as the Flagship of the Commander in Chief China Station. The older ship took a historic part in the Falkland Islands battle, and later sank the *Dresden* off Juan Fernandez Island. He was a surgeon in the RNVR before the war, and has maintained that connection ever since, being the Surgeon-Commander of HMS *Flying Fox* at Bristol still (1932). We can therefore claim as a family to have seen fighting in the air, on the sea, on the ground and under it and, although we had no direct connection with the submarine service, my brother had many a flight observing for signs of U boats, whilst one of us came into touch with that department at the Admiralty later on, as will be narrated in another chapter.

A Commander Harvey was on the *Flying Fox* two years ago, and his name reminds me that I told General Harvey at that lunch that I was really a distant relation of his.

'How's that? Why didn't you tell me in France?'

'Well, Sir, it wasn't true then, and if it had been I should never have had the nerve to tell you. But you see a niece by marriage of my eldest brother married your first cousin.' [*Dixon's handwritten annotation here:*

'On asking a small boy to whom I read this chapter what relation I was to the General, he replied, "An ancestor"!']

The father of that lady must be my excuse for the rambling nature of this chapter. Whenever he took his family to Thurston for their summer holiday, he always kept one large trunk open for the odd parcels left over at the last minute, and he used to say that this trunk invariably contained the real essentials for the holiday, and was well filled on every occasion.

It is to be hoped that in this long chapter will be found sidelights on the Tunnelling Companies which will enable the reader to appreciate certain aspects of their work, which are essential for the full story of their small but important part in the war in France.

During the Fifth Army retreat the Tunnellers took a full share in the fierce fighting, forming a part of the famous Carey's Force, which staved

With the opening of the anticipated German offensives of 1918, the war of static, heavily fortified successive defensive lines came to an end. Successive German attacks between late March and July put the allies under severe strain, but each offensive was brought to a halt, even if the situation of the allies was frequently very precarious. Here British and French troops combine to defend a hastily prepared temporary line during the retreat of Gough's Fifth Army on the Somme.

off the last desperate attacks before Villers Brettoneux [*this ad hoc Force included 253 Tunnelling Company*] and at the Battle of Lys in April. Two Tunnellers who had been captured by a German officer on the front of the XIX Corps [*which took part in the First Battle of the Somme 1918 and formed part of Fifth Army*] were reported as having escaped to safety by hitting their captor in the eye with first time shots with the tins of bully beef carried as iron rations.

In the autumn of that year at the long German tunnel at Bellicourt, some of them got a little of their own back. The tunnel was captured in the attack on the Hindenburg Line, and I was shown over it later on. In the power house of the tunnel were two of our men taking their ease, while two German prisoners, taken the day before, were polishing the Tommies' boots before being sent on to the prison cages in the rear. At this Tunnel occurred an incident that must be set down. When it had been surrounded and captured it was left, as usual, to the Tunnellers to report it safe for occupation before being used by the infantry. The German in charge was requested to show them the working of the various switches in the power house and from which the lighting was obtained, but he seemed strangely reluctant to close two switches, and under cross examination confessed that if they had been closed the demolition charges placed in concealed positions at the entrances would have been fired.

[*The Bellicourt – or Ricqueval – Tunnel is a very long (almost six kilometres) canal tunnel, part of the St Quentin Canal and formed an important part of the Hindenburg Line defences. In September 1918 it came under attack by Monash's Australian Corps (along with a couple of American divisions, the 27th and the 30th) and to its immediate south the British 46th (North Midland) Division. The Germans made extensive use of the protection that the tunnel offered.*]

The 'Kadaver' boiling factory of mythical renown was near this point, and I am glad to be able to add my small mite to the weight of evidence against this war lie. Undoubtedly the spot had been a central kitchen which had been hit by a heavy shell, with the results that gave rise to that very unsavoury and equally untrue story.

It has been explained that the Adjutant General was one of the few generals who lived in a chateau outside Montreuil. Coming out to France with the original Expeditionary Force as Chief Engineer, he remained at GHQ throughout the war and was one of the very few officers to do so. Lieutenant General Fowke* was a striking figure of an AG. I had heard a lot about him before catching sight of him, and expected to see the last word in beaux brummels. But my first sight of him revealed a tall and slightly stout figure, minus Sam Browne belt, a pipe in his mouth and his hands in his pockets. Only a great AG could dress like that! His interest in the Tunnellers was always profound, and we had him to thank that their strength was fully maintained when the shortage of manpower in 1918 called for such drastic reductions in the case of many other branches of the Army.

A job we did for him brought me into personal contact with him on a number of occasions. It happened in this way. During one of the frequent air raids the Germans dropped a bomb in the grounds of the chateau and killed a large cow. When the news reached the ears of Colonel Danford he made his expected but disrespectful remark. 'Quite a pardonable error on the part of the bomb dropper.'

Whether this was ever passed on to the AG I do not know, but he would have laughed if he did hear it. At all events he was persuaded to

Lieutenant General Sir George Fowke. Engineer in Chief of the BEF until February 1916. A physically big man with a personality and intelligence to match; he was a man who knew his own mind and was notably successful in adapting the Royal Engineers to the requirements of the war – not least in developing the tunnelling companies. His move to become Adjutant General of the BEF (up to and beyond the Armistice) was not entirely welcomed by him, but he made a success of it and Haig made full use of his wisdom and decisiveness.

have a pair of dugouts built in the chateau grounds, and probably they are still there, in use as wine cellars or mausoleum, for it was the latter they chiefly resembled when they were finished.

As the chateau stood on rising ground it was expected that there would be no difficulty in putting down an ordinary dugout with thirty feet of cover, but to the dismay of Danford and myself a spring of water was struck about ten feet down and there was a lot of discussion between him and the AG as to what should be done. The section of a Tunnelling Company who were then making various dugouts at Montreuil were finally instructed to turn the job into a pair of concrete dugouts, the roof to be level with the grass, and after weeks of labour it was decided by General Biddulph that the new French idea of having steeply pitched concrete roofs above such structures was to be followed out, so that finally the appearance was that of two large tombs in a churchyard. Over forty tons of cement alone went into each dugout.

Danford went on leave for several weeks in September, as he had not previously been home that year, and he was away when they were being finished. I wonder what the AG really thought of them.

One of our Companies, who were being helped by Chinese labour in the construction of dugouts, were unable to get the air pumps they needed for ventilation. They were working in made ground and the air was very foul, and to their surprise they found one day a Chinese working away at a wooden pump of their own design, which was giving all the air needed, and was in fact nearly as good as the proper ones we used. I was very interested in the design of this pump, which was subsequently circulated in 'Mining Notes', the circulars which were sent out from the I of M.'s office, and was particularly amused to see the construction of the piston, the packing of which was made from feathers. Perhaps the French farmers' suspicions were more than justified. It was of exactly the same pattern as the pumps in use for the fires under all the cooking pots in food shops all over China but, knowing no better, at the time we gave them the credit of having produced something really original.

The air raids over back areas became so serious as the last year wore on that we had a section of Tunnellers at work at the big munition dump at Abbeville for some weeks to provide shelter for the staff there. This must have been a pleasant job for the section, for Abbeville was a restful old town in the war days.

Lieutenant General Sir Travers Clarke. Quartermaster General of the BEF. He succeeded Lieutenant General Maxwell, who was very successful in his post but had reached the age of 65, at Christmas 1917. He faced the challenges in 1918 of large scale retreat and the subsequent advance, with all the impact these had on logistics, with considerable success.

When Lieutenant General Travers Clarke* became Deputy Adjutant General there was much speculation as to how long it would be before he succeeded General Fowke, and it was a surprise to most people when the former suddenly became Quarter Master General instead. The effects of the energetic new broom were soon felt in the E-in-C's department, for instead of the whole of RE Stores being dealt with from that office through a CRE at Les Attaques, a new branch of the QMG's department was created under the title of the Directorate of Engineering Stores. As this was a brigadier general's appointment, it was necessary for him to have a considerable staff, one at least of whom had very few ideas on the subject of engineering stores. A subaltern from the E-in-C's office was sent for by this gentleman one day, who asked him a question so elementary as to have been the jest of our office later. 'I say, can you tell me what a joist is? I'm always being asked for them.' 'Certainly, Sir,' was the answer, 'there's one up there', and he pointed to the rafters above the officer's head. No doubt this staff officer had other sound qualifications, but he must have found it difficult for a long while to deal with the mass of detail which such work involved.

On another occasion, Captain Hart*, who was for some years in the office of the Controller of Mines First Army, and later became Water Supply officer in the same Army, had indented for a deep well pump for one of the sub-artesian wells that were sunk at many points. A senior officer queried this indent, and asked whether a trench pump would not do instead. On being told that the lift was over ninety feet, and that the hole was only of 6″ diameter, and that a trench pump was not designed either for high lifts or for deep wells, he remarked that it ought to be possible to suck it. What a boon it would be to engineers if somebody would invent such an impossibility.

From water to water seems a natural sequence, and this carries me on to an intelligence report over which Colonel David, as he then was, and I laughed together. An aviator reported that there was serious flooding in the low lying ground to the east of Calonne and that the water appeared to be coming out of the top of a pit shaft. Knowing the vast extent of the colliery workings in that area, and that water does not run up hill, we thought it a very absurd statement. But David began to puzzle over it, and eventually we had to admit that the report was quite correct. But for his prolonged study of the water levels in the chalk areas he should never have hit on the right explanation. He had established the fact that the vast volumes of water in a chalk country do not take up a simple horizontal level as might be expected, but that the level follows to some extent the contour of the surface. There were many shafts in that area of coal mines which were inter-connected below ground. David suggested that the retiring Germans had probably blown in the tubbing [*ie the water tight, cast iron lining of a circular shaft*] of one of the shafts on the rising ground at a point above ground level at the lower shaft, from which the water had been reported as coming. The result, he said, would be that the water in the chalk, previously held back by the steel tubbing, would flow down the shaft, fill the workings, and so in time reach the top of the lower shaft and cause the floods. The explanation, which he worked out from theory, was found to be absolutely true when the area was recaptured and the shafts could be examined.

David put in a lot of work in the latter part of 1918 in London and Paris, going into the question of the geology of the Rhine, for it then looked as though the Germans would never throw up the sponge without a last stand on the Rhine. And so he worked patiently at the important problem of the best sites for tunnelling operations underneath the river, all his working meeting with the same fate as 'Z' Scheme in due course, dying a natural death.

He was always a source of anxiety to us, for whenever he could get up to the line, he seemed to make for the nearest big 'strafe', and on more than one occasion he was found in a front line dugout, perfectly happy, while enquiries were being telephoned all over the area to ask if anything was known of our very precious geologist. After several happenings of this nature, General Harvey issued a written order that 'No geologist shall go within one mile of the front line trenches'.

It was among the collieries of this area, though slightly further to the south, that Colonel Logan had his adventure. The details are somewhat hazy now, but I think it was about Fosse VIII it occurred. It was well known to us that pit-shafts on either side of No Man's Land were connected by underground workings, and the colliery owners had been asked to put in concrete stoppings in the galleries so as to block off completely the portion in German hands. This however was never done, though we were assured that it had been, but a post was maintained of French troops as soon as this was realised.

It was rumoured at the time that the colliery was being used as a means of access for spies to our lines, and this may easily have been the case before we had the post there. The nearest shaft in the enemy lines had originally been the upcast shaft of the colliery ventilation system, but with the complete destruction of the pit-head it was feared that the direction of the air current might be reversed, and it was pointed out to the colliery authorities that there was a danger of the Germans sending gas down their shaft.

It was not long after the French troops were in the mine before sounds of approaching men were heard, and shots were exchanged between the parties. Two days later the prophecy as to gas attack was verified and a number of French soldiers were overcome. It was then that Logan led a party of Tunnellers, I believe with Ball and Smart of the First Army Mine School, down the ladders of the derelict shaft on our side, along many hundreds of feet of underground roads, down an underground shaft again by ladders, only to find the bodies of the victims. When

THE INCIDENT AT FOSSE 8

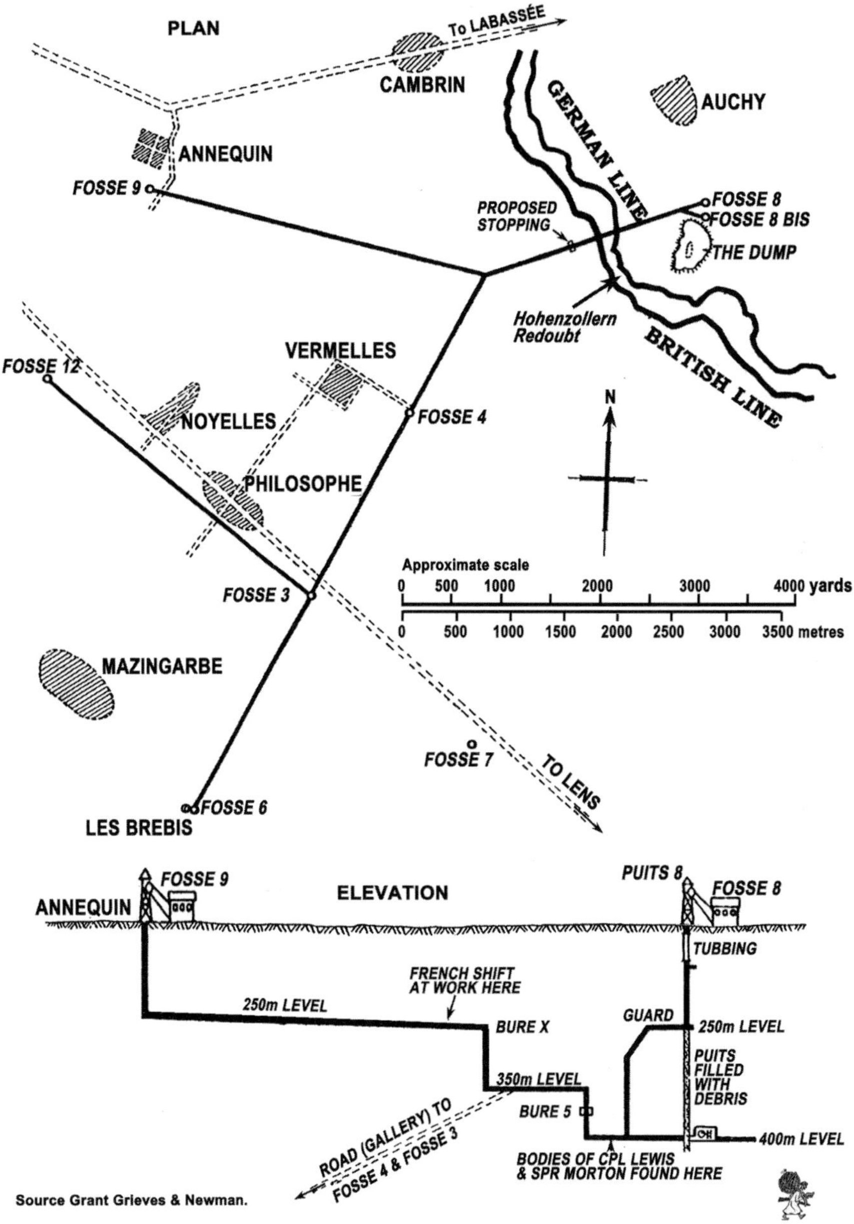

Source Grant Grieves & Newman.

it is added that the whole journey was inside in gas masks, and that heavy rescue oxygen cylinders and other aids for the gassed men were carried, it will be agreed that this exploit, coming on top of his other splendid work in Mine Rescue organization, thoroughly earned the DSO he bears.

[*The incident at Fosse VIII (8) occurred in September 1917. At the time there was an underground defence post manned by an NCO and six men of 170 Tunnelling Company (although CWGC records give them a variety of unit affiliations, which is not particularly unusual) and four French miners. On the night of 26 September the Germans flooded the system with cloro-picrine, a highly lachrymatory gas. A French working party managed to escape but the sapper NCO and a signaller were overcome. Over the next three days several rescue and recovery attempts were made, in the course of which Lieutenant Thirwell and two more men of 170 Tunnelling Company were killed. This complex saga took place in shafts and tunnels going to a depth of around 400 metres.*

Lieutenant TA Thirwell, who died at the age of 33 on 1 Oct 1917 as a consequence of mustard gas poisoning, is buried (his headstone has him as captain) in Calais Southern Cemetery in Plot B Row Officers Grave 10. Other British soldiers involved in the same incident were all buried in Noeux-Les-Mines Communal Cemetery Extension. Corporal DE Lewis DCM (aged 35), died on 26 September 1917, is buried in I C 12; Lance Corporal HG Hall MM (aged 21), died on 30 September 1917, is buried in II B 21 and Sappers WW Morton (died on 26 September 1917, buried in II B 16) and J Shanks (also died on 26 September, aged 33, buried in I C 13).]

I wonder if Logan ever has time to spare from his busy practice at Newmeins to play cricket, as he used to before the war, for the West of Scotland Club?

Members of 173 Company at least, and most Tunnellers too, will need no introduction to Major Lowry, Cornishman and South African mining engineer. His name always recalls to me the formation of a Tunnelling Company for the Italian front, for which command he volunteered, and was later selected. By the summer of 1918 most Tunnellers were ready for a change of scene, and when it was announced that this Company was to be formed, there was at first quite a rush for the job. Danford was on leave, and the then I of M, General Biddulph, was away, but he had told me that he wished Major Lowry* to get the job if I could arrange it in his absence. In order to wangle this I had to put off the other applicants by telling them that the personnel of the new unit were to be raised from Maltese miners, which I believed was the case, and in due course a bluff and irate Major Lowry arrived in my office at Montreuil, having heard this rumour. It was a strict rule that no line officer came to GHQ, but that mattered little to Lowry. Having heard that Danford was on leave, he asked to see the I of M., and when he was told that he too was absent, he appeared to be defeated.

But not Lowry. Could he see the officer in the AG's office who was dealing with the matter? Driven back on my last defences, I told him that if he went across there he would at once be taken before the Deputy AG and be severely strafed for coming to GHQ without orders. That scared even him a bit, and he went back to his Company, and in due course to Italy.

Not long after his departure for his new command, I had a communication from the Director of Mechanical Transport, who stated that the casualties among the motorcycles allotted to 173 Company RE had risen to alarming proportions, and asking for an investigation and report. When next in their area I called on the Adjutant and mentioned the matter.

'Well, it's like this, if you want the real truth. You remember Lowry went to Italy last month. The night before he left we gave him a farewell dinner, having just received two weeks arrears of liquor rations from the Canteen.' 'Yes', I said, beginning to see a little daylight, but not much, 'what has that got to do with the motor-bikes?'

'Do you see that field over there?' And looking out of the window I saw a perfectly good Flanders field, complete with trimmings, fittings and a small-cultivated garden attached. And out it came at last.

'Well after mess we had races in the dark.'

Here was the required light. I hope I relieved his mind by enquiring what make of cycle they preferred, and how many new ones they really wanted.

On my return I wrote to the DMT as follows:

'173 Company RE Casualties to Motor-cycles.

> This matter has been carefully investigated, and it has been established that the old cycles at present allotted to this unit are quite unsuitable for the arduous conditions under which their work is carried out. The roads in that area being in very bad repair, and the nature of the work is such that cycles are in use at all times of the day and night. It is therefore recommended that the present equipment be withdrawn altogether and be replaced with new Triumphs.'

I heard later that this was done. After the Armistice a lieutenant colonel strode into the office, his broad chest bright with foreign ribbons, beside the DSO and MC which he had worn before. It was Lowry, who told me he had called on his way through on leave, that he had made Tunnellers out of his Maltese, and that he was shortly returning to Italy as Officer in Charge of War Graves. Presumably that did not last indefinitely, as I last heard of him as being in business in London.

During General Biddulph's absence I came automatically under the orders of the other Deputy E-in-C, General Edmonds, of whom little mention has been made so far, for he has a chapter to himself at the end of this book.

But it is time to say something more about General Harvey's successors. General McInnes only held the post of Deputy E-in-C for a few months at the end of his brilliant career, and they were the most anxious and difficult of his life. His was a very attractive personality, and his energetic efforts to repair the political blunders which led to the great attack on the Somme, were fully appreciated by all who know how hard he worked to get defences erected in time. [*This refers to the Kaiserschlacht offensive in March and April 1918.*]

General H. Biddulph was a real Sapper, and it was an honour to work under him. One of the finest instructors in military engineering the Corps has known, he had a capacity for thoroughness and hard work little short even of General Harvey's. He kept very much in the background as far as the Tunnelling Companies were concerned, leaving the outside work to the mining staff, but he was none the less a very good friend to them all on many occasions, and worthily upheld the high standard set by General Harvey. His duties included many other RE activities beside those of the Tunnellers, and in some of these we helped when we could. But he will always be remembered by me for one thing above any other.

When the demolition scheme in the back areas was being discussed he asked me how it was proposed to keep the detonators and dry gun cotton primers safe from damp, and I replied that it would be done in the usual manner customary among Tunnellers. As mentioned in Chapter VI, this was 'by the use of a small rubber bag'. Accordingly he told me to arrange for a supply of these from Ordnance, which I did, but not before some humorist on the staff there had started a correspondence which caused the General and the rest of us considerable amusement. On that occasion I must have told General Biddulph the story of Major Lowry's visit to a shop in Amiens in April 1918, when he asked for two dozen of these for urgent demolition work. The lady behind the counter was filled with astonishment and admiration, and remarked: 'Deux douzaine, Monsieur, DEUX DOUZAINE!!'

Of the various drivers of cars who were attached to the E-in-C's office there were two in particular whose names and faces are still clear. Taysom of the cheery smile took me over many thousands of miles of Flanders roads in 1918, and was an excellent driver. Phillimore was more cautious and his car was the least likely of all, except the old Rolls, to break down twenty miles from nowhere on a bitter night. His was a Vauxhall, while Taysom drove an old pre-war Daimler. Both had acetylene lamps, and present day motorists may be grateful for their electric no-trouble headlights.

Phillimore was an interesting character. As an old Etonian, and a nephew of the well known judge of that name, he could have taken a commission at any time, but he was perfectly content to serve throughout the war as a driver, and doubtless he acquired a lot of knowledge useful to him as a motoring correspondent of one of the leading London papers. He had been at Eton with Colonel Mackintosh, and it was said that on occasion rank was forgotten and that the two would foregather in some quiet estaminet and discuss a *plat du jour* together. It was always a pleasure to go in his car, as he was excellent company on those long drives, but he never forgot a punctilious salute when in the presence of any other people, which made him into an ordinary driver again until we were alone on the return journey. I only remember one night when he failed to get back to GHQ. Other cars would often fail us, and lifts had to be cadged and lorries jumped but, except for the night when his main transmission shaft snapped in two outside St Pol, his car always rolled through the gateway sometime in the small hours. I believe it was Taysom who Colonel Sankey thought should be wearing his gas helmet when driving the General.

In the cold winter weather the offices at the École were only heated by small stoves, and some of the chillier among the Great Ones started an agitation for central heating. Long afterwards I came across the file of minutes on the subject and bitter were the comments of some of those whose opinion was taken. One general of a mordant wit put his views very briefly as to the suggested scheme. 'The heating arrangements now recommended appear suitable. At all events they will be better than the present ones, which in other offices are said to be as overleaf.' Turning the page I found the well known picture from *La Vie Parisienne* of the Lady of the Muff. Any of those who inhabited a dugout will know it, and the author of the minute will remember it.

'The Lady in the Muff' appeared in La Vie Parisienne in 1917. The magazine, founded in 1864, was a weekly review that was well known for its slightly risqué content: all too much for General Pershing, who warned the members of the AEF against it. Needless to say, his strictures only ensured that its circulation increased.

Some time in 1918 we brought an officer from one of the Fourth Army companies to Montreuil to do some special work in the office and it was arranged that I should pick him up at his HQ. That day the driver was a man who did not know the roads or his driving too well, and the car was the oldest of the Daimlers. When the officer produced his kit I had fears for that car. Apart from the ordinary collection of clothes and bedding, he had a sack full of German shells and bombs, two of their rifles, and sundry oddments, which must have brought the total weight up to a ton. He was so obviously attached to them all that we piled in on top of them somehow, and set off about eight o'clock from somewhere beyond Péronne.

Carefully watching the map at first, we managed to keep the driver from heading for Constantinople, but once we reached a turning too late for me to warn him, and could only shout 'Right!' as we were nearly on it. We were doing about twenty-seven miles per hour, a good gait for that ancient vehicle, and the driver made a wild clutch at his wheel, and made the turn on two wheels. but it was too much for the tyres, and within a hundred yards we had two punctures. Having changed the two tubes, the spare tyre being flat already, we got under way again, only to have three further punctures before we finally reached Montreuil at 4 a.m. The last three punctures had to be mended in the old time cyclist's way with patches, and it was a relief to get out of the car at last.

Towards the end of the War I spent a night with a Company in Valenciennes. The next chapter deals with the work of the Tunnellers in regard to traps and land mines, and at this period they were usually well housed because they were the first troops to enter towns as fast as these were surrounded by the infantry and so selected decent billets for themselves. Company HQ at Valenciennes was in a house belonging to a wealthy Frenchman, and was decorated in the extravagant but chilly style so dear to the French nouveau riche. There was no stove in the large room used as a mess, so two batmen were told to bring down the big one from a bedroom upstairs. For some time there were the usual sounds of batmen removing stoves up above, but it was shortly realised that quiet had supervened, and after ten minutes or so an officer was asked to investigate. Lying on the floor of the room he found two batmen, paralytic, and very nearly dead, so potent was the absinthe of which they had found a dozen bottles hidden behind the stove, and, taking it for white wine, had taken a very long Tunneller's swallow without apparently tasting it at all. Certainly that absinthe was powerful stuff, but only a well-practised Tommy could have got so much over his throat as those two did without choking.

Another picture comes to mind of Maubeuge, where the Germans had blown the big road bridge over the river, and this had been replaced by a new Hopkins bridge by the Tunnelling Company there. But the twisted girders of the old bridge were lying in the river collecting all the refuse brought down by the stream, and threatening to dam the river altogether. In the Grande Place I noticed a caterpillar tractor as we came into the town, behind which was a long steel hawser to which we found the Tunnellers were harnessing huge sections of the derelict bridge. These were cut through by a party with acetylene torches, working from a raft in the stream. At the signal, the old caterpillar charged away across the square and up the timber ramp, which had been built for the purpose, and up would go another long length of first class ruin.

As the Hazebrouck drive, known as the Battle of the Lys, came to a standstill in the late spring, the Tunnellers found a lot of work to do along the famous line of hills south of the Cassel-Poperinghe road, known as Mont Rouge, Mont Noir and the Mont des Cats. This line now became the northern flank of the great salient the Germans had driven into our lines. This gave us observation over all that area of the utmost value, and the enemy casualties must have been enormous. At Sailly-sur-la-Lys, after they had again been driven back, I saw a cemetery which had formed an adjunct to one of their casualty clearing stations. They only held that area for some five months, but the last number on those serried graves was 14,009. The figure sticks still.

The fullest value was made of the observation facilities afforded by the hills, and the Tunnellers were at this time very busy erecting concrete O.Pips [*observation posts*] for this purpose, as well as all manner of reinforced concrete defences in the threatened area.

It was no uncommon thing at that time to go into what appeared to be a very slightly damaged house, and find fifty tons of concrete in the drawing room, a concealed strong point. One of the officers engaged on this work, who was at great pains to explain its good points to me, impressed me with his knowledge of concrete construction, and on my return I turned up his civilian record in the files. He was the General Manager of one of the largest mines on the Rand, and it seemed absurd to me at the time that I should be inspecting his work. At that time very little was known as to the best form of construction to resist the effect of heavy shells. In the captured pillboxes on the Messines Ridge and elsewhere we had noticed many enemy dead, although they were unwounded, and they must have been killed by the concussion of a direct hit, even though the shell failed to penetrate the concrete. These pillboxes always struck one as being most unhealthy places once their position was spotted by the gunners, and most people preferred to be in the open trenches, where at least they could relieve the tension by moving about. It brought home to me something of what the Navy must have experienced in action, for to be in a cabined and confined space forming a definite target for all manner of nasty big guns was their lot too, though the thrill of the throbbing machinery and the sense of motion of the ship possibly helped them a lot.

A battered, but essentially sound, German bunker on the Hindenburg Line after its capture. By this stage in the war, indeed by later 1917, bunkers were mainly used as shelters and did not have a firing slit or aperture. Machine guns could be mounted on the roof and there was often a ledge, equivalent to a fire step, at the rear. Recent research on bunkers in Flanders has been unable to find any reference to the use of the acronym MEBU (Mannschafts-Eisen-Beton-Unterstand – reinforced concrete shelter for troops) by the Germans, although it was commonly used by the British.

When I recall that the old *Kent* was hit fifty-seven times in the duel with the *Nürnberg* off the Falklands, readers will agree that while the Navy did not get the continuous experience of shelling that was the common lot of the infantrymen right through his stay in the line, and often while he was supposed to be resting behind it, yet while they were in action they certainly had a concentrated spell of existence. Comparisons are odious, and the Army were never jealous of the sailors, for to them the Navy was father, mother and best friend in their existence overseas; but there must have been moments when foot weary Tommies longed for the clean baths and clean clothes which the naval men always enjoyed.

But now it is time to turn to the last great field of activity and opportunity for high service which came to the Tunnelling Companies and which found them ready as ever to turn their hands and their wits to defeat the plans of our friend the enemy.

Chapter Thirteen

Mopping Up

Of Sherlock Holmes disguised in Tunneller's kit,
And of risks he ran doing it.

One of the most memorable days recorded in British history was 8 August 1918, when at last the tide turned definitely in our favour. [*This day marked the opening of the allied offensive on the Somme and the start of what has become known as The Advance to Victory.*] The new technique of attack with massed tanks and without the old-style revealing artillery preparation beforehand, was a triumphant success, and Rawlinson's Fourth Army began the victorious progress which never halted again until the bridgeheads of the Rhine were held by Allied troops.

To Lord Rawlinson and the Fourth Army Staff is due the highest credit for showing how men could be used effectively in the attack without the sacrifice of lives out of all proportion to the advance secured. Not that other armies did not do equally well when their turn came, but Fourth Army led the way this time. The victory must have been welcome to the Chief of the General Staff at GHQ, Sir Herbert Lawrence*, who had succeeded Sir LE Kiggell* earlier in the year; he was a soldier and then a civilian before the war, and is now a civilian again, gaining equal distinction in both capacities. I saw him on many occasions at Montreuil and he seemed a fitting colleague for our great C in C.

The immediate effect of this initial victory was very marked for the Tunnelling Companies. Instead of preparing to demolish roads and bridges behind Armies, they had to remove as best they could the booby traps and landmines left in their wake by the retreating enemy troops. In other words their work in this respect was exactly reversed.

Bridging of course became increasingly important too, but their main duty from then on until the end of the war was to act as detectives of

General Rawlinson was an infantryman, commissioned in the KRRC and later transferred to the Coldstream Guards. He commanded a division in 1914, a corps in 1915 and was made GOC of the newly created Fourth Army in March 1916, tasked with commanding the field army for the Somme offensive in 1916. Relative failure there led to him playing no important part in the major offensives of 1917. He came into his own once more the following year, his Army launching the first of the BEF's counter-offensives in August 1918. Of the BEF's Army commanders at the end of the war, only he and Horne failed to be promoted field marshal. It is likely that his early death in 1925, when commander in chief in India, prevented him getting the rank.

buried death, to remove the devilish devices when found, and when they had satisfied themselves that a house was safe to mark it accordingly.

Of their work in this direction I cannot write too enthusiastically, but it was never my job to share in the practical and very dangerous work involved, but only to keep in the closest touch with the whole front, so that information regarding new contraptions, and new methods of discovery could be circulated at once, and thus the danger to the troops and to our Tunnelling detectives could at least be minimised.

When it is remembered that the whole area through which our advancing Armies passed was thickly populated and that every house in every hamlet, town or city held the possibility of death in scores of ways, the magnitude of the work may be realised. No town was occupied by infantry if it was possible first to surround it and to send the Tunnellers in to 'vet' it as safe.

What this involved may be better understood if we take an imaginary walk into such a recaptured village. The bridge over the little river as we approach had not been blown, and all our worst suspicions are aroused, for this would be a likely spot for a delayed action mine. A party is detailed at once to search the surrounding ground for any sign of disturbance, and we press on to the village well. There are various possibilities here. A delayed action mine may be placed nearby, or a contact mine be fixed

Sappers replacing a destroyed bridge, autumn 1918. One of the principal tasks of the Royal Engineers during the 1918 'Advance to Victory' was the replacement of the numerous bridges that the Germans destroyed during their hasty retreat. Many of the tunnelling companies were deployed to undertake this work.

up to explode when the winch handle is moved, or when the bucketful of water is set down on the cobbles beside it. Here we look for loose stone in the path, for wires or strings, or in fact anything at all unusual in appearance. The principal buildings and best houses in the town meet with very special attention. It may be of course that the turning of the door handle will be the end of all the party, and if a window is tried that too may have the same result.

However entrance has to be obtained somehow, and the cellar is examined with special care for delayed action mines, the treads of the stairs looked over for any sign of loose boards, the pictures and furniture approached with the greatest respect before a thing is touched, and in fact all the wiles of Sherlock Holmes, Lecocq, Poirot, Thorndyke and the other mere amateurs are employed. Finally, if nothing has been found, the house is marked with chalk: 'SAFE 174 Company R.E'.

Then for the next, and so throughout every house in turn. In the case of a big town the inhabitants often gave very valuable information, but in the many abandoned and ruined villages it was just a case of wits against guile. No house was occupied by infantry until the magic chalk of the Tunnellers proclaimed it safe; and on very few occasions only had they any reason to regret their faith in the thoroughness and ability of the searcher.

At first we were more concerned with the smaller type of trap with only a few pounds of explosive involved in its construction, or perhaps a small shell or bomb. But as time went on we became more and more unpleasantly conscious of the fact that the whole of the German back area had been strewn with delayed action mines laid at leisure and most cunningly concealed. As the Districts passed into our possession the mine would go off at one important point after another, and caused us great damage and loss of life. It was impossible in the time available to search every yard of the enormous area, and that it was no fault of the Tunnellers that some went undiscovered may be readily understood for, after the Armistice, when (as is related in the next chapter) the Germans handed over every possible information regarding the mines laid in our front, their own officers who had laid them were often unable to find them again, even with their own plans of the site in their hands.

The Allied troops faced numerous hazards in their move forward in the autumn of 1918. Amongst these were mine charges deep underground that had not been fired. One is left with the feeling that a modern approach to this hazard would not be content with the restrictions imposed by this sign.

A road and rail demolition on the approaches to Cambrai, autumn 1918. In retreat, engineers of both sides were detailed to make conditions for the enemy as difficult as possible in their advance. Thus bridges were demolished, sections of railway were torn up and (usually small charge) improvised mines were placed under road junctions, railway lines and other infrastructure key points and blown. In turn, the engineers of the advancing army had the task of restoring them to functional use.

The railway authorities became increasingly apprehensive after the experience of one or two of these mines, and the search of track and stations, sidings and sheds grew ever more expert and successful. But it may be as well to give a better indication of the construction of a delayed action mine before continuing the story of their discovery and removal.

The standard practice of the Germans was not to use clockwork mechanisms for this purpose, although a few of such types of fuse were detected by the skilled listeners of the Companies. The usual device was similar to one found in the Fourth Army area in 1917, as described in an earlier chapter [*Chapter 7*]. It consisted of a short tube containing a detonator and primer of explosive, together with a steel striker. This was held up against the action of a strong steel spring by a fine steel piano wire, which passed through a cork in the top of the tube, above which was fixed a small copper vessel. The wire passed through this to a clamp at the top and as long as the wire was intact the striker could not be driven down by the spring on to the detonator. The copper vessel had a little filling cap to which a special liquid was introduced, according to the length of delay intended. The liquid was a mixture of copper sulphate, slightly acidified, and of glycerine, and it set up an electrical action on the wire and by very slow degree this was eaten through and the charge fired. We discovered the liquid before the fuse. It was made up in a glass tube with tapered ends, and these could be easily snapped off and the liquid put into the fuse. The tubes were marked with paper bands of different colours signifying the number of weeks of delay this would give. Actually a number of mines went off more than four months from the time of laying, as taken from the Germans' own record.

These fuses could be used with any form of explosive or shell. It was only necessary to insert one of these into a big dump for the whole lot to go up in due course. The chief use was in heavy shells buried in the ground

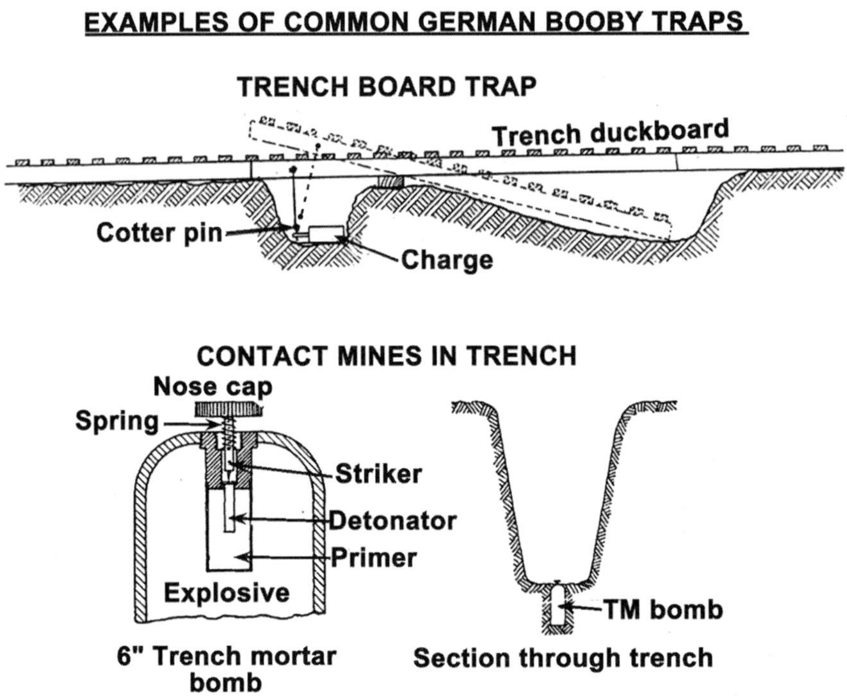

Examples of common German booby traps. Although the German retreat in the autumn of 1918 was rapid, it was never a rout and they usually had time to leave a wide variety of booby traps to disrupt the progress of the advancing allies.

under likely points and carefully concealed, a fact that led to the visit to the Admiralty described in the next chapter. The cleverest adaptation of this type of fuse was in connection with ammunition dumps which the enemy had to abandon. Patterns were made which were outwardly identical in every respect with the ordinary shell fuses, except for the colour of the gaine [*Gaine: An explosive extension that screwed into the base of a fuse to convert the flash from an initiator into a detonation wave.*] which could not be seen when the fuse was in the shell, and for a tiny imprinted star, the significance of which did not strike either the Gunners or ourselves for a long time. It was only necessary for the retreating enemy to replace one ordinary shell fuse with one of these devices to ensure the explosion of the whole dump weeks later. It is obvious that the longer a delay action mine had been laid the more nearly would the wire have been eaten through, and the more sensitive it became to anyone attempting to remove it. It was therefore a job calling for that special kind of cool courage and skilled precaution for which the Companies were already famous.

In connection with these dumps, a few days after the Armistice had been signed I was in the Fourth Army area, and inquired of a company commander what his men were doing, and was told that they were defusing forty truckloads of German shells to make sure that no delayed action fuse was in any one of the thousands of shells involved. It seemed to me a wicked shame that our good fellows who had survived the war should still be risking their lives in this way, and I asked the Controller of Mines whether it was not possible to employ a few of the many idle German prisoners on this work, of course under supervision of our own men. He said that the Army staff considered it against the Geneva Convention to do so. At that stage of the war it seemed to be stretching things to a very unnecessary length to insist on the last letter of the famous Convention, which had been flagrantly broken by the enemy on innumerable occasions, and as soon as I got back I saw General Biddulph, and pointed out that under the Armistice conditions the Germans were bound to assist in the removal of traps and landmines. He at once went across to the operation section of the General Staff, who issued a telegram as follows:

> To all Armies. Reference Clause VIII(a) of the Armistice conditions, a proportion of German prisoners may be used to assist in the removal of mines and traps.

This resulted in such work being done very largely by the Germans thereafter, and on a number of occasions this action undoubtedly reduced British casualties from the infernal things.

It may be mentioned that we received a lot of help from the Signallers in regards to telephone exchanges, which were a favourite objective for German Machiavellis. At Lille, in particular, matters were so arranged that the connection of two numbers likely to be in frequent use together would have blown the whole exchange to bits.

The finest example I can recall of the instinct for these mines which the Tunnellers developed was in the case of an important cross road, near which they found a patch of disturbed ground, which suggested that a shaft may have been sunk there, from which a gallery could have been driven under the road. Accordingly they started to dig, and at about three feet they came across a dead mule. 'Ugh', said one of them, 'it's only an adjectival mule, let's chuck it, and try the next place.' The other straightened his back, took off his hat and scratched his head thoughtfully for a moment, and said, 'Half a minute, Bill, did you ever know the Bosch to go to the trouble of burying a mule more than six inches deep? This here blighter's three feet down, and it don't look right to me somehow.' Persevering through that not too recently deceased animal, they found the expected gallery and removed the mine.

The tubes of copper sulphate were packed in sawdust, and this proved a clue in a large number of instances, particularly along the railways, where it was more easily detected. Any sign of sawdust meant that the neighbourhood received specially close scrutiny for disturbed metal along the track, or other indications of excavation. The actual digging necessary was bad enough when something was found, but must have been dreary work in the many cases where holes were dug with a negative result. It had to be done with the greatest care least a pick should strike a charge unexpectedly, and so cause the weakened piano wire to break.

The finest tribute to work done by the Tunnellers was paid by Lord Horne in the First Army. The Controller of Mines, Colonel Yuill, had submitted, weeks after the Armistice, a list of officers and men for decoration with the MC and MM, and he was sent for by the Army Commander.

'What's this about, Yuill? Don't you realise that the war is over and that no decoration can be given now?'

Yuill explained in a shy but determined way that the work was of a most dangerous character, and that he had only put forward a few cases of exceptional courage and good work.

'Well', smiled the Army Commander, 'I won't accept this, you can take it away. Also please note the you may turn all the MCs into DSOs and the Military Medals into DCMs and I want another list of twelve more officers whom you can recommend for MC, and as many names of men for the MM as you like.' This was a great man's opinion of great work.

General Sir Henry Horne, GOC First Army from the early autumn of 1916 until the end of the war. Horne is described in the title of the one and only biography as the 'Silent General' – that is he has a low profile in accounts of the war, despite being a successful commander at all levels. The Canadian Corps was in his Army at Vimy in 1917 (Horne was a gunner; the Canadians were certainly not short of massive quantities of artillery for the attack); he held his right flank during the German attacks on Arras (March 1918) and the left flank on the Lys (April 1918); and contributed to the Advance to Victory. An unflashy, under-rated commander, who had the gift of selecting a talented staff.

Chapter Fourteen

Admiralty and Armistice

The Navy offers us a helping hand,
And seems a bit at sea in that strange land.

During most of September Colonel Danford had been home on leave, and on his return I took the opportunity of going for a few days to Paris, as we felt the end of the war was near. Staying in a hotel somewhere in the Boulevard des Italiens I felt lost for a while, until I met a charming French Canadian officer, who knew his Paris well. With him I learned to enjoy the luxury of first class French food as served in the obscure restaurants known only to the real inner circle of Parisian gourmets. We went one night to see Sacha Guitry in one of his plays, and greatly enjoyed his brilliant acting, although most of the finer points of his dialogue escaped me.

There was a Victory Loan procession one day and I saw the French light tanks for the first time, racing along the road, wheeling like lightning, and generally conveying to the civilian crowds that there was a lot of fight in the men of France yet.

On my return to Montreuil, Colonel Danford told me that there were to be changes in the establishment of our office. In place of the two A I of M. there was to be only one, a staff major. He said he had been appointed to the command of a new tank bridging battalion, then being raised at home, and regarded as one of the most important of the new schemes for the final drive that was being prepared for the next year. Even then it seemed too good to be true that the German nation would throw up the sponge within a few weeks, and that a fugitive Kaiser would be seeking refuge in Holland. So Danford departed, and bequeathed me his own red tabs. The war was over before my appointment as staff major came through, and I never wore those tabs, but somewhere in my home in England they are still preserved as a memento of the year we spent

Bertram William Danford DSO, mentioned in dispatches four times. He was Controller of Mines Fifth Army and appointed Assistant Inspector of Mines in spring 1918. At the opening of the German spring offensive in late March 1918 he was appointed OC GHQ line, then subsequently responsible for the GHQ line behind Hazebrouck when First and Second Armies were attacked in April.

together; and of Danford's honour and humour, and unfailing cheery companionship. He has risen high in the Corps since then, and recently retired from the post of Chief Engineer Egypt. Soon after the war he was taken prisoner by Sinn Feiners in Ireland while in a car with General Lucas, and was seriously wounded while trying to escape.

[*The incident, in June 1920, is indicative of Danford's resolution. As reported in the Times: 'The raiders, who had arrived in two motorcars, took possession of General Lucas's car and set off with their prisoners in the direction of Cork. Soon afterwards Colonel Danford made a courageous but unsuccessful attempt to escape. The prisoners had not been bound in any way, and, seizing a moment when his captors' eyes were not upon him, he jumped out and ran in a direction opposite to that in which the cars were travelling at a fairly high speed. There was an order to halt, and the republicans opened fire on Colonel Danford, who after a few rounds fell prostrate on the highway with serious wounds in the head and shoulder. Observing his serious condition, the raiders took counsel and decided to liberate Colonel Tyrrell, so that he could attend to his wounded fellow-officer. The raiders left them on the roadside and drove away with General Lucas. General Lucas incidentally escaped from his captors a few days later. It was some six months before Danford could return to duty.*]

Colonel Danford's medals (the foreign decoration on the right is the Khedive's Silver Medal, with the Talodi (2-15 June 1905) clasp). He was awarded the DSO in June 1916. He was released from staff duties later in 1918 and by September he was the CO of a Tank Bridging Battalion. Post war he was taken prisoner by Sinn Feiners in Ireland but was released when badly wounded when trying to escape. He later became the Chief Engineer, Egypt.

With Colonel Danford's departure, General Biddulph and Colonel L E. Hill of the Fourth Army became the only regulars left in the Tunnelling service. But without the help and good offices of our regular friends we should have fared ill in Army circles and, while to the temporary men full credit may be given for the work they did, we should never forget what men like General Harvey, General Biddulph, General Edmonds, General Heath, and the many other senior men did for us. Nor are we ungrateful to the many field company officers for their help on diverse occasions, and to others in every branch of the Army.

But it was not until the last ten days of the war that we asked for help from the Navy. The Engineer in Chief, General Heath, had been Chief

Major General Sir George Heath KCMG CB DSO (April 1901) was appointed Engineer in Chief at GHQ in October 1917 and held the post until the end of the war. He had seen active service in South Africa and at the outbreak of war was the Chief Engineer in South Africa. He had been Chief Engineer First Army since May 1915 and thus Haig would have known him well. When at GHQ he noted: 'My duties were chiefly administrative, but entailed much travelling about on inspection work. Before and after the great German offensive of 21 March 1918, my work was chiefly bound up with the construction of lines of defence, by Armies, Corps and Divisions. After our retreat to the line Amiens-Ypres, we constructed 5,000 miles of lines of defence between us. After that came our advance; road making, bridging, water supply became the order, and my chief duty was to see that everyone got what they wanted to enable them to make a rapid advance.'

Engineer First Army in the days when mine fighting was at its height, and was very keenly interested in anything that affected the Tunnellers. With the continued menace of delayed action mines causing scores of casualties, he was greatly concerned to search out every avenue which might lead to quicker detection, and so reduce the risk to our men. He sent for me on 2 November (the date is memorable to me as the date of birth of my first son) and said that he thought that the Admiralty might possibly be able to lend us some of their instruments for the detection of submarines, or to suggest new methods of detection. His brother, Admiral Sir Herbert Heath*, was then Second Sea Lord, and on the next day I crossed over and entered the famous portals, feeling not unlike the man who went to the War Office in Bateman's unforgettable cartoon in *Punch*.

I AM BIDDEN TO THE WAR OFFICE
I DEPART FOR IT
I APPROACH IT
I ENTER
I AM NOT OBSERVED
I AM STILL NOT OBSERVED
I AM OBSERVED
I AM SPOKEN TO (AND STILL LIVE)
I CONTINUE TO BE SPOKEN TO
I AM SPOKEN TO QUITE NICELY
I AM SHAKEN HANDS WITH
I TAKE MY LEAVE
THE CIVILIAN WHO VISITS THE WAR OFFICE
HM BATEMAN 1917

Professor John McLennan OBE (1917), knighted 1935, was an outstanding Canadian research physicist. He worked on the use of helium in airships and was a scientific advisor to the Admiralty, working in particular on combating the 'submarine menace'.

Not only was I taken notice of, but I was shaken hands with and very kindly received by a cheery admiral, then passed on to Captain Smith. He took me along to see the Director of Equipment and Research, Professor McLennan*, formerly, and still, of Toronto University, whose latest work has been the development of methods for the recovery of helium from natural gas, which has already revolutionised the outlook for large airships, as the gas, though heavier than hydrogen, is not inflammable, and the greatest danger to these leviathan of the upper air, has been removed by his discoveries. [*Sir John McLennan, 1867–1935, knighted in 1935.*]

McLennan said that the only hope lay in an instrument he might be able to design which would detect masses of buried metal; as shells were often used by the Germans for these charges it seemed the best line to pursue. He said it would take him a couple of days to get it made, and would I come back on the Monday. This suited me very nicely indeed and I was soon in Birmingham beside my wife, looking with awe at the curiously wrinkled red thing alongside her, which was my first-born.

On the Monday we went out to Woolwich and collected the instrument, described later on, and tried it out roughly. I was not very sanguine of its success, for reasons which will appear, but it was most ingenious, and to have produced it in a couple of days showed what the Navy could do when they tried. McLennan asked me to go and see Professor Fleming* at University College, as the thermionic valves entered into its construction, and Professor Fleming is of course the inventor of the wireless valve.

Wandering through the Engineering Department, I came across a little man in a white jacket, working away at a bench in the laboratory. I asked him if he could tell me where the professor could be found, whereupon he pulled a long rubber tube from his pocket, and fixing one end in his ear, asked me to repeat the question into the other. I did so. 'I am Professor Fleming.' It is surely one of life's strangest ironies that the man who has given new worlds of delight to many millions of wireless enthusiasts and talkie fans all over the world should himself be afflicted with almost total deafness. He approved the principles of the instrument, and I took it over with me the next day.

Its design was most interesting to me, as at that time I had never even heard of thermionic valves. It consisted of a wooden rod about eight feet long, on which were mounted at opposite ends two similar pairs of coils of wire. One coil of each pair was connected up to the corresponding coil in the other, and through this circuit an alternating current was passed from a buzzer in the instrument box, which accompanied the detector. The other two coils were connected in opposition to each other to the valves and so to the telephone headpiece. So long as the induced currents in the secondary coils were equal, nothing was heard in the telephones, but if one end was bought anywhere near a mass of iron or steel, the induction effect at that end was increased, and a singing sound was heard. By keeping one end still and swinging the other about, it was possible to tell at which end the steel was. The general idea was simple and excellent, but electricians and mathematicians will appreciate the limitations of the apparatus when the professor informed me that the effect would vary inversely to the 6th power of the distance. The result was that while it gave a loud noise when a key was held close to one end, a mass of steel a few feet away hardly gave any indication at all.

Professor McLennan had never then been to France and I asked him if it would be possible to come over for a few weeks or so and see the conditions for himself. It was not easy for him to get away at that time, but after the Armistice he spent ten days with us, as he told me he still remembers in a letter a few months ago. The instrument was taken to the Australian AEMMCB Company for testing, and very lurid were the comments made upon it by Major Morse and his brother Australians. There is nothing like seeing a job, and Professor McLennan entirely shared their views when he did come over.

These events brought us to 10 November, the last Sunday of the war, and at eight o'clock I was sent for by General Biddulph, and ordered to go at once to Chantilly, where Foch had his Grand Quartier Général. With a staff major from the railway branch of the Quartermaster General's Department and two expert drivers, the finest Rolls Royce in France picked me up, and we started out on our long drive, brimming over with excitement, for our instructions were to bring back, from the British mission attached to GQG, full details of the delayed action mines laid by the enemy, which their representatives had actually brought with them when they came to Foch to ask for peace. They were handed over that Sunday, and therefore we knew that this was the end and that the war at long last was over.

The Rolls was the one reserved for Lloyd George on his visits to the Western Front and therefore it is with regret I have to record that it broke down somewhere beyond Abbeville. One of the tyres was punctured and the spare wheel, for some unknown reason, would not fit, and the two drivers had to take the good tire off the spare wheel and change it over. At last it was done, and while we ate a few sandwiches in place of forgotten dinner we rushed through France and eventually drew up at the British Mission, where a night-capped Frenchman put his head out of the lodge and opened the gates. The brigadier general came down in his pyjamas and found us a drink and some sandwiches. It was then 1 a.m. Forty draughtsman, collected from all the various departments, were set to work to copy and print the plans of mines laid in each Army area, and by the time the Last Great Hour of the war arrived, I had contrived to snatch a bite of breakfast, and at the 11th hour of the 11th day of the 11th month I was shaving! By 2pm dispatch riders were making their way to the different Armies with 900 copies of drawings of mine sites.

When it became clear that the war was over, the question of returning to civil life loomed large, but just then a notice appeared in Orders regarding a certain course at Chatham for candidates for the Ordnance Service. They had to have technical qualifications and to be Regular Officers unless specially recommended for a Regular Commission. General Biddulph was good enough to speak to General Heath on my behalf, and in due course my name was sent in, backed by separate references from General Edmonds and Colonel David. A friend in the AG's office told me that there were seventy applications from France alone and that there were only seven vacancies. So as it was my imperative that there should be enough income very soon, I wrote to an old friend, the father of Eric Parsons, and told him what steps I had taken. There the matter rested, while the question of the remaining delayed action mines occupied me very fully.

Professor McLennan duly came over and we set out on a tour of the front which lasted for a week or so. We passed through Arras, Albert, Bapaume, Cambrai, Douai, Lens, Lille, Tournai, Tourcoing, Messines and Béthune, and it was particularly interesting to me to see, for the last time in most cases, the scarred battlefields that were so familiar and some places never within reach before.

At Bapaume we went straight to the town hall where the first delayed action mine of the war had exploded in 1917. This was the first time that the professor had been able to visualise the actual problem. We looked down into the crater on the site and I asked him whether he thought he could tell us if there was a second delayed action mine there. Bapaume had of course been in German hands again for six months during 1918, and it would have been like them to lay a mine on their second retreat at the same point.

McLennan shook his head and smiled. Certainly his instrument would have had difficulty in detecting anything except a few tons of old iron that lay in the crater. We passed on to Cambrai, and met Colonel Laws, and went with him to a point on the railway, where the sidings of that important railway junction branch off from the main line. Colonel Laws informed us that the German officer who had been sent over to Third Army HQ to assist in the search knew that two mines had been laid near this spot, and according to their information they were due for explosion within a couple of days.

McLennan realised how hopeless it would be to use the instrument at such a spot, as a constant stream of railway traffic prevented the rails being taken up for a search; 'Q' had actually decided that it was better to risk a whole train being blown up rather than interrupt the supply of food and stores to the Armies in front, who so badly needed them.

I do not know whether McLennan was glad to move elsewhere, but I was. Delayed action mines due to go off with trains thundering over them do not make a combination which I appreciate. Colonel Laws, with his experience of the worst days on Gallipoli, probably thought it was all a picnic.

In Douai we found a Company who had just succeeded in restoring the water supply to this ghost of a town. Lens was a mere heap of bricks,

The Mairie in Bapaume, left, on 18 March 1917, with Australian soldiers passing before it, the town recently having been liberated when the Germans withdrew to the Hindenburg Line; and, on page 160, a contemporary photograph of it. The Mairie was probably the most notable of the buildings that the Germans booby trapped in their withdrawal. A delayed action mine had been hidden in the building and was not discovered. During the night of 26 and 27 March the mine (detonated by the use of a delayed action chemical fuse) went up, eight days after it had been set. The Germans possibly intended to catch a higher formation HQ that might have made use of the large building; on the same day (26 March) a large dugout on the outskirts of Bapaume, in use by the HQ of 7 (Australian) Brigade, also went up, though fortunately all but two signals clerks were out of it at the time. The Mairie mine killed, amongst others, two French deputies of the Nord, Briquet and Taillandler, who were sleeping in the building when the mine went off. Interestingly, Briquet was instrumental in forcing mine owners to give face workers paid time for a lunch stop – some have suggested (somewhat dubiously) that the word 'break' derives from his name.

The detonation of these two sophisticated booby traps provoked a series of warning orders about the dangers of booby traps and considerable engineering resources, not least from the tunnelling companies in the sector, were devoted to neutralizing them.

but Lille was more like a normal town than any of the others. It was never shelled by us, and had therefore not suffered at our hands. I had visited it with Colonel Logan a couple of days after its capture by Lieutenant General Haking's* Corps. The little flag which adorned his car had been given to the city and when I was in Paris it was displayed on the statue to Lille in the Place de la Concorde.

But the most impressive aspect of Lille was the entire absence of all copper and brass of every description. Imagine a city as big as Manchester, with not a single copper tram wire, brass door plate, door handle or electric fitting. It was as though these familiar metals had been wiped off the list of stores of the Universe by the Great Architect. The Germans in their thorough way had even collected all the copper coinage, so short were they of copper for the driving bands of their shells and of brass for fuses, and a thousand other purposes. I still have at home paper notes for five and ten centimes and cardboard discs to the same value, worth then about a half penny and penny respectively. This was before the days when the great flood of small paper money set in across the world, and at the time it made a strange impression. The Germans had forced the inhabitants to surrender all their cherished copper and brass ornaments, and when the professor said that he would like to buy a souvenir of the visit I jokingly suggested a pair of brass candlesticks from Lille. But he took me up on this, and spent half a day ferreting round all manner of shops and houses, until he actually succeeded in finding a pair, which their owner had kept stuffed up a chimney all through the war. They are the most cherished things on my mantelpiece at home still.

We stayed several days in Lille with Colonel Bland enjoying his pleasant company and then drove out on a bitter frosty morning along the Wytschaete to Messines Ridge, and almost to St Eloi, before the sun thawed the road so quickly that we were nearly bogged in the awful shell holes a score of times, and had to abandon our intention of getting right through to Ypres. While the driver was getting the car out of the last bog, we stood on the road looking across the completely deserted battlefield, and McLennan tried to picture it as we had known it for so long, peopled by patient, mud smeared and cold defying infantry. He turned away at last with a sigh, and said: 'Yes, a fortnight of these

The utterly devastated industrial town of Lens, photographed in 1919. The French, in particular, were faced with the monumental task of rebuilding hundreds of similarly flattened villages and towns, replacing destroyed infrastructure and bringing thousands of square kilometres of agricultural land back into productive use.

conditions must have been worse than all the Navy ever went through. Even the men on destroyers and submarines never endured such hardship.' Coming from one who knew the splendid work of our Navy as few could have done, it seemed the finest of all tributes to the men who held the Salient.

Down at the foot of the long ridge the craters of the famous day in 1917 were visible as huge frozen lakes; there was not a living being in sight except ourselves, and yet the whole vast scene seemed peopled with actors in the greatest drama there was ever staged. Perhaps they were there yet, and we were but three among the countless host, whose presence could impress itself by some wireless system beyond human ken. At least it seemed so to me then, and this leave-taking of that land of horror and glorious defiance of death's terrors remains one never to be forgotten moment while I live.

At Christmas we designed a card illustrating some of the main activities of the Tunnelling Companies during the year, and I spent a few days at home.

As there was no news of the Ordnance course, my friend in Birmingham wrote and said that if I would indicate the salary I wanted he would try and get me fixed up with a job. I replied at once and then went to Third Army for a night or two, spent with Colonel Laws in Cambrai. On my return on the Sunday night, there was a letter from Birmingham asking me to try and get leave, in order to meet the Chairman of a well-known Midland firm. By Tuesday night I had reached home and sent a cable on Thursday withdrawing my Ordnance application. This arrived at the same time as my orders to go to Chatham for the course, and some other candidate doubtlessly benefited.

On this leave I was given a foretaste of domesticity, and a different kind a civilian life from any I had known hitherto. My wife was in rooms, and our No 1 was an obstreperous infant who insisted on being fed four times every night. He was by no manner of means a properly trained modern babe. On my first night, the thermos broke, and four times did I have to descend into a strange kitchen, and with measuring tin and saucepan of milk, prepare the youngster's bottle. The next morning I bought a new extra strong Thermos, a gas ring, and a special fitting for fixing it to the pipes in our bedroom. That thermos lasted until No. 2 arrived four years later, when my wife insisted on the principle of one new thermos for one new baby.

I returned to Montreuil, and made use of a regulation which, for the benefit of the Companies, I had succeeded in getting the AG to make as regards demobilisation. Miners were badly needed at home and were soon classed high up in the priority list, but mining engineers, as most of our officers were, had not been included. As they were even more anxious to get home in many cases than the men, they fared not too badly by comparison with some of their home comrades. It was decided that officers who had jobs to go to could be released under the same category, and I packed my kit for the last time.

The last of my fourteen crossings of the Channel was by far the worst. The saloon in that ship ran fore and aft, and along the settees lay a very sick lot of men, each with his basin beside him. As one of the lucky good sailors, I had no need of one, though was glad enough to lie down that night. Once a great wave lifted the bows high in the air, and all the basins moved down one end. But it made no difference to the busy fillers.

It seemed strange that the name of the place at which I finally said 'goodbye' to the Army has passed entirely out of my mind. It was somewhere in Berkshire, I think, and thousands must remember it. The story is nearly ended, but I have reserved for a final chapter a short account of one of the grandest of men, and of his work during and since the war.

Chapter Fifteen

The Official Historian

A glimpse of famous history, and a friend
Who brings this story to a fitting end.

The name Brigadier General Sir James Edmonds is familiar to every student of the War as the compiler of the official history of the Land Operations. When I first went to Montreuil there was a tall staff officer who frequently came in to see General Harvey, and his enigmatic smile lightened the terror which I then used to feel on entering the Inspector of Mines' own office. Throughout the next two years and more, he was uniformly charming and kindly in his treatment of me, no doubt largely because I did not come directly under him, and he did not have to tolerate my mistakes, as General Harvey managed to do before long.

At the end of 1917 Colonel Edmonds became a brigadier general and deputy Engineer-in-Chief, conjointly with General Harvey, who handed over his work at GHQ a few weeks later. After this I saw a good deal more of the former, particularly in connection with our work on dugouts. On one occasion I had been asked to prepare a map, or series of maps, for the artillery, showing all the dugouts constructed by the Companies in areas where they would be of use for the gunners. The latter often had a number of alternative gun positions, and it frequently happened that the position of certain dugouts was not handed over to the relieving batteries, with the result that excellent cover that had taken weeks of work to make was abandoned to the rats and the encroaching mud; for without proper maintenance, a dugout, at least in the clay areas, soon filled up and became utterly uninhabitable.

General Biddulph asked me to let General Edmonds have the maps, and I took them into him. 'What's this? … Dugout maps … Who for? For Gunners! But no gunner can read a map! Don't you know that at Chatham [*he probably said Woolwich and not Chatham*], of the men who pass their exams, the top half are made Sappers, and the rest Gunners?'

Brigadier General James Edmonds was an extremely talented Royal Engineer officer, who was instrumental in developing Britain's counter intelligence prior to the war. In August 1914 he was GSO 1 of the 4th Division; but the strain of the opening weeks of the war led to a breakdown. On his recovery, he was sent to GHQ and stayed there for the remainder of the war, ending as deputy engineer-in-chief. When it became apparent that Sir John Fortescue was incapable of writing a satisfactory Official History for the army, Edmonds took on the role of editor himself. Through sheer determination he overcame numerous obstacles and saw the project to a conclusion (the last volume for France and Flanders was published in 1947), when he was eighty-six years old.

His sarcastic wit was famous in the higher circles of the Army, and the better appreciated because of his known kindly nature, but on occasion he could be very deadly in his criticism.

Once in the Mess Major David told me that General Edmonds had been particularly scathing about a certain individual much in the public eye just then, who had the faculty for getting the ear of politicians at home and securing fat jobs, where his misdirected energy caused quite a lot of trouble. [*This paragraph appears to be about Norton Griffiths.*] General Edmonds concluded his remarks by saying, with his well known smile to soften all he had said before, 'Ah! Shouldn't I like to write his life.' General Sankey, who was almost the equal of the General in cynical remarks, answered, 'Well, General, why not? You have your very able pen, and – er – your bottle of vitriol.'

After the Armistice had arrived and the men were looking forward to early demobilisation, General Biddulph was away for a few days, and I suggested to General Edmonds that it might perhaps be a nice thing if the Engineer-in-Chief sent a letter out to them thanking them for their services as Tunnellers. There was a good deal of unrest at home in the coalfields, and it seemed possible that it would give our own steady fellows more weight and influence among the stay-at-homes if they had a document of this kind to show their friends.

The General said at once, 'Yes, good idea, you draft something and let me see it.' Accordingly this was done, and I took the draft in. He scrutinised it with his usual meticulous care, and altered one word, a small one. He read it through again with even greater care, and then looked up with a smile. 'Yes, that'll do very well. Leave it with me.'

Three days later the document was returned to me, with one of the familiar buff slips attached, on which was written:

'A.I.-of-M

You may like to see this.

J. E.'

Across the foot of the draft itself was written, 'Approved. Special Order of the Day. D. H.' [*See end of chapter.*]

General Edmonds had passed through the Staff College in the same year as Earl Haig, and this may have helped to suggest to the General the wonderful notion of transforming my draft of a letter from the Engineer-in-Chief into that highest of all honours, a special Order of the Day above the signature of the C-in-C. It was naturally a matter of the greatest gratification to us all that this single mark of favour was extended to the Tunnelling service, an honour unique in the Corps at that time.

The Companies whom I visited thereafter seemed equally delighted, and I hope it did some good at home too. But the essential kindly genius of General Edmonds could not be better illustrated. He had seen the initiation of the Tunnelling Companies under Sir John Norton-Griffiths and, fittingly enough, gave them this last great reward. On many occasions, behind the scenes, quite unknown to most Tunnellers, he had fought for their interests in support of General Harvey and General Biddulph, and he may fittingly be described as their godfather, attending the christening of the infant, watching it grow to lusty manhood, and sending it out with his blessing into a wider world.

Before adding the final paragraphs to this chapter I must refer to my last leave in London, when I stayed a night or two at the Rubens Hotel in Buckingham Palace Road. There was a big crowd outside the Palace one afternoon, and I pushed my way through to see what was happening. Out on the balcony I saw a memorable group of people. Their Majesties stood beside President and Mrs Wilson, who had just arrived. Mrs Wilson was handed a little Union Jack by Princess Mary, and stood there waving it, while the crowd cheered and cheered again.

It was seven-and-a-half years since I had seen our royal family, when the King reviewed the OTCs of the public schools in Windsor Great Park in 1911. As a very small boy I had seen the Great Queen, a little figure all in black, driving in a carriage across Blackheath. Some years later I had seen King Edward pass through the West End, and the review at Windsor was memorable as my first sight of our present Sovereign, but I never expected in my wildest dreams that I should one day stand outside his Palace, an officer in his Army, and see him there on the famous balcony beside the President of the United States, for ever to be one of the tragic figures in history, the progenitor of a great ideal, which is still struggling along under the hopeless handicap of the defection of the nation that sent him to Europe to make peace in the world.

* * *

The hands of the clock turn quickly, and they are now in the spring of 1930: two-and-a-half years ago I walked along the Embankment to a tall building overlooking the river that has seen so much history and, ascending in the lift, and met by a commissionaire, was taken through long, silent corridors. An officer in mufti, a namesake of mine, give me warm greeting, for did I not serve, centuries ago it seems to me, with his beloved Chief? Yes, the General was expecting me, and I went on along more corridors, past a large notice board on the way. On it was written: 'Visitors are warned that any time wasted in frivolous conversation may delay the completion of the Official History'.

And thus prepared, I was ushered into the presence of that familiar and distinguished soldier, whose works will be read by our children's children, and their descendants for countless generations, until the Great War becomes a legend and myth to some fine and higher type of humanity. General Edmonds' welcome was as kindly and as genial as in the old days at Montreuil. Over a cup of tea he asked how he could best be of assistance to me in a matter about which I had written to him, and finally gave me a valuable introduction to the late Lord Thomson, the Secretary of State for Air, himself once a Sapper. He reminded me of many things that had almost passed from my memory, and then

I asked him how he even began to carry out his stupendous task. As he explained it, there was not too much in it, but that was always his way. The impression I came away with was that the main outlines originated in his wonderful store of personal memories, and that by following these out and referring to the documents available in such overwhelming bulk, other events and aspects suggested themselves to his fertile brain, his assistants filled in the essential details, and their history thus took shape.

Volume after volume continues to flow out from that hive of industry, and it may be years before it is completed. The jealous care of him taken by all his helpers was a very good thing to see, and the British public will pray with them that the work may be finished before he answers the Last Call and lays down his pen.

SPECIAL ORDER OF THE DAY

A large number of men are now being withdrawn from Tunnelling Companies for urgent work at home.

Before they leave the country I wish to convey to the Controllers of Mines and to all ranks of Tunnelling Companies, both Imperial and Overseas, my very keen appreciation of the fine work that has been done by the Tunnelling Companies throughout the last four years.

At their own special work, Mine Warfare, they have demonstrated their complete superiority over the Germans, and whether in the patient defensive mining, in the magnificent success at Messines, or in the preparation for the offensives of the Somme, Arras and Ypres, they have shown the highest qualities both as Military Engineers and as fighting troops.

Their work in the very dangerous task of removing enemy traps and delay-action charges, on subways, dugouts, bridging, roads and the variety of other services on which they have been engaged, has been on a level with their work on the mines.

They have earned the thanks of the whole Army for their contribution to the defeat of the enemy. Their fighting spirit and technical efficiency has enhanced the reputation of the whole Corps of Royal Engineers, and of the Engineers of the Overseas Forces.

I should like to include in the appreciation the work done by the Army Mine Schools and by the Australian Electrical and Mechanical Mining and Boring Company.

D. Haig, F.M. Commander-in-Chief
British Armies in France

General Headquarters
4 December 1918.

Haig, his Army commanders and other senior officers photographed on Armistice Day at the end of a meeting to discuss how the BEF was to implement the terms of the armistice in the short term; whilst Haig was also concerned how the troops were going to be meaningfully occupied in the uncertain months that would follow.
Front row: Plumer (Second Army), Haig and Rawlinson (Fourth Army).
Second row: Byng (Third Army), Birdwood (Fifth Army) and Horne (First Army).
Third row, left to right: Lawrence (Haig's chief of staff), Kavanagh (Cavalry Corps), White, Percy, Vaughan, Montgomery, Anderson, the chiefs of staff of the five British Armies on the Western Front.

'VALETE'

The tale is told, the years a-growing long,
Yet shall we keep our memory ever strong
Of those who helped along a mighty work,
Who ever scorn to falter or to shirk
This simple duty, and who are enduring passed
Onward and upward and to That Great Last.

Appendix I

Plan Showing Mining Areas on the BEF Front

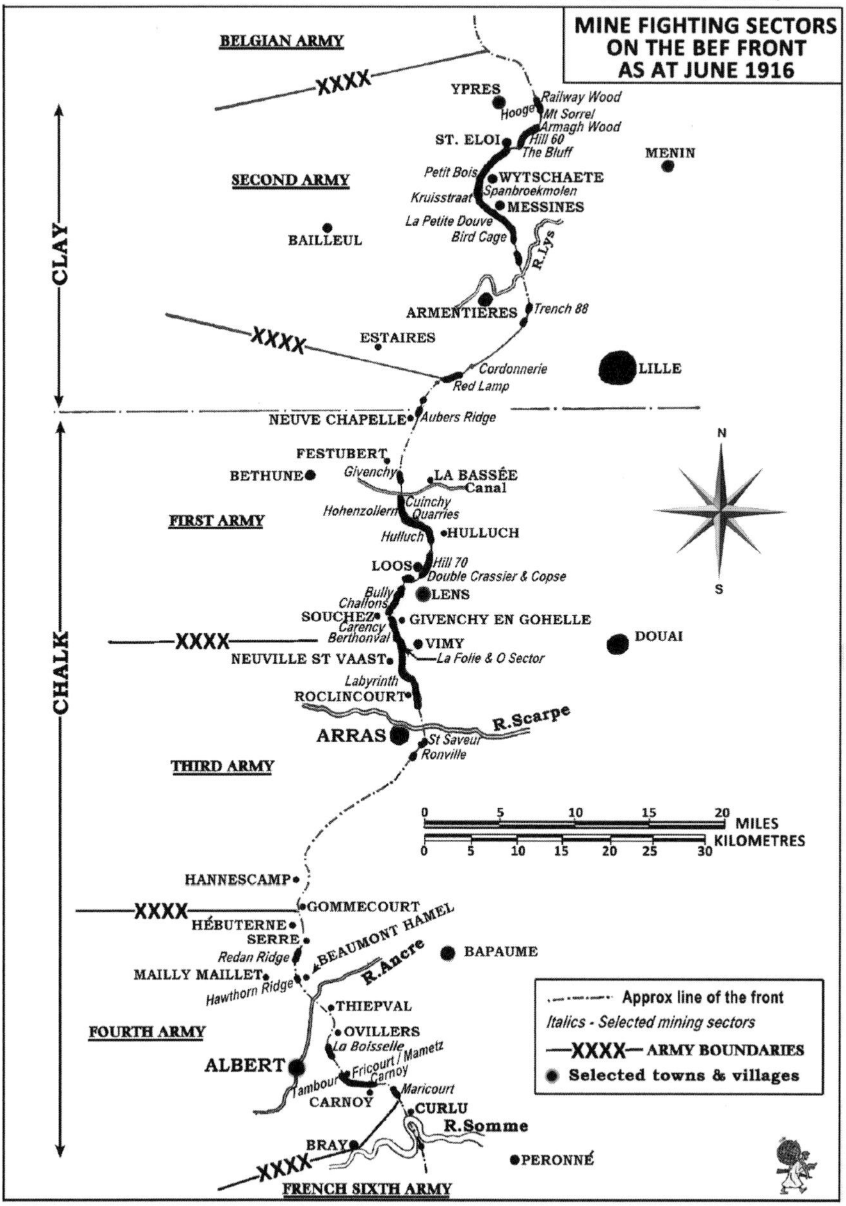

Appendix II

255 Tunnelling Company

Strength as at 18 Nov 1916

	Personnel		*Animals*		*Carriages & transport*							
						Horsed		*Mechanical*				
DETAIL	*Officers*	*Other Ranks*	*Draught*	*Heavy Draught*	*Ammunition wagons / limbers*	*4 wheeled*	*2 wheeled*	*Motor cars*	*Lorries*	*Motor cycles*	*Bicycles*	*REMARKS*
Effective strength	21	533	4	6	2	2	1	1	1x 30cwt 3 x 3 ton	11	6	4 men due transfer & 164 att infantry
ASC		16										
RAMC		2										
TOTAL	21	551	4	6	2	2	1	1	4	11	6	
Attached – Batman		1										
Temporarily att infantry	1	152										
Infantry att for rations		10										Rations only
TOTAL Rations	22	718										
War Establishment	15	335	2	8	2	2	1	1	4	11	6	

Effective strength includes Regular RE 7, Tunnellers 154, Tunnellers Mates 193.
Signed by Thomas P Farth, 2/Lt. 18 Nov 1916

Appendix III

Composition of 3rd Australian Tunnelling Company as at March 1917

EXAMPLE of the COMPOSITION of a TUNNELLING COMPANY
(3rd Australian Tunnelling Company March 1917)

COMPANY HEADQUARTERS

Officer Commanding	Major
Adjutant	Captain or Lieutenant
Medical Officer	RAMC
Company Sergeant Major	Warrant Officer Class 2 Company Quartermaster Sergeant
36 Other Ranks, including:	Draughtsmen, Clerks, Drivers, Cooks, Storemen and Batmen

MINING SECTIONS

	Sections				
	1	*2*	*3*	*4*	*Total*
Section Commander. (Captain or Lieutenant)	1	1	1	1	4
Section Officer (2/Lieutenant or Lieutenant)	3	3	3	3	12
Blacksmiths *	1	1	1	1	4
Carpenters *	1	1	1	1	4
Storekeepers	1	1	1	1	4
Cooks	5	6	6	5	22
Listeners	8	8	4	8	28
Permanent Protomen	2	2	2	3	9
Other trades	7	8	8	6	29
Miners	82	86	94	77	339
Labourers	46	42	41	47	176
TOTALS (all ranks)	157	159	162	153	631

Total Company strength: 19 Officers and 653 Other Ranks
* Blacksmiths and Carpenters temporarily employed at Company HQ.
Each Section, with its own motor transport, drivers, cooks and other administrative personnel could be detached to operate in a semi independent role, or to reinforce another Tunnelling Company.

Appendix IV

Extract from 255 Tunnelling Company Weekly Mine Report on 10 November 1916

EXAMPLE OF PART OF A 255 TUNNELLING COMPANY WEEKLY MINING REPORT PROBABLY ABOUT THE DATE THAT DIXON DEPARTED FROM THE COMPANY.

A. F. W 3404.

SECRET.

Date 10/10/16.

WEEKLY MINE REPORT.

2 Officers and 134 O.R. at present working in XVII Corps area.

IV Corps.

37th Division.

255th Tunnelling Company, R.E.

Strength of Company (From A.F. B-213).	Officers.	O.R.
R.E. ...	21	402*
Attached Infantry	2	323
Total ...	23	725

* 10 pending transfer.

Designation of working. 1.	Trench No. or name. 2.	Map reference. 3.	Shaft or Gallery. Depth. 4.	Shaft or Gallery. Size inside timbers. 5.	Shaft or Gallery. Total footage. 6.	Footage for week. 7.	No. of days worked. 8.	Nature of ground. 9.	REPORT. Circumstances affecting progress. Results of listening. Mines and camouflets. General information. 10
Railway Cutting, Shaft. No.2.F.8.	Roman-os.	M.15.b 46.55.	43'		87½'	nil	nil	chalk	Enemy working about 40 feet away on right front.
Pit-prop Corner. Shaft.No6.Rt.Lat	Moon-light.	M.14.d 98.15.	55'		425'	71'	7	"	Lateral progressing.
" " L.P.15.			"		100'	19½'	2	"	L.P. finished.
" " " 16.			"		79'	37'	4	"	New L.P.
Shaft.No8 Main.	Sunlight		"		8'	8'	2	"	New incline shaft started.
Calonne. Shaft.No3.R.H.1.	Staf-ford.	M.20.b 37.70.	54'		101½'	nil	nil	"	Distant sounds of enemy working.
Dives. L.H.1.			"		84'	"	"	"	" " " " ".
Shaft.No2.R.H.2.	"	M.20.b. 33.57.	51'		62'	"	"	"	) Enemy working heard during the week.
Little Willie. L.P.4.					53½'	"	"	"	)
Lat.bet.1 & 2.LP.1.	"		54'		80'	"	"	"	Distant sounds of enemy working.
Shaft.No.1.RH.3.Rt.	"	M.20.b. 14.47.	53'		61'	"	"	"	Enemy working about 30 feet away.
Big Willie.RH.2.					89'	"	"	"	" " " 30 to 40 feet away.
" " RH.1a.					70'	16'	1½	"	We sprung mine 3.20.pm.7/10/16.Charge 2,100 lbs ammonal. Enemy working about 15' away at time of blow.Gallery since recovered to 54' & new L.P. started.
Shaft.No.7.Main.		M.20.b. 15.51.	70'		333'	30'	3	Hard chalk.	) Deep level system progressing.
Proto. R.G.1.			"		101'	18½'	2½		)
" Lat from R.H.1.					29½'	29½'	4	"	)
" 2nd Con to B.W. Lateral.					34½'	34½'	4	"	)
Proto Dug-out.	Boyau.209.				45'	17½'	3	"	)

ARMY PRINTING AND STATIONERY SERVICES A—8/16—G279—13,000.

Appendix V

First Army Report on Mining Situation on Taking Over from the French in the Artois in March 1916

Inspector of Mines, General Headquarters.

Attached is a short statement asked for yesterday by First Army regarding the enemy mining in line taken over recently from the French. It includes the steps that have been taken to meet the situation.

I believe these notes were required for a conference.

Captain R.E.,
for Lieutenant Colonel,
Controller of Mines,
First Army.

In section of line taken over from the French M 9d 8.8.to M 25b 9.8. There are 5 sectors where energetic mining must be carried out at once.

(1) MAROC MINE SECTOR M 9d 8.6 to M 9d 6.1
A main incline has been constructed to 140' from parapet,and branch galleries to protect the salient are being driven. This work is being done by a section of 40 men from 1st Division. Sounds of enemy mining have not been heard since taking over.

(2) RAILWAY CUTTING SALIENT M 15b 5.5.to M 15b 2.2.
The French had a listening gallery here which we are extending. Two other shafts are being sunk and a system of defensive galleries will be started as soon as possible,because this is rather an important salient and is exposed to enemy underground attack. Sounds of underground work have been heard but these may be due to the enemy constructing deep dug-outs.

(3) RAILWAY EMBANKMENT M 15c 1.2 to M 20b 8.9.
Requires a small protective system. Listening galleries will be constructed to detect any underground activity.

(4) CALONNE SECTOR M 20b.4.7. to M 20b.1½.3.
Several French listening galleries are being used here. The enemy are working underground in this sector and not far from our trenches. We have put down shafts in the 2nd line trench and shall drive out under his galleries if possible. This work is being done at high pressure because the French listening posts are not deep enough to be effective for destroying the enemy galleries.

(5) ANGRES SECTOR M 20b 1.0. to M 25b 9.8.
This section has three salients to be protected,underground. There are several French listening galleries in use. We are extending some of these and also starting a deeper system to fight the enemy mining which is suspected. No definite sounds have been heard since we took over from the French.

At sectors Nos. 2,3,4,and 5,the work is being done by the 23rd Divisiona Tunnelling Company (300 men) assisted by 200 Infantry from the 2nd Div. Until this Divisional Tunnelling Company is approved as a proper Tunnelling Company,it is liable to have to move with the Division and leave this sector without any miners.

Continued-

Report to First Army continued 2

In the line from the ETONNOIRS M 25b.9.9. to BOYAU ERZATZ the southern boundary of 1st Army Front, the 176th Coy., is employed in constructing the listening and protective galleries. The work is divided into 3 main sectors.

(1) TRENCH FERRACOL M 25d 9.4 is opposite a German salient and is a junction of several communication trenches. The distance between the lines is small, therefore a defense should be constructed at once. No mining noises have been heard since we took over.

(2) SULPHURINO & SEBASTOPAL SALIENTS are exposed to underground attack. We have 4 listeners, but except on one occasion sounds have not been reported. The trenches in these two sectors are in very bad condition, which may explain the fact of the enemy not mining there at present.

(3) CARONCY SECTOR south of SOUCHEZ S 9a 1.0 to S 15a 1.7. is on the ridge of the hill. The French had 7 or 8 galleries, 5 of which are useful as listeners. They had also started 4 shafts in the second line trench with a view to driving a deeper system of galleries out to counter the German workings. The French reported the Germans to be working in 3 places, but we have detected only two since taking over the line. Systematic listening is being carried out and a comprehensive scheme of shafts and galleries for the underground protection of this sector is now in progress. 3 sections of the 176th Coy., are detailed for this work ; while one section is on the other two sectors north of SOUCHEZ.

****

24/3/16 H.H. Guill Capt R.E.
a/Controller of Mines
1st Army.

Appendix VI

Nieuport 1917

The BEF's strategic objectives for the Flanders offensive in mid 1917 aimed at breaking through the German defences in the Ypres Salient, coupled with a linking drive up the coast along with a seaborne assault by a division near to Ostend – Operation Hush. Accordingly, in June, the Fourth Army (General Rawlinson) replaced the Belgians and French on the coastal area at Nieuport (Nieuwpoort). Innovative preparations were simultaneously put in hand for the seaborn operation.

The front on the coast was cramped between the sea and inundations inland. The forward line lay to the east of the Yser canal and river amongst extensive sand dunes, the support line on the western side. The 2nd Australian Tunnelling Company was deployed in support. On the eastern side of the Yser they at once began offensive mining towards a feature close to the coast known as the Grand Dune; and on the construction of subways and dugouts, a complex task in the sandy ground. They overcame doubts as to the feasibility of tunnelling and dugout construction in the sand by keeping just above the ground water level, fifteen to twenty feet below the surface, and by close timbering their work throughout.

A group of 3rd Australian Tunnelling Company miners at the entrance to a dugout or tunnel amongst the dunes.

The Germans foresaw the possibility of imminent attack and launched a spoiling offensive, Operation Strandfest (who says that the Germans do not have a sense of humour? Strandfest translates as Beach Party). On 10 June the elite Marines Corps Flanders attacked between Lombartzyde and the coast, supported by a ferocious bombardment that destroyed the three bridges across the canal in that sector and, amongst other things, used for the first time, certainly against the British, Yellow Cross (mustard) Gas, against which the defenders had little protection. The 2 Brigade, 1st Division, taken by surprise, were swiftly cut off and overwhelmed, although isolated parties fought on through the day. In addition to fatalities, just over 1,300 all ranks were captured. Of the 1st Battalion Northamptonshire Regiment, only nine junior ranks escaped back across the canal.

No. 1 Section of the Australian Tunnelling Company were cut off on the eastern side of the canal. Trapped in their underground workings, most were forced to surrender when the Germans dropped smoke bombs down the vents and in some cases played flame projectors down the inclines. In addition to two fatalities, one officer and forty miners were captured (many of them wounded), along with most of their attached infantry.

There were heroic episodes but none more so than that of Sapper James O'Connell, who was in the Company Cookhouse near the front line when the enemy attacked. He retreated, bombing as he went, until he reached the canal bank, at which point he was hit in the head by rifle fire. He fell into the canal, but managed to drag himself out and make his way to a nearby dugout, gathering a handful of bombs and again making a determined stand. He was then severely burnt by a German flame projector and found his way back to the canal. After lying in the water for about half an hour he struggled out and crept into a dugout, where he found Second Lieutenant Hargraves (also of 2 Australian Tunnelling Company), who tended his wounds. As the enemy approached, he decided to take a chance and swim the canal. In spite of his wounds he succeeded in getting across but, just as he was emerging from the water, he heard cries for help from men who were in danger of drowning. Without hesitation, James O'Connell returned to the water and rescued one of the soldiers. It was only after reaching the western bank of the canal for the second time that, collapsing from exhaustion, he allowed himself to be taken to a dressing station. Recommended for a VC, he was awarded the Distinguished Conduct Medal for his actions.

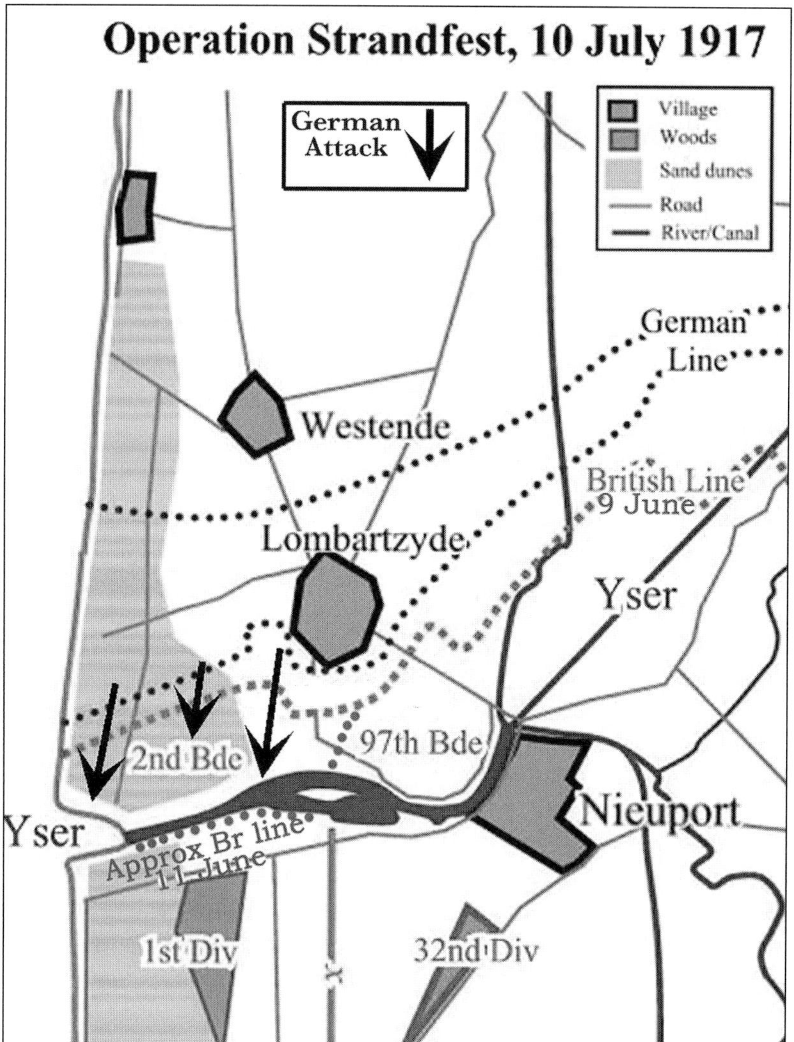

To supplement the depleted Australians, 257 Tunnelling Company deployed to Nieuport (Nieuwpoort) on 21 June and together both companies were employed on driving subways in and around Nieuport. They suffered severely from continued German artillery fire and in July lost heavily from the effects of mustard gas shells. The 257's war diary for 22 July reported:

German Marines light mortar section in action amongst the sand dunes.

> 'Germans used new Mustard Gas shell on Nieuwpoort during the night. One officer and 23 other ranks admitted to hospital and a large number of men suffering from effects may have to go later. This shell apparently bursts with a very small report and the effects are not felt for several hours after which it effects eyes, voice and skin, even through the clothes.'

The following day sixty-one other ranks were admitted to hospital as a consequence.

In late June, 184 Tunnelling Company arrived, followed in mid July by 256 Tunnelling Company, both to work on the provision of shelters in the dunes, artillery positions and the sinking of wells. They also suffered from shell fire; but their greatest problem was that of working in the fine sand that percolated through the timbers and into machinery, whilst percussion from shells would often bring down the working face on the miners. Consideration was given to tubbing down to the blue clay that lay about eighty feet below the surface and tunnelling below the river; but on further consideration of the resources required, the scheme was abandoned.

With the loss of the British positions on the eastern side of the Yser Canal, and the failure to achieve an early break out of the Ypres Salient, Operation

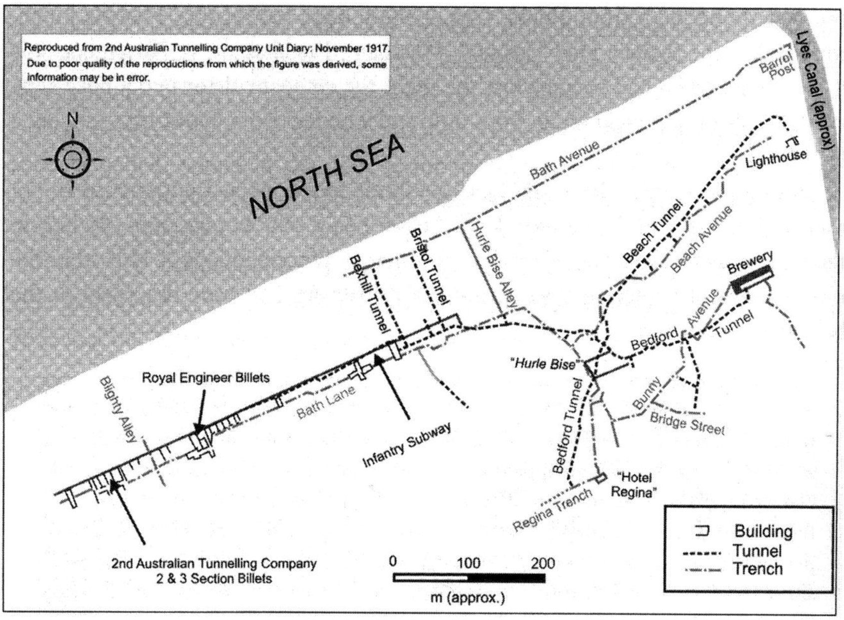

Hush was abandoned. In November the coastal sector, now well endowed with subways and shelters, was handed back to the French and the tunnelling companies moved elsewhere.

In recent years, notably in the the 1990s, it has been claimed (the evidence has been disputed) that timber supports have rotted in some of the extensive subways and dugouts constructed by the British and the French and that this has led to subsidence problems and consequent damage to buildings in areas of Nieuwpoort.

Appendix VII

Biographical Notes on Selected Personalities

Not all those mentioned in the text have a biographical entry here; we have produced a selection that we think reflects the varied careers of the men with whom Dixon came in contact during the war. Some people have lengthy captions by their photograph in the text and are not included. Some well known personalities have relatively short entries, given their fame during the war. In some cases we have included considerable information, partly because their careers (often before or after the war) are both interesting and unusual, partly to illustrate the depth of experience that was deployed in the conduct of the war at GHQ and Army level. In numerous entries we have included citations for gallantry decorations, the majority of which relate to acts whilst the officer concerned was working in a tunnelling company. Amongst other considerations, these awards underline the fact that many of the 'despised' staff performed heroically in the field.

Allenby, Sir Edmund, General: GOC Third Army until the end of the Arras Offensive of 1917; then C-in-C Palestine. Known in the army as 'The Bull'. A cavalry officer. He has enjoyed mixed reviews from military historians and has possibly been under-rated; he certainly commanded the Palestine Campaign with great success, whilst he showed himself to be tactful in a very volatile political, religious and cultural situation.

Atkin, Keyser, Captain, RAMC: A prisoner of war (whilst attached to 2/S Staffs: PoW from 22 September 1917 – 23 February 1918, one of ten RAMC officers repatriated on that date). Killed in action on 6 June 1918. He is buried in Marfaux British Cemetery, VIII.G.7

Ball, H S, Captain, later Major: OBE, 4 x MiD: 170 Tunnelling Company and then Commandant First Army Mining School, later Assistant Inspector of Mines, GHQ, after the Armistice. Born in 1888, he was educated in South Africa and took a second degree in Canada; specialised as a mining engineer and petroleum technologist. Won a Research Scholarship. Wrote an article on the 'Work of the Miner on the Western Front' in Transactions of the IMM. Pre war worked in South Africa, Canada, Trinidad and South America. He died in South Africa in 1941.

Bellamy, C: Experimental Officer on the Engineer in Chief 's staff. In Chapter nine there is mention of his invention to stop armour piercing bullets by the use of spaced cement-asbestos fibre plates set on armoured cars, a surprisingly modern technical solution.

Biddulph, H, Colonel, T/Brigadier General: DSO, gazetted January 1917, CMG, 1919, 5 x MiD. Inspector of Mines – succeeded Major General MacInnes at or close to the end of the war. Dixon claimed that he was one of only two regular RE officers serving with the tunnelling companies at the end of the war. Born in 1872, he was commissioned in 1892. He served in the Tirah Campaign, 1897-1898 and later on the NW Frontier, in operations against the Waziris, in 1902. At the outbreak of the war he had been chief instructor at the School of Military Engineering since September 1912. Post war he was the Chief Engineer in Southern Command and later became Director of Buildings at the Air Ministry, 1928-1931. He retired from the army in 1929 and died in 1952.

Bloom, Alan: A tunnelling officer in 255 Tunnelling Company. A South African.

Bryant: At the time, probably a major. Assistant to the Camp Commandant, Montreuil

Buchan, John: Author and propagandist during the war – the 'Official Eye Witness'. He had an extraordinary career – ending up as Governor General of Canada and ennobled as Lord Tweedsmuir. He was a noted author; amongst other books related to the war, he wrote the history of the South African Brigade and of the 15th (Scottish) Division.

Buchanan, Jim, Lieutenant: Cameronians and then 180 Tunnelling Company. Killed in a railway accident on 18 February 1918. He is buried in Cathcart Cemetery, c.12.A

Buckingham, William, Captain: MC, gazetted 14 January 1916, 4 x MiD. 180 Tunnelling Company. He replaced Major Stokes for a time as Assistant Inspector of Mines. He subsequently commanded an RE Field Company. Post war he saw service in the Sudan.

Cadman, Sir John (later Lord): (1877-1941) Professor of Mining at Birmingham University. He was brought up in a mining family, was a DSc, having studied Mining and Geology at various universities and by 1903 was HM Inspector of Mines in Staffordshire. He became an expert in the oil industry and was the leading British expert on oil in the country during the war. He was also involved in the development of television and of Imperial Airways and commercial air travel. KCMG 1918, GCMG 1929, elevated to the peerage as Baron Cadman of Silverdale, 1937.

Clark, Sapper, in time promoted to sergeant. A draughtsman in the office of the Inspector of Mines; he assisted with the preparation of defence plans in early 1918.

Clarke, Sir Travers E, Lieutenant General, GBE (1926) KCB (1920 – CB 1917) KCMG (1920) and numerous decorations from the Allied powers: Quartermaster General to the BEF, 27 December 1917-1919 and then to the Forces (and a member of the Army Council), 1919-1923. Commissioned in Royal Inniskilling Fusiliers (1890), served India (NW Frontier), and South African War 1900-1902. Physically a giant of a man. Only in his mid 40s when appointed; continued the run of very efficient QMGs to the BEF, even in the logistically very challenging months of retreat and advance of 1918.

Collie, A, Sergeant Major: Chief Clerk in the Inspector of Mines office at GHQ. Died of wounds received during an air raid on 3 June 1918 and is buried in Étaples Military Cemetery, LXV.E.26.

Conner, C: An officer in 255 Tunnelling Company. Wounded, as a result of which he lost an arm.

David, Sir T W Edgeworth, Major later Lieutenant Colonel: KBE, gazetted September 1920 for services during the war; CMG (1910), DSO, gazetted January 1918, 2 x MiD. Australian Mining Corps, attached to GHQ as Geologist BEF, November 1916. Professor of Geology at Sydney University 1891 – 1924. MA, DSc, FRS. Born in Wales (1858), moved to New South Wales in November 1882. A mountaineer, he made the first ascent of Mount Eurebus, Antarctica. He reached the south magnetic Pole in 1909 and claimed it for the British. Agitated for the founding of an Australian Mining Corps in 1915 and was commissioned as a major in October 1915. Awarded a state funeral on his death in 1934.

Davidson, Sir JH ('Tavish'), Major General: DSO (with 1st KRRC, South African War), CB 1917, KCMG 1919 11 x MiD. General Staff. BGGS First Army on its formation; MGGS GHQ when Haig became C-in-C in December 1915. Retained his position at GHQ until the Armistice. An advocate of 'bite and hold' operations. Became MP for Fareham in 1918 (resigned 1931) and worked hard to improve the lot of ex-servicemen. He published in 1953 *Haig: Master of the Field*, an impassioned defence of Haig (and to some degree GHQ) at a time when criticism of both was reaching new heights. The book (2017) is still in print. He died in 1954.

Dickson, Edward JQ (Birdie), Captain: MC, gazetted 17 September 1917, 'For conspicuous gallantry and devotion to duty on two occasions, in entering a dugout which had been wrecked by hostile shell fire, extricating the victims and carrying them to the dressing station, three hundred yards away, under heavy and continuous shell fire. By this prompt and gallant action he and his NCO were the direct means of saving many lives, as the place was again hit directly after his work was completed. He has frequently proved himself an extremely gallant officer, with an utter disregard for danger when assisting others.' 255 Tunnelling Company. Killed in action on 26 October 1917 by a sniper during the Battle of Passchendaele. Buried in Lijssenthoek Military Cemetery. XXVII.A.19

Dixon, CD: Shanghai Volunteer Corps, Somerset Light Infantry, commanded a Chinese Labour Company. Brother of HR Dixon (the author). Wounded on the Somme whilst with the SLI.

Dixon, HR, T/Major: MC, gazetted June 1918. The author.

Edmonds, Sir James E, Brigadier General: CB. CMG, Knighted (KB) 1928, 5 x MiD, DLitt. GHQ and then Deputy Engineer in Chief there from late 1917 – 1918. The British Official Historian. A brilliant mind, a polyglot; head of MO5, later MI5, 1904-1909. GSO1 of 4th Division at the outbreak of the war but broke under the strain of the Retreat, September 1914. Sent to GHQ; he was well regarded by Haig. In 1919 became director of the military branch's historical section; ended up writing many of the Western Front volumes of the British Official History himself (1922–1948; Volume II 1917 was the last to be published), finally completing it when he was 87 years old. Despite criticism, the Official History has much to commend it, both in scope and contents. He died in 1956, at the age of 94.

English, AA, Captain: MC, gazetted I January 1917. Tunnelling officer in 255 Tunnelling Company. South African. Transferred to the RFC. He was wounded in the Salient when flying in a Bristol F2b as the observer during an offensive patrol on 25 September 1917; his pilot made a forced landing.

Fidoe, JW, Captain. 251 Tunnelling Company, then Office of Inspector of Mines, GHQ. Replaced Smyth.

Fleming, Sir John, Professor, FRS. University College, Professor of Electrical Technology. Invented the first vacuum tube, often considered the beginning of electronics. He played a major role in the development of radar. Generations of school pupils will know him for Fleming's Left and Right Hand rules. He died in 1945, at the age of 95.

Ford, T/ Captain. Initially Assistant to Camp Commandant, Montreuil, then ADC to Sir Eric Geddes

Fowke, Sir GH, Lieutenant General: KCB (1916), KCMG (1918), 11 x MiD. Engineer-in-Chief at GHQ 1914 – February 1916 and then the Adjutant General at GHQ (-1919). A brilliant linguist, with a capacious memory and a serious professional soldier, despite appearances. Had a dominating personality; was a good problem solver and was decisive. Had an outstanding personal knowledge of the officers of the army. Served in the South African War, was attached to the Japanese Army in Manchuria during the Russo-Japanese War, 1905. Retired in 1928 and lived in France; he died in February 1940.

French, Charles John, Major. OC 255 Tunnelling Company in 1916 (originally 5th King's Shropshire Light Infantry). Killed in action on 2 July 1916. Buried in Noeux-les-Mines Communal Cemetery, I. L. 13.

Geddes, Sir Eric, Major General; then Vice Admiral. Inspector General of Transportation at GHQ, 1916 – May 1917; then transferred to the Royal Navy. Brought in to reorganise the BEF's transportation system. Had been a go-ahead and innovative General Manager of the North Eastern Railway in 1914. Born in 1875, he was notably young for such high responsibilities. His brother, Auckland, was an equally effective administrator; he served in the Government as Minister of National Service in 1917.

Gort, Viscount [from 1902] (John Vereker), Lieutenant Colonel: VC, DSO and two bars, MC, 8 x MiD. On General Staff for a time, then CO Grenadier Guards. In August 1914, ADC to Haig (I Corps); then GSO3, same Corps and then a brigade major (4[Guards] Brigade) Then GSO2 at GHQ and moved within GHQ to be part of what was effectively the first planning staff without other duties. In April 1917, CO 4th Grenadier Guards. Wounded on 31 July 1917 (Bar to the DSO awarded in early 1917). Wounded at Cambrai, November 1917. As commander of 1st Grenadier Guards, awarded a further Bar to his DSO for his actions at Arras during the German spring offensive. Awarded the VC for actions near the Canal du Nord, when temporary GOC of 3 (Guards) Brigade, in which action he was again wounded. Chief of the Imperial General Staff, 1938. Commanded the British field force in France 1939-1940; Governor of Gibraltar, April 1941, Governor of Malta, May 1942, High Commissioner and C-in-C Palestine, 1944-1946. Died of cancer in March 1946.

Gough, Sir Hubert, General. GOC Reserve Army, 1916, which became Fifth Army in October 1916. Mainly associated with the fighting on the southern flank of the British Arras Offensive of April-May 1918; and then with the northern flank of the Third Battle of Ypres 1917. Sacked on 28 March 1918 after the defeat of Fifth Army in the opening phase of the German spring offensives (although many would argue that his Army's performance was actually quite good, given the circumstances). One of the great survivors (he died in 1963), he lived long enough to be interviewed at home (but no interview was broadcast) by John Terraine prior to the broadcasting of BBC 2's much admired Great War series.

Grant Grieve, W, Captain. Tunnelling officer 255 Tunnelling Company. Author of Tunnellers, with Bernard Newman; until Alexander Barrie's War Underground was published in 1961, this was probably the most useful single volume book on the tunnellers, with all the advantages (and some disadvantages) of being written by a tunneller of the Great War.

Haking, RCB, Lieutenant General. Promoted from a brigade (September-December 1914), division (the 1st, December 1914 – September 1915) to a Corps (XI, until the end of the war) commander. Commanded at Fromelles, July 1916; sent to Italy in November 1917 and then returned to the Western Front in March 1918. Wounded in September 1914 (the Aisne). Regarded by many as a 'butcher', not least for his command of the Fromelles operation (a judgement marginally qualified by modern military historians). His Corps performed well at the Battle of the Lys 1918 and Haig was keen to promote him to Army command.

Haig, Sir Douglas, Lieutenant General (I Corps) then General (First Army and as C-in-C); Field Marshal January 1917. C-in-C BEF from 19 Dec 1915 to the end of the war. Created Earl Haig of Bemersyde after the war; the remaining ten years of his life were largely devoted to the welfare issues of ex-servicemen. Only recently, maybe within the last twenty years or so, has it seemed possible to have a nuanced opinion about Haig both as a man and as regards his qualities – or otherwise – as Commander in Chief of the BEF. From the fifties and for forty plus years afterwards, certainly, admirers and detractors (at their worst) had often seemed to engage in polemics.

Haldane, Richard, Viscount. Secretary of State for War, 1905 – 1912. Lord Chancellor 1912 – 1915. Probably one of the greatest Secretary of States for War in British history; on paper a rather unlikely outcome at the time of his appointment in a noticeably unwarlike Liberal administration. A great reforming minister and largely responsible for the formation of the Territorial Force and the British Expeditionary Force amongst other achievements. He made Britain as prepared for war as possible in the political circumstances. He was hounded from office on the spurious grounds of being a German sympathiser, principally by the Northcliffe Press (eg the Daily Mail).

Hart, Captain. Office of the Controller of Mines, First Army, then Water Supply Officer First Army.

Harvey, RN, Major General: CB (1917), CMG (1916), DSO (gazetted 19 April 1901) 6 x MiD. He was Assistant to the Engineer in Chief at GHQ from January 1915. Appointed the first Inspector of Mines at GHQ from about December 1915 to late 1917 (succeeded by Major General MacInnes). At the beginning of 1918 became Chief Engineer to IV Corps. Post war, he was the Engineer in Chief of the Indian Army, 1924-1928. He was appointed Colonel Commandant RE in 1935. Commissioned in 1888. He died in 1937.

Heath, Sir Herbert, Vice Admiral. Second Sea Lord 1917-1919 (responsible for naval personnel matters). Brother of Major General GM Heath

Heath, Sir Gerard, Major General: KCMG CB DSO, gazetted 8 February 1901, 6xMiD. Born 1863, commissioned in 1882. He had extensive campaigning experience, starting with the Bechuanaland Expedition (1884-1885), then the Chitral Expedition (1895); he served in South Africa throughout the war 1899-1902. He had experience in command on active service of a pontoon train, a telegraphic section, a balloon section and a field company RE as well as a period as an intelligence officer. He was an instructor in field fortification at Chatham, followed by further service in India and Burma. Soon after the outbreak of war (he was in South Africa at the time), in September 1914, he was appointed as Inspector of Engineers. He went to France as Chief Engineer II Corps (May 1915), then the same in First Army (November 1915), then Engineer in Chief as successor to Major General Spring Rice at GHQ in October 1917. He was slightly wounded by a shell fragment in 1917 whilst inspecting at the front. He died in 1929.

Hill, LC, Major, possibly T/Lieutenant Colonel for a period: DSO, gazetted 3 June 1919, MC, whilst with 177, 3 January 1916; 4 x MiD. 174 and 177 Tunnelling Companies and Assistant Controller of Mines, Third Army. Dixon shows him as Colonel (ie Lieutenant Colonel) and Controller of Mines Third Army; but post war list has him only as a major and the Assistant. He might have been holding the post temporarily. Before the war he was working for Rio Tinto Spain (since 1912), having qualified from the Royal School of Mines, South Kensington.

Hill, LE, Lieutenant Colonel: OBE, MC, gazetted 14 January 1916 when a lieutenant with 171; 4 x MiD. 171 Tunnelling Coy (attached from East Yorkshire Regiment), then HQs of Second, Fourth and Fifth Armies. Probably went from OC of 171 Tunnelling Company to Assistant Controller of Mines at an Army HQ and finally Controller of Mines Second Army. Before the war he had been a mining engineer in Forfar.

Hopkins, N J, Captain, ultimately Lieutenant Colonel. Engineer in Chief's Staff at GHQ; he had been severely wounded on 2 September 1914. A bridging specialist. Designer of the 'Hopkins Bridge' system in early 1917, which provided spans from 60 to 120 feet.

Kiggel, Sir L E, Lieutenant General: CB (1908), KCB (1916), KCMG (1918). Chief of the General Staff GHQ BEF under Haig until January 1918, when he was removed, partly for reasons of exhaustion, partly for the failures of Third Ypres and Cambrai. An infantryman, his forte was as a staff officer; he was commandant of the Staff College at the outbreak of the war. He was an early advocate of a War School for middle ranking staff officers – eventually to come about as the Imperial Defence College; and he was unusual amongst military men in his appreciation of political considerations in determining strategy. By the time he left his post he was exhausted through working very long hours and had outstayed his usefulness to the BEF. Despite his health issues, he lived to be over ninety.

Lawrence, Sir H A, Lieutenant General: KCB (1917), GCB (1925). Chief of the General Staff GHQ BEF from 24 January 1918 until the end of the war (having served for only a few weeks immediately previously as the replacement of Charteris as Director of Military Intelligence). He had an unusual military career, resigning in 1903 and then proceeded to make his fortune in the City. Called back to the army in 1914, he performed well in Gallipoli and Sinai, less well as a divisional commander (the 66th (2/ East Lancashire) Division) at Third Ypres. He was an effective presence at GHQ, was a sound support for Haig, sharing his views on the war and, crucially, got on with the French. Both his sons were killed on the Western Front, Oliver, on 26 May 1915 (8/ London Regiment), at the age of 21;and is buried, appropriately enough, in Post Office Rifles Cemetery, Festubert, I.C.9). The other, Michael, a captain in 1/ Coldstream, was killed, also at the age of 21, on 16 September 1916 (Battle of Flers Courcelette) and is buried in Grovetown Cemetery, I.C.38. In both cases the epitaphs comprise the respective date of birth, followed by Pro Deo et Patria. He returned to an industry and City career at the end of the war.

Laws, H W, (Temporary) Lieutenant Colonel: CMG, DSO, gazetted 8 November 1915 (for services in Gallipoli); 4 x MiD. He served as a staff officer with VIII Corps on Gallipoli (starting in the RN Division). On arrival on the Western Front he found employment in 254 and then 250 Tunnelling Companies before becoming Controller of Mines, Fourth Army. According to Dixon he was one of only two regular RE officers in the Tunnelling Branch of the RE at the end of the war, the other being Biddulph. The Army List of 1918, however, has him appearing in the Supplementary List for the RE.

Logan, Dale D, Major, then Lieutenant Colonel RAMC: DSO, gazetted 4 June 1917. He was attached to the Inspector of Mines office at GHQ as the resident expert on tunnelling medical matters.

Lowry, T M, Major, later Lieutenant Colonel: DSO, gazetted 3 June 1918, MC (gazetted 14 January 1916), 3 x MiD , Order of the Crown of Italy. Croix de Guerre (France). He commanded for a while an ad hoc Mining Company, largely comprising members of the Maltese Labour Corps on the Italian Front in late 1917. British divisions under Plumer were sent there after the disaster of Caporetto in November 1917. He was a pre war graduate of the Camborne School of Mines and was attached to the RE from the Duke of Cornwall's Light Infantry.

Mackintosh, E E B, (Temporary) Colonel: DSO, gazetted 1 January 1917, Légion d'Honneur, 2 x MiD. He was ADC to the Sirdar and Governor General of the Sudan, 1908-1911 (and was seconded to the Egyptian Army for a while in 1916). After a time with a field company in France, was a staff officer (RE) at Fourth Army until December 1916. Assistant Engineer in Chief, GHQ, October 1917 to the end of the war.

MacWilliam, K J, Captain: MiD. Tunnelling officer in 255 Tunnelling Company. Like so many tunnelling officers, he was a South African, with mining experience in that country.

Manning, Robert Charles, Major: DSO, gazetted 4 June 1917, MC, gazetted 14 January 1917 when a temporary lieutenant, 2 x MiD, Légion d'Honneur. Enlisted in the Canadian army at the outbreak of the war (educated in Ireland) as a lance corporal, thanks to his OTC experience at Trinity College, Dublin. Commissioned in the field for conspicuous bravery when serving with a mining section. OC 170 Tunnelling Company. Killed in action on 6 September 1918, aged 29. Buried Pernes British Cemetery, VI.A.38.

Macinnes (sometimes rendered as MacInnes), Duncan S, Brigadier General: DSO (gazetted 19 April 1901 1900), CMG (January 1917), 4 x MiD, twice during the South African War, Légion d'Honneur. A Canadian, commissioned in RE in 1891. Saw service in the Ashanti Expedition and was responsible for constructing the fort at Coomassie; South African War (noted particularly at the defence of Kimberley), staff in Canada from 1905, thence to UK (Shorncliffe and Staff College). Involved in development of the RFC, then member of staff at Camberley; Retreat from Mons (wounded 26 November 1914), OC 54 Field Company RE; War Office, latterly as Director of Aeronautical Equipment. Resigned in 1917 to go to France; March 1917 CRE 42nd Division (particularly noted for his work when the Division was at Nieuport (Nieuwpoort), September – November 1917); succeeded Harvey as Inspector of Mines at GHQ, December 1917 (as well as sharing the duties of Deputy Engineer in Chief with Edmonds)

– his duties were extended to responsibilities for preparing defences in the light of both the anticipated German attack of 1918 and the German spring offensives themselves; accidentally killed 23 May 1918, buried 25 May 1918, Étaples Military Cemetery XXVIII.L.2.

McLennan, J C, Professor of Physics, University of Toronto: (OBE 1917) KBE (1935), FRS. Worked with Rutherford at Cambridge on X Rays; chair of Physics in 1907. An outstanding research scientist. During the war his work on helium took him to England. There he served in the Admiralty (staff of the Second Sea Lord), in charge of the Admiralty research laboratory 1917-1918 and later as Scientific Adviser to the Admiralty, 1918-1920. His work and the group he gathered about him on the magnetic detection of submarines aided greatly in reducing this menace to British shipping. In his latter years he was a pioneer in the field of radiation treatment for malignant tumors.

Morgan, W H, Major: DSO, gazetted 4 June 1917, 4 x MiD. Arrived in France in 1915, trained as a civil engineer. An officer in 170 Tunnelling Company before becoming OC of 255 Tunnelling Company on the death of Major C French in July 1916. Post war became County Engineer of Middlesex and a Vice President of the Institute of Civil Engineers. He died in 1966. His oldest son was killed as a Pilot Officer in the RAF (VR) in June 1942 at the age of 21; he has no known grave.

Morton, Herbert L, Captain: MiD. Adjutant 255 Tunnelling Company and the taker of several of the photographs in this book. Born in Stanford, Cape Province, 13 June 1890. Educated at Oundle and the Royal School of Mines. Returned to southern Africa (1911) and worked in the Rand and South Rhodesia. After the war he worked on copper mines in Ireland and then with the Bengal Iron Company – invalided home. In later life he worked for Shell. Died in 1979.

Norton-Griffiths, Sir John, Major, later Lieutenant Colonel: DSO, gazetted 14 January 1916, 6 x MiD (three times during the South African War), Commander Grand Star of Roumania, Légion d'Honneur; KCB 1917, created a Baronet 1922. 'Empire Jack'. Largely responsible for the formation, organization and deployment of British tunnelling companies at the start of 1915. Tasked in mid 1916 with the destruction of oil wells in Roumania. An MP (Conservative) 1910-1924. Died by a shot in the head whilst swimming off Alexandria in Egypt in September 1930.

Parsons, Ernest, Lance Corporal 8th London Regiment (Post Office Rifles). Born in Bloomsbury, enlisted in Holborn. A friend of Dixon's. Died of wounds on 20 April 1918 and buried in St Pierre Cemetery, Amiens, XII.E.4.

Poate, F W, Lieutenant, Light Armoured Motor Battery, Machine Gun Corps (Motors) [Quite a mouthful!]: MC, gazetted 27 June 1919, 'At Altun Keupri

[Mesopotamia], on 27th October 1918, when on reconnaissance, he left his armoured cars and went on alone to the brow of a hill. Seeing a party of the enemy coming up the other side, he called up his cars and directed one into action himself, to very close range, standing on the running board of the car so as to see better. He inflicted numerous casualties and then, with great skill, withdrew his cars from a dangerous position.'

Rees, B E, Lieutenant: MC, gazetted 16 September 1918. 'For conspicuous gallantry and devotion to duty in reconnoitring roads on several occasions and preparing them for demolition under very heavy shell fire. In one case he persisted until his only means of access was blown up by shell fire, and at another he successfully blew up a road within 300 yards of the enemy.' He was a member of 255 Tunnelling Company.

Richards, D G, Captain: MC, gazetted 31 May 1916 (then a second lieutenant), 'On the explosion of an enemy mine he organised and led a rescue party, making three journeys into our galleries, which were full of foul gas. On the last journey he was himself overcome while endeavouring to rescue a sapper and got out with great difficulty. On another occasion he did similar gallant work'; C de G. An officer in 173 Tunnelling Company.

Rogers, P A, Second Lieutenant. 170 Tunnelling Company, died of wounds 27 May 1918 at the age of 30. Buried in Noeux les Mines Communal Cemetery Extension, III.C.13. Sapper J McDonald was killed in the same incident and is buried next to him, C.12.

Runciman, A W, Captain, later Major. MC, gazetted 1 January 1918. An officer in 251 and then 255Tunnelling Companies. By the end of the war he was the OC of a Tramway Company. These companies were responsible for the forward, trench tramway system. In February 1918 they were absorbed into the new Foreway Companies RE.

Sanderson, A, Major: DSO, gazetted 1 January 1919, MC, gazetted 26 September 1916, 'He showed great coolness and pluck under heavy shell fire when exploding 'Push Pipes'. When the leads were cut by shell fire he went out regardless of danger to light the fuse. Finally his work was entirely successful.' (this took place at Fromelles), Bar to MC, gazetted, 17 September 1917, 'For conspicuous gallantry and devotion to duty during a raid upon enemy trenches. He did excellent work in reconnoitring and destroying the enemy's mining system and blowing in two dugouts, and very largely contributing to the success of the operation.' (this took place at Hill 70, Loos). Sanderson ended the war as OC 3rd Australian Tunnelling Company. Born in New Zealand in 1881 (Oamaru, South Island, NZ), he moved to Perth, in Western Australia, where he was a consulting engineer and mine manager.

Sankey, C E P, Temporary Brigadier General: DSO, gazetted 23 June 1915, 'for distinguished service in the field'; Bar to the DSO (as CRE 1st Division), gazetted 4 October 1919, 'For great gallantry in making personal reconnaissances of the Sambre-Oise Canal, south of Catillon, during the period 28 October – 3 November 1918. Owing to the able way in which he carried out his work the crossings over the canal were negotiated with comparatively few casualties in the face of a large number of machine guns and heavy shell fire. The success of the operation may be very largely credited to the skill and personal gallantry of Lieutenant Colonel Sankey.' 4 x MiD. Commissioned in the RE in 1896; served in the South African War and in France from the outbreak of the war. He was Assistant to the Engineer in Chief BEF, January 1916 to June 1917.

Shepherd, S, Captain: MC, gazetted 3 June 1918. Served in 173 and 255 Tunnelling Companies.

Skeats, T G, Major (QM): MiD, OBE. Served in the Ashanti Expedition. Involved in the office administration of the Chief of Staff, GHQ, along with Major Evans, who was chief clerk to the Chief of Staff.

Smart, R C, Lieutenant: MC, gazetted 14 November 1916, 'For conspicuous gallantry in action. He, in charge of a party, after thirty-six hours of strenuous work, succeeded in charging a mine in close proximity to the enemy. It was due to his skill, courage and endurance that the mine was successfully fired in time.' Officer in 176 and 251 Tunnelling Companies; and then First Army Mine School.

Smyth, GM, Captain. Worked in the Office of the Inspector of Mines at GHQ and was transferred to the War Office in late 1917. Won a DCM whilst serving in the ranks during the South African War.

Stevenson, A G, Lieutenant Colonel, later Colonel, finally (1925) Major General and Colonel Commandant Royal Engineers 1935 – 1939 (his death): DSO, gazetted 15 November 1898, '… Lieutenant, Royal Engineers. In recognition of services in Egypt and the Sudan, including the Battle of Khartum [sic]'. [Strangely enough, the insignia was presented to him in Nigeria by the High Commissioner of Cyprus.] CMG, 1917, CB, 1918, 10 x MiD (three of these times prior to the Great War). Commissioned in 1891. Seconded to the Egyptian Army for several years, fought in the South African War (Railway Staff Officer, South Africa). Then worked on railway survey in Uganda and the East African Protectorate; then Inspector of Iron Structures in Aldershot and the War Office. During the war he was CRE 6th Division – 18 December 1915; Controller of Mines Second Army 19 December 1915 – 28 November 1917 (replaced by Lieutenant Colonel LC Hill, qv); to Italy 3 December 1917 to 28 March 1918, before returning to France. His final post war appointment was as Engineer in Chief, Army HQ India.

Stokes, Ralph S G, Major (later Colonel): DSO, gazetted 4 June 1917, MC, gazetted 14 January 1916 (when a lieutenant), OBE (promoted to CBE), Order of St Anne, 5 x MiD. Initially served in 174 Tunnelling Company; then Assistant Controller of Mines; mid 1917, Controller of Mines First Army. In 1918 he was sent to Murmansk (allied operations in Russia after the Russian Revolution and Peace with Germany). There he served as a Colonel on the staff of General Ironside. Born 1882 in Windsor, fought as a trooper in the South African War and then went into gold and diamond mining, working in South Africa, Canada and the USA (Arizona); he was in Alaska when war broke out. Post war, a highly successful and very senior manager for de Beers, amongst others. Rejoined the RE at outbreak of war in 1939, sent by Ironside to Narvik and then went to North Africa with responsibility for airfields as a Brigadier at GHQ. After the invasion of Italy, to the War Office. Continued working until 1959, retired to the UK and died in Sherborne in 1979. His management mantra was encompassed as: Articulate, Brief, Courteous.

Thresher, J H, Lieutenant Colonel (Rifle Brigade): CMG (1919), MVO (1917), MiD, Légion d'Honneur. Served in France and Flanders throughout the war (he was an early arrival, landing on 14 August 1914). Bar the first two weeks after arrival, his entire service was as a Camp Commandant, most of that at Montreuil.

Vickerman, M H, Major (New Zealand Engineers Tunnelling Company): DSO, gazetted 1 January 1918, OBE, 2 x MiD. From 9 January 1917 he was OC of the Company until the end of the war. Educated in New Zealand and had worked as a civil engineer pre war.

Williams, G C, Lieutenant Colonel, later Brigadier General (in 1941 General): DSO, gazetted 29 October 1915, '…173rd (Tunnelling) Company. For conspicuous gallantry and initiative in France. He pushed his advanced galleries through those of the enemy, thereby successfully carrying out mining operations. From the commencement of this difficult and dangerous work, Major Williams directed and controlled the work with great daring and forethought, which alone enabled an almost unique result to be obtained.' CMG (1919), 5 x MiD, Order of St Stansilas, 2nd Class, with swords. OC 173 Tunnelling Company; Controller of Mines First Army 14 December 1915 – 11 June 1917; CRE 66th Division 12 June 1917 – 16 March 1918; GOC 199 Brigade [in the rank of Brigadier General] 16 March 1918 (just before the German Michael Offensive opened – the Division was on the Somme front) to the end of the war. Williams was born in Bangalore in 1881 and was commissioned in 1900. Served until 1904 in Bermuda; from

1909 he was engaged in survey work in the East African Protectorate until 1914 (Director of Surveys 1912). Post war stationed in India, with a four year break at the War Office; commanded a Brigade 1927–1928, then chief instructor at the Imperial Defence College; Chief Engineer, Aldershot; Commandant Staff College, Quetta, 1934-1937; GOC 5th Division 1937-1938, GOC-in-C Eastern Command, 1938-1941, Military Adviser to the NZ Government, 1941. Colonel Commandant RE, 1940–1951; Chief Royal Engineer, 1946–1951. CB (1935), promoted KCB 1939. Died February 1959.

Yuill, H H, Major, later Lieutenant Colonel: DSO, gazetted 4 June 1917, MC, 'For conspicuous gallantry and devotion to duty on several occasions: On 29 May 1915, at Cuinchy, when one of the leads broke close to a charge, he at once untamped the top of the charge and crawled into the mine to find and mend the break, although the Germans were working so close he could hear them talking. On 24 and 29 June, at Cambrin, at great personal risk, he charged mines, well knowing the Germans to be charging against him, and managed to fire his charges before they succeeded in doing so. Again, on the night of the 21st-22nd August, at Cuinchy, Second Lieutenant Yuill exhibited great skill and bravery in directing mining operations. The enemy were working within a few feet of our galleries, opposite No. 5 and 7 mines, and it became a race which mines would be first exploded. The situation was critical, but owing to his splendid example and energy two shafts were sunk in time, charged and tamped. The resulting explosions must have blown in the German galleries and the miners in them.' C de G, 4 x MiD. Assistant Controller of Mines and then Controller of Mines First Army (mid 1918), replacing Colonel Stokes, qv. He was a Canadian, born in Nova Scotia, a mining engineer pre and post war. He died in Vancouver in 1935.

Appendix VIII

Analysis of Tunnelling Companies Fatal Casualties

FROM THE TUNNELLERS OLD COMRADES ASSOCIATION

The Roll of Honour in the Tunnellers Old Comrades Register dated February 1925 lists 181 tunnelling officer fatalities in the course of the conflict, of which 24 are from Dominion Companies.

Tabulation of Tunnelling Company Fatal Casualties.
Derived Over Selected Periods As Shown.

Company	*OFRS*	*OR*	*Source*
172	3	53	CWGC – Whole war – but this probably refers only to RE casualties and not other attached personnel.
174	3	35	Somme. 5 March 15 to 31 March 17
176	2	44	Vimy. 13 March 16 to 30 April 17
178	3	92	Somme. 3 August 15 to end April 17
179	4	62	Somme. 24 August 15 to 17 January 17
180	3	76	September 1915 to October 1916 Hohenzollern & Hulluch areas then Somme until June 1917
181	2	25	Ecurie 15 April to 19 Aug 16 & Somme 19 Aug 16 to 15 Jan 17
183	1	19	Somme 9 September 15 to 13 March 17
184	1	23	Somme 26 October 15 to 4 March 16 & Roclincourt & Ecurie 1 April 16 to 23 June 17
185	3	18	Somme 4 November 15 to 29 February 16.
252	2	27	Somme 21 November 15 to 12 April 17
256	0	10	Somme 29 October 16 to 31 March 17
NZETC	2	49	Whole War. Data derived from NZET History.
Aus Tun Coys (1, 2, 3 & ABC)	12	327	Whole war. Data derived from Crumps & Camouflets – although this shows 8 officer fatalities against 12 listed by the Tunnellers Old Comrades Association.
TOTAL	41	860	

ANALYSIS

Ratio of other ranks killed to officers killed is 21 OR to 1 officer.

On that basis and given 181 officers killed or died, the number of other rank fatalities = 3,800.

COMMENT

Without more data on the Royal Engineer Tunnelling Companies it is uncertain whether those in the NZET and Australian Companies distort the ratio. In the periods for the RE Companies there are 27 officer fatalities against 484 OR fatalities, a ration of 1 to 17.9.

Glossary

AEMM & B or AEMMB	Australian Electrical, Mechanical, Mining & Boring Company, commonly referred to as the Alphabet Company or ABC Company.
AG	Adjutant General responsible for all BEF personnel matters.
AI of M	Assistant Inspector of Mines. Officers working for and reporting to the Inspector of Mines at GHQ.
Ammonal	Ammonium nitrate based explosive with a strong lifting effect, three and a half times more powerful than gunpowder. Inert and safe to handle. Adopted in mid 1915 as the standard British mining explosive.
ASC	Army Service Corps (BEF)
Batman	A junior rank appointed to care for the personal administration and equipment of an officer. Often called an officer's servant.
BEF	British Expeditionary Force. In the context of this book, the BEF refers to British, Dominion and British colonial troops serving in France and Belgium.
C in C	Commander in Chief. In the BEF from 19 Dec 1915, this was General Sir Douglas Haig (Field Marshal from 1 Jan 1917).
C of M	Controller of Mines. Army HQ post. Normally a lieutenant colonel.
Camouflet	A contained underground explosive charge that does not break surface. Most often employed to destroy enemy tunnels.
Carbon Monoxide (CO)	A colourless and odourless gas released on detonation of explosives. If inhaled it combines with the haemoglobin of the blood, displacing the oxygen. If not swiftly treated it is invariably fatal. A very serious hazard for the Tunnellers.
CGS	Chief of the General Staff.

Clay kicking	Method of digging small tunnels quickly through clay used by sewer tunnellers. Advantage of being relatively silent. Adopted by the British tunnelling companies.
CO	Commanding Officer. Normally a lieutenant colonel commanding a battalion or equivalent unit and large logistic units; sometimes a major was appointed as CO. Accorded significant disciplinary powers.
CRE	Commander Royal Engineers – found on the staff of divisions, corps and Army HQs.
Detonator	Copper or aluminium tube, about the size of a cigarette, containing one of several very sensitive explosives. Used to initiate detonation normally via a 'primer'. Two main types, igniferous (initiated by a burning fuse) or electrical.
DRLS	Dispatch Rider.
E in C	Engineer in Chief.
Fosse	A mine shaft and / or workings at the head of the shaft.
Gaine	An explosive extension that screwed into the base of a fuse to convert the flash from an initiator into a detonation wave.
Gallery	One of several terms describing a tunnel, most commonly one running towards the enemy lines or tunnels.
Geophone	A listening instrument with two microphones, constructed on the principles of a stethoscope. Sound waves through the ground are magnified and transmitted separately to each ear of the listener. By exactly balancing the pitch a bearing could be taken on the source of the sound.
GHQ	General Headquarters. At Montreuil-sur-Mer from early 1916 (St Omer previously).
GQG	*Grand Quartier Général*. French equivalent of GHQ.
HAC	Honorable Artillery Company.
I of M	Inspector of Mines (Brigadier General at GHQ). Responsible for the overall direction, deployment and resourcing of the mining units and their activities.
Lateral	Defensive tunnel dug parallel to the front line trench. Used as a starting point for listening and attack galleries and interconnection between galleries. Effectively a deep underground 'trench'. Also called a transversal.
Mine	Explosive charge laid underground. Optionally, the tunnel in which that charge is laid.
NZET	New Zealand Engineers Tunnelling Company.
OC	Officer Commanding, normally at company level. Usually a major or captain. Limited disciplinary powers.

OHL	German General Headquarters *(Oberste Heeresleitung).*
OTC	Officers Training Corps.
Proto apparatus.	The most commonly used of several British self-contained breathing apparatus, combining an oxygen supply with a recycling system for absorbing the carbon dioxide exhaled by the user. Endurance up to two hours with experienced users but usually limited to forty-five to sixty minutes. Also known as the Fleuss Apparatus.
Puits	French for a vertical shaft.
QMG	Quartermaster General. Responsible for all stores, equipment, rations and munitions.
RE	Royal Engineer, or (plural) Royal Engineers.
Russian Sap	Either a deep trench covered and concealed, effectively to form a tunnel, or a shallow underground gallery, usually below No Man's Land. Used for communication and placing of weapon positions close to the enemy line. Sometimes converted into a trench by breaking down the top cover. Nicknamed daisy-cutters by tunnellers
Safety fuse	A slow burning fuse. The British Bickford fuse burned at a rate of 38 seconds per foot (125 seconds per metre).
Sap	A trench dug towards the enemy. The term was often used for a mine gallery driven towards the enemy.
Sapper	The most junior of the engineer trained ranks in the Royal Engineers; but also used as a generic term referring to all Royal Engineers regardless of rank (and sometimes to military engineers in other armies). The same applies, for example, to the Royal Artillery and 'gunner'.
Seismomicrophone	An electrical sound detector, usually linked to a Central Listening Station covering an area of the mining front.
Subway	A communication tunnel providing concealed and protected access to front line positions. Most also included command and signals centres, accommodation and logistic facilities.
Tamping	In a mining context, backfilling the gallery leading to a mine charge to prevent the force of the explosion being directed back along the tunnel.
TCO	Train Conducting Officer.
Tubbing	Steel cylindrical sections used for sinking shafts in wet or loose ground.

References and Recommendations for Further Reading

Dixon was writing mostly from memory and so far as can be ascertained without much research into the limited publicised material at the time. Hence there is no apparent Bibliography for his memoirs. The editors however have drawn on a number of specific sources for reference as well a benefiting from some of the publications listed below.

Captain W Grant Grieves and Bernard Newman. *Tunnellers.*

Institute of RE. *Work of the R.E. in the European War 1914–1919.*

Jones, Ian. *Malice Aforethought. A History of Booby Traps from World War One to Vietnam.*

National Archive (PRO). War Diary 255 Tunnelling Company.(WO 95/245)

National Archive (PRO). War Diary 252 Tunnelling Company. (WO 95/406)

National Archive (PRO). First Army Weekly Mining Summaries. (WO 158/196)

The Tunnellers Old Comrades Association. *Register dated February 1925.*

RE Library / Museum. *GHQ Mining Notes.*

RE Library / Museum. *Inspector of Mines Circulars.*

Various private papers held by the editors.

Readers who wish to delve more deeply may be interested in some of the following publications, additional to the Tunnelling Company War Diaries at the National Archive and the RE Museum.

Alexander Barrie. *War Underground, The Tunnellers of The Great War.*

Peter Barton, Peter Doyle and Johan Vandewalle. *Beneath Flanders Fields. The Tunnellers War 1914–1918.*

Tony Bridgeland and Anne Maorgan. *Tunnel-master & Arsonist of the Great War. The Norton Griffiths Story.*

Adolf Buchner. *Der Kampf um La bataille deVauquois / The Battle of Vauquois.* [Tri lingual – German, French & English]

Will Davies. *Beneath Hill 60.*

Hugues C. Dewerdt, Guillaume Paques, Frédérick Willman. *Les Muches. Souterrains-Refuges De La Somme.* [French language only.]

Damien Finlayson. *Crumps and Camouflets. Australian Tunnelling Companies on the Western Front.*

Jean-Marie Girardet, Alain Jacques, Jean-Luc Duclos. *Somewhere on the Western Front. Arras.*
Ian Henry. *Subterranean Sappers. A History of 177 Tunnelling Company RE.*
Les Amis de Vauquois et de sa Région. *La Butte meurtrie Vauquois. La Guerre des mines 1914–1918.* [French language only]
Simon Jones. *Underground Warfare 1914–1918.*
Robert K Johns. *Battle Beneath The Trenches – The Cornish Miners of 251st Tunnelling Company RE.*
Matthew Leonard. *Beneath the Killing Fields.*
J.C. Neill. *The New Zealand Tunnelling Company 1915–1919.*
Pas de Calais City Council. *Vimy 1917. La Guerre Souterraines Des Canadiens.* [French and English. Predominantly about graffiti and covers other areas of the front.]
Ian Passingham. *Pillars Of Fire. The Battle of Messines Ridge June 1917*
Phillip Robinson & Nigel Cave. *The Underground War, Vimy Ridge to Arras.*
Jack Sheldon & Nigel Cave. *The Battle for Vimy Ridge – 1917.*
Captain H.D. Trounce, ERC. *Fighting the Boche Underground.*
Captain H.D Trounce. *Notes to Military Mining.*
Alexander Turner. *Messines 1917. The zenith of siege warfare.*

Index